Architecting Generative AI Applications

Build, deploy, and scale production-ready GenAI systems with LLMOps best practices

Leonid Kuligin

<packt>

Architecting Generative AI Applications

Portfolio Director: Gebin George
Relationship Lead: Ali Abidi
Project Manager: Prajakta Naik
Content Engineer: Mark D'Souza
Technical Editor: Rahul Limbachiya
Copy Editor: Safis Editing
Indexer: Manju Arasan
Proofreader: Mark D'Souza
Production Designer: Prashant Ghare
Growth Lead: Nimisha Dua

First published: March 2026

Production reference: 1270326

Published by Packt Publishing Ltd.
Grosvenor House
11 St Paul's Square
Birmingham
B3 1RB, UK.

ISBN 978-1-80667-865-5
www.packtpub.com

To my wife, Ksenia, whose unwavering love and optimism have been my constant support throughout the years; to my father, Evgeny, who showed me how to be a person of both strength and love; and to my mother-in-law, Tatyana, whose belief in me, even in my craziest endeavors, has been an incredible source of strength.

– Leonid Kuligin

Contributors

About the author

Leonid Kuligin is a staff AI engineer at Google Cloud, working on generative AI and classical machine learning solutions (such as agentic AI, demand forecasting, and optimization problems). Leonid is also an associate researcher at TUM University Hospital, Technical University of Munich. With over two decades of experience, Leonid has a track record of building B2C and B2B applications and solving users' problems in domains such as search, maps, knowledge extraction, and investment management in industry-leading German and Russian technological, financial, and retail companies.

I am deeply grateful to the many colleagues and exceptional people I've encountered throughout my career who shared their wisdom and passion. I owe a special debt of gratitude to Slava Rubaev, my first manager and a lifelong mentor, for teaching me the essentials of entrepreneurship and critical-thinking. My thanks also go to Thomas Cliett, for showing me how to thrive in the corporate world, and to Maximilian Tschochohei, for demonstrating how to lead with both ambition and empathy.

Also, a big thank you to my colleagues and friends, Alex, Grigory, Maximilian, and Thomas, who took the time to review this book, and to Ali and Mark from Packt for their relentless support while working on it.

About the reviewers

Alex Blinov is a senior engineering manager at Oracle, focused on building and scaling complex cloud and healthcare applications. At Oracle, he has worked on cloud migration services and on Oracle Health products including *Patient Administration* and *Patient Portal*. His background spans cloud infrastructure, distributed systems, enterprise architecture, and engineering leadership. Alex is especially interested in the practical use of GenAI to improve developer productivity, platform effectiveness, and large-scale product delivery.

Max Tschochohei advises enterprise customers on achieving their AI and ML goals with Google Cloud. As an engineering manager in Google Cloud Consulting, he leads teams of AI engineers delivering mission-critical projects, with a focus on agentic systems, MLOps, and healthcare AI.

Before joining Google in Munich, Max worked as a consultant at KPMG and the Boston Consulting Group, where he led large-scale digital transformation initiatives, including for NTUC Enterprise, a Singapore government-linked organization. He holds a PhD in Economics from Coventry University.

Thomas Zettl is a Munich-based AI engineer at Google, where he develops state-of-the-art Cloud AI solutions and frequently speaks at local community events. He holds a PhD in Physics and has an academic background spanning Ludwig-Maximilians-Universität Munich, the University of Cambridge, and Stanford University.

With over a decade of experience in machine learning, data science, and data engineering, Thomas brings a strong track record across NLP and computer vision. He began working with generative models at their inception, following the release of BERT and GPT-1, and has continued to build expertise with today's most advanced architectures.

Previously, he held key technical roles at Steadforce GmbH and Allianz. He combines deep theoretical knowledge with extensive industry experience in debugging, testing, and productionizing AI applications, ensuring they meet complex business requirements while adhering to responsible AI principles and robust security standards.

Grigory Movsesyan is a senior infrastructure engineer at Google Cloud PSO. He helps enterprise-level organizations to streamline their journey to Google Cloud, specializing in the design of secure landing zones and the automation of infrastructure via Terraform. An expert in CI/CD, logging, and monitoring, Grigory focuses on creating seamless, automated environments that allow businesses to scale efficiently and reliably.

Table of Contents

Preface xiii

Free benefits with your book ... xvii

Chapter 1: Building a Prototype 1

Secrets of a successful AI prototype ... 2

Starting a proof of concept at a large company • 5

Starting a proof of concept as a start-up • 8

What GenAI has changed ... 9

The reality of developing AI products ... 12

Misconceptions when developing AI products ... 15

Summary ... 18

Further reading ... 19

Chapter 2: Evaluation 21

Evaluating GenAI applications ... 22

Generalization in ML • 22

ML development lifecycle • 26

Metrics-based evaluation ... 28

Binary and multi-class classification • 28

Binary classification • 29

Multi-class classification • 31

Comparing texts ... 32

Retrieval ... 34

Using an LLM as a judge ... 38

Grade an answer reference-free, or without providing an expected answer • 38

Grade an answer relative to an expected solution (often called a referenced, or a golden answer) • 40

Perform a pairwise comparison, or task an LLM to express its preference on which answer is better • 40

Consensus • 42

Human-in-the-loop 43

Implementing HITL • 43

Scaling and operationalizing human evaluation • 46

More complex evaluation scenarios 48

Evaluating RAG applications • 48

Evaluating an agent • 50

Summary 51

Further reading 52

Chapter 3: Key Architectures 55

Organizing and versioning prompt templates 56

Storing and retrieving embeddings with vector databases 58

Hybrid search and re-reranking 61

Inverted index • 62

Re-ranking and merging results • 64

Query expansion 66

Dealing with a limited context window with MapReduce 67

Exploring agentic architectures 69

Tool calling • 70

Task decomposition and tree of thoughts • 73

Multi-agentic systems • 75

External orchestrator • 77

Operationalizing the tool-calling pattern • 78

Agentic memory • 79

Summary 81

Further reading 82

Chapter 4: From Prototype to Production 85

Why operationalization matters 86

Code readability 89

Making your code easy to read in Python • 91

Making your code easy to extend • 92

Single Responsibility Principle • 93

Don't Repeat Yourself • 94

Loose coupling • 95

Testing 96

Unit testing • 97

Unit testing in Python • 99

Unit testing GenAI applications • 99

Integration testing • 101

Load testing • 102

Keeping it simple! 105

Taking the quick-fix path 106

Onboarding users 107

Summary 109

Further reading 110

Chapter 5: Moving from DevOps and MLOps to LLMOps 113

DevOps 114

Automation of code delivery processes • 114

What is CI/CD? • 115

MLOps 117

ML pipelines • 119

What are success metrics? • 124

LLMOps 124

How has GenAI changed the developer's experience? • 125

What is the value behind LLMOps? • 126

Choosing LLMOps tools • 126

Case study: CI/CD job for RAG • 127

Summary 130

Further reading 131

Chapter 6: Deploying Your Application 133

Stateless and stateful applications 133

Deployment best practices 135

Infrastructure as code • 135

Secret management • 137

Configuration management • 138

Deploying an application 139

Wrapping code as a web API • 139

Deploying your container on Kubernetes • 143

Deploying with a managed service such as LangSmith • 147

Best practices for scaling your application 148

Caching • 148

CAP theorem • 151

Context caching • 152

Failing gracefully • 153

Request throttling • 153

Cascading failures • 154

Summary 156

Further reading 157

Chapter 7: Ethics and Security 159

The basics of Responsible AI 160

Fairness 162

Improving fairness • 162

Fairness in GenAI • 163

Explainability 164

Improving explainability • 165

Explainability of LLMs • 167

Safety and security 168

Safety in the classical ML era • 168

GenAI safety • 170

Privacy 172
Improving privacy • 172
Additional privacy concerns in GenAI • 175
Summary 176
Further reading 177

Chapter 8: Observability and Reliability 181

What is site reliability engineering? 182
Achieving reliability 182
SLIs, SLOs, and SLAs • 183
Error budget • 185
Other SRE principles • 187
Managing production application 189
Telemetry data • 190
Logs • 190
Metrics • 192
Traces • 193
Monitoring • 194
Alerting • 195
Observability 196
GenAI observability 198
Instrumenting your application 199
Summary 200
Further reading 201

Chapter 9: Maintaining Your Application 203

Life after deployment 203
How are platform teams different? 204
What differentiates GenAI platform teams from regular platform teams? • 205
GenAI platform building blocks • 208
Model gateway • 208
Prompt store • 209

Tool registry • 210

Execution sandboxes • 211

Session store • 212

Feedback service • 212

Human-in-the-loop • 213

Serving infrastructure • 214

Training infrastructure • 214

Product strategy and roadmap **215**

Summary **218**

Further reading **219**

Chapter 10: A/B Testing and Online Experiments 223

What are A/B tests? **224**

Statistical testing **226**

Type I and Type II errors • 227

Conducting statistical analysis **228**

Myths about p-value • 230

Good metrics for online testing **230**

Increasing the power of your tests **234**

Common errors when running A/B tests **236**

Summary **238**

Further reading **240**

Chapter 11: Unlock Your Exclusive Benefits 243

Unlock this Book's Free Benefits in 3 Easy Steps **244**

Other Books You May Enjoy 248

Index 251

Preface

Generative AI (GenAI) is changing the world and how we all operate. We can debate the scale of this change and how far it will go, but it is undeniable that the transformation is already underway. This book explores these changes and their implications for software development processes. Rather than focusing on vibe coding, it emphasizes the first principles of software development—principles that evolve slowly (almost adiabatically, one might say) and remain foundational over time. Understanding them is key to building great products for your users.

At the same time, we now have the ability to use vibe coding to quickly put together exciting prototypes and even launch products. When in doubt, we can turn to Gemini, ChatGPT, Claude, or other advanced assistants. So, why do we still need a book about software architecture and best practices? Why not rely entirely on these tools for guidance?

I believe the shift that GenAI has introduced makes it even more important to know what to ask. A solid grasp of fundamentals enables us to ask better questions, provide clear instructions to AI assistants, and critically evaluate their outputs. Agents are only as effective as the instructions they receive.

As a result, we are moving toward broader, more horizontal expertise, developing a foundation that spans multiple aspects of software development. For many, this may signal a move away from deep vertical specialization in a single domain. Instead, application developers increasingly act as coordinators of highly capable coding assistants.

This book is designed to help you take the first steps on that path.

Who this book is for

This book is for data scientists or ML developers who, when bringing their prototype to production, suddenly realize that they need to think about the security and reliability of their applications. It is also for application engineers who start developing their AI applications, as well as for engineering managers, product and technical leaders, and business owners who wish to enter the GenAI space and wonder what implications it would bring for their teams and businesses.

A basic understanding of GenAI and LLMs is assumed, along with some Python knowledge, since this is the language of choice for many developers in this space. However, only a few examples in this book are Python-specialized (but they can be easily generalized for any language); everything else would be relevant to any programming language. The Python snippets provided should be easy to read and understand even if you are not familiar with Python. The principles are the same across all computer languages.

What this book covers

Chapter 1, Building a Prototype, introduces how to develop a prototype by first defining the critical problem. It also provides guidance on GenAI adoption across different types of organizations and highlights common misconceptions around data, evaluation, and production-readiness.

Chapter 2, Evaluation, explores the challenges of evaluating open-ended GenAI outputs. It covers the development of offline evaluation metrics, the LLM-as-a-judge approach, and the integration of human-in-the-loop processes into the evaluation of RAG systems and agentic workflows.

Chapter 3, Key Architectures, discusses design considerations for production-ready GenAI systems, including organizing prompt templates, often-overlooked aspects of vector databases and hybrid search, applying MapReduce to large-scale data processing, and designing robust single- and multi-agent systems.

Chapter 4, From Prototype to Production, focuses on core engineering best practices for transitioning from experimental prototypes to reliable production systems, including testing strategies and practical approaches to managing technical debt.

Chapter 5, Moving from DevOps and MLOps to LLMOps, introduces the concept of operational excellence, tracing the evolution from DevOps and CI/CD through MLOps and continuous training to LLMOps, with a focus on evaluation, cost management, and code-data coupling challenges in modern GenAI applications.

Chapter 6, Deployments, covers stateless application design, implementing repeatable infrastructure using **infrastructure as code** (**IaC**) with Terraform, orchestrating containers with Kubernetes, and ensuring high performance through semantic caching and graceful failure strategies.

Chapter 7, Ethics and Security, examines the ethical responsibilities involved in building powerful AI systems. It covers Responsible AI principles such as fairness, explainability, safety, and privacy, as well as key security risks associated with GenAI.

Chapter 8, Observability and Reliability, introduces Site Reliability Engineering concepts, including measuring acceptable levels of unreliability using service-level objectives, balancing technical debt with error budgets, and implementing observability in GenAI systems through logs, metrics, and traces.

Chapter 9, Maintenance, focuses on evolving from a single successful application to a scalable GenAI platform. It highlights the role of platform teams and key LLMOps components such as model gateways, tool registries, execution sandboxes, and feedback services, along with guidance on product strategy and roadmapping.

Chapter 10, A/B Testing and Online Experiments, covers statistical testing concepts such as Type I and Type II errors, the design of online experiments, and common pitfalls to avoid when running A/B tests.

To get the most out of this book

You can skip chapters or sections that are not relevant or are too easy for you. This is inevitable since we touch on many aspects, and if you are an expert in some of them, you would know them much deeper than this book covers. But if something is new, go deeper and beyond the content of this book. After each chapter, I share a list of relevant links, books, and papers that I have been collecting for years, which should serve for further exploration of the topic. Some topics might be completely new and puzzling, and that's a good sign! Spend more time on them, go into additional materials, consult your AI assistant of choice, and enjoy the learning process.

Download the color images

We also provide a PDF file that has color images of the screenshots/diagrams used in this book. You can download it here: `https://packt.link/gbp/9781806678655`.

Conventions used

There are a number of text conventions used throughout this book.

`CodeInText`: Indicates code words in text, database table names, folder names, filenames, file extensions, pathnames, dummy URLs, user input, and Twitter/X handles. For example: "The only reason to change the `summarize_webpage` function is when the business wants to change the logic."

A block of code is set as follows:

```
async def summarize_webpage(state):
    web_page_content = _fetch_webpage(url=state["web_page"])
    summary = await _summarize_text(web_page_content)
    return {"page_summary": summary}
```

Bold: Indicates a new term, an important word, or words that you see on the screen. For instance, words in menus or dialog boxes appear in the text like this. For example: "GenAI uses special types of ML models, **large language models** (**LLMs**) and their extensions, for example, **large vision models** (**LVMs**)."

> **Note**
>
> Warnings or important notes appear like this.

> **Tip**
>
> Tips and tricks appear like this.

Get in touch

Feedback from our readers is always welcome.

General feedback: If you have questions about any aspect of this book or have any general feedback, please email us at `customercare@packt.com` and mention the book's title in the subject of your message.

Errata: Although we have taken every care to ensure the accuracy of our content, mistakes do happen. If you have found a mistake in this book, we would be grateful if you reported this to us. Please visit `http://www.packt.com/submit-errata`, click **Submit Errata**, and fill in the form.

Piracy: If you come across any illegal copies of our works in any form on the internet, we would be grateful if you would provide us with the location address or website name. Please contact us at `copyright@packt.com` with a link to the material.

If you are interested in becoming an author: If there is a topic that you have expertise in and you are interested in either writing or contributing to a book, please visit `http://authors.packt.com/`.

Free benefits with your book

This book comes with free benefits to support your learning. Activate them now for instant access (see the "*How to Unlock*" section for instructions).

Here's a quick overview of what you can instantly unlock with your purchase:

How to Unlock

Scan the QR code (or go to `packtpub.com/unlock`). Search for this book by name, confirm the edition, and then follow the steps on the page.

UNLOCK NOW

Note: Keep your invoice handy. Purchases made directly from Packt don't require one

Share your thoughts

Once you've read *Architecting Generative AI Applications*, we'd love to hear your thoughts! Scan the QR code below to go straight to the Amazon review page for this book and share your feedback.

`https://packt.link/r/1806678659`

Your review is important to us and the tech community and will help us make sure we're delivering excellent quality content.

Join our Discord and Reddit Space

You're not the only one navigating fragmented tools, constant updates, and unclear best practices. Join a growing community of professionals exchanging insights that don't make it into documentation.

Join our Discord at `https://packt.link/z8ivB` or scan the QR code below:	Follow us on Reddit at `https://packt.link/0rExL` or scan the QR code below:

1

Building a Prototype

I've been working in software engineering and data analytics for more than 20 years, 12 of which I spent developing **machine learning** (**ML**) products. I have worked in small start-ups and large corporations, developing new products and scaling existing ones, expanding into new markets, and combating newly emerging competitors. Multiple times, I've come across technology that I find to be overrated. We often hope that some cool technology developed by the engineering team will help solve the problem of falling sales, unsatisfied users, and decreasing customer base, but this remains wishful thinking.

We always need to first understand the problem we wish to solve. Quite often, I've seen engineering teams diving into the implementation before clearly identifying the challenge and the problem that users are facing. All this does is delay the inevitability of failure.

Generative AI (**GenAI**), a subfield of ML, is on the rise, and more and more applications and product engineering teams are developing GenAI applications. GenAI uses special types of ML models, **large language models** (**LLMs**) and their extensions, for example, **large vision models** (**LVMs**). These foundational models are trained on a large amount of data and on different input and output modalities (text, video, audio, etc.); they exhibit excellent reasoning and other capabilities for solving tasks that they were not specifically trained for. This makes it possible to create a broad range of applications in almost any domain with the use of GenAI. This, therefore, means that almost any product engineer should master GenAI. You are not expected to be able to train an LLM, but you should be able to incorporate it in your application. This book will help you understand the fundamental design principles that you should be familiar with, which will help you develop production-ready GenAI applications.

In this chapter, we will start with a discussion on how to build a successful GenAI prototype (surprisingly, it's not much different from starting a successful prototype in ML). We will look at situations when AI works and when it doesn't, and how the implementation of AI in big corporations differs from that in small start-ups.

We will discuss what business leaders need to understand about AI and GenAI in particular. This chapter will be useful for a business leader, of course, but it might also help a product manager or a technical leader to understand the perspective of their colleagues. In the end, it's our task as engineers to educate the business part of the organization, and help them to use new technologies to grow the business and improve customer experience!

Of course, I will be simplifying things a little bit and avoiding discussing nuances. Don't judge me too strictly on that, please.

You will find book recommendations at the end of this chapter, and if you're interested in the topics discussed, I highly encourage you to check them out!

In this chapter, we'll be covering the following topics:

- Secrets of a successful AI prototype
- What GenAI has changed
- The reality of developing AI products
- Misconceptions when developing AI products

> Note
>
> **Your purchase includes a free PDF copy + exclusive extras**
>
> Your purchase includes a DRM-free PDF copy of this book, 7-day trial to the Packt+ library (no credit card required), and additional exclusive extras. See the *Free benefits with your book* section in the *Preface* to unlock them instantly and maximize your learning.

Secrets of a successful AI prototype

First, let's briefly discuss how AI is different from ML, since these terms are frequently used interchangeably. AI is a broad field of computer science that aims to create computer programs that can solve complex tasks that would typically require human intelligence. ML is a subdomain of AI; in other words, all ML problems are AI problems, but not all AI problems are ML problems. ML focuses on solving tasks by training models on large labeled datasets, so we can say it's a different way of programming compared to writing an algorithm. We've seen the rise of ML in the recent decade, as various ML algorithms have been applied to different real-world problems with a large business impact. From a practical standpoint, most AI systems developed by enterprises in the decade from 2013 to 2023 were ML systems (for example, recommendation engines, fraud detection systems, demand forecasting and planning engines, etc.), and we learned a lot about the practical applications of ML throughout this decade.

Complex rule-based systems, Monte Carlo simulations, and greedy search algorithms are examples of AI systems that are not ML systems. With the rise of GenAI, we have gotten access to a new way of designing AI solutions, and these solutions are based on pre-trained LLMs. Technically speaking, training an LLM falls into the ML domain, but many engineering teams just use a pre-trained LLM to solve business problems. As we will see throughout this book, some core principles of developing ML systems apply to GenAI applications too, and the importance of such principles (such as writing clean and readable code, designing systems for reliability, maintainability, and AI safety, etc.) is often underestimated by engineering teams.

Now that we've established the difference between AI and ML, let's get back to our topic at hand. Developing a prototype is very similar to starting a business, even if you're working at a large company with plenty of resources and a stable user base.

The most important step is to determine the problem the business is trying to solve. If I were to summarize the main point of this chapter in a single sentence, it would be "Don't be afraid to ask yourself difficult questions and make it clear what problem you're going to solve and why." Put another way, focus on the problem, not on the cool technology that you'd like to use to solve some potential problem that you're not really clear about. Defining the product you're building is one of the core tasks of a product manager, and you, as a business or technical leader, might take on this role. If you're new to the product manager role, a great book to read is *Inspired: How to Create Tech Products Customers Love* by Marty Cagan.

Before jumping into implementation and starting to think about cool technological problems, ask very specific questions about what the core problem is that you're solving. Can you solve it with heuristics? Is the problem worth solving? How would your solution be used in the field?

At the same time, sometimes businesses have concerns of being disrupted by a new technology (we'll discuss this further later in this chapter), and they ask a fair question: "Is this the right time for us to start using GenAI (ML, chatbots, and so on)?" Sometimes it's a good idea to take a fresh look and try to adopt a new technology. In practice, I've seen AI deliver real value in only three types of situations:

- **When a business wants to replace a set of heuristics in a product that has grown too complex over time with an ML model**: The increased complexity would make the product very difficult to maintain and improve in its current state. Also, typically, when we try to fix one problem, another functionality degrades. This makes it very difficult to measure the quality of our product. In such a scenario, the problem is clear: we need to replace a bunch of heuristics with an ML model and introduce a common evaluation approach to measure whether the new version is better than the previous one.
  Another scenario in which a company might like to replace existing heuristics and the humans behind them with ML would be when the business is expanding, and increasing manpower is not feasible. Their product might have a lot of manual work

under the hood that prevents them from scaling. Imagine you have a start-up that helps small and medium-sized businesses with accounting. You have developed a shiny mobile application that allows your customers to easily upload their bank transactions and related documents, and you have hired a few accountants to help businesses with their reporting. You're doing extremely well, but now you're facing a problem: you started with a small human team performing manual operations, but it's extremely difficult (or often almost impossible) to scale such a team 100 times—you just can't hire new good people at the pace that the growth of your business requires.

- **When businesses want to optimize performance in a product that has scaled to millions of users**: At such a scale, a small increase in conversion rates can justify weeks of engineering effort because the improvement multiplies across a large user base and generates a strong return on investment.
  For example, improving a conversion rate from 1.0% to 1.05% is usually irrelevant for a small startup. First, the company would likely lack enough data to measure such a small improvement reliably (we will discuss evaluation in more detail in *Chapters 2* and *10*). Second, the potential revenue increase rarely justifies the engineering effort. Early-stage companies should focus on finding product–market fit rather than optimizing small metrics. However, the situation changes dramatically for large companies. At scale, a seemingly minor improvement can translate into millions of dollars over time.

  In these scenarios, the problem is clearly defined: you have a large amount of usage data, a specific metric you want to improve, and a well-defined component of the product to optimize. This is a classic setting where ML performs extremely well.
- **When businesses want to leverage new technology to unlock previously impossible opportunities**: This is the most common reason to start a start-up, but in most cases, you should start lean, use an existing mostly available technology (that hasn't reached mass adoption yet), and begin with multiple heuristics. As your product grows, your logic becomes more and more complex, and you onboard more and more users (which means you'll gather a lot of labeled domain-specific data); you reach a point when you start replacing your heuristics with a more advanced AI solution (we discussed this previously). That's the time for custom AI development!
  A good example is GenAI start-ups that are part of the recent Y Combinator batches. Y Combinator is a prestigious and highly successful start-up accelerator. It is famous for investing in start-ups such as Stripe, Coinbase, and Airbnb. They run four cohorts per year, and you can browse through different cohorts on their website. Most of them do not develop LLMs from scratch, but they start by building thin wrappers on top of ChatGPT, Gemini, or other foundation models, and invest their time in finding a problem that is worth fixing. That means the problem should be narrow to begin with,

while at the same time representing a large enough market worth VC investment. A brilliant book on this topic is written by Peter Thiel, *Zero to One: Notes on Startups, or How to Build the Future.*

Of course, there are examples of start-ups, such as Mistral and Anthropic, that build LLMs themselves, but there are many more business-oriented start-ups that start with finding the customer segment, developing a business model, and gradually improving the product. Typically, they begin with heuristics and rule-based systems, but as they mature, they collect their own dataset and evaluation mechanisms, and their tech becomes more and more advanced and sophisticated. To keep it short, don't be afraid to start small and find a good problem to fix.

If you want to use AI (and GenAI in particular) but you feel like you don't fall into any of these three categories, then you may be operating within a larger organization. In this environment, it's not uncommon to encounter situations where the broader context or rationale behind certain initiatives is not fully visible, which can introduce additional challenges.

Once leadership decides that the company should explore AI or GenAI, the natural next step is to launch a proof of concept. However, before jumping into implementation, it is worth taking a step back and preparing carefully.

Starting a proof of concept at a large company

At a large corporation, it's common for a member of the senior leadership (a CEO, a board member, a CPO, etc.) to decide that the company should start adopting ML, GenAI, or something else because everybody around is telling them that it's a very important opportunity that the company can't miss. There's nothing new here – in recent decades, the same story has played out multiple times with other new technologies.

You may be very keen on starting to develop an AI solution. You immediately want to call a meeting with your team and start planning the launch. But don't jump too soon. Before you begin implementing AI within your organization, do the following:

- **Understand your stakeholders and what they really want**: Remember that talking to your stakeholders is like interviewing your users. They might tell you what you want to hear, and not what they really care about. You can read more about this in the brilliant book *The Mom Test: How to Talk to Customers & Learn if Your Business is a Good Idea When Everyone is Lying to You* by Rob Fitzpatrick.
  Here's a very simple example: you might be told, "We want to use GenAI to serve our users and make the world a better place," but what they mean is, "Right now, we urgently need to demonstrate that we're not behind the GenAI wave, and we need to show at least one working use case before the next investor call." These statements don't necessarily contradict each other, but they are still quite different. Your job is to

find this out and align short-term needs with the long-term roadmap and product strategy.

- **Spend time with your users and understand their needs**: If, for example, you're developing an enterprise assistant (that's where most GenAI use cases start), I'd strongly recommend spending some time in the field, looking at what the actual work involves, trying to grasp the details of business logic, and identifying the core problem. For example, if you are developing an agent to automate support operations, spend some time in the call center and get an idea of what support engineers are doing on a regular basis, what the challenges of their daily routines are, what tools they use, and so on.
- **Question all assumptions**: There's a famous Russian proverb, "Trust but verify." People might misunderstand what you need and misguide you unintentionally. For example, in my more than a decade of working on ML projects with dozens of teams and companies, I have only heard a few times that the data is not in good shape. In most cases, I was told that clean and high-quality data was available, and we could start developing a model right away. As you can guess, I have never (ever!) seen a dataset that is clean and ready to use for starting ML development.
- **Put together a short document that summarizes all your preparation work**: Invest your time in this document. Don't make it too long; try to keep it concise and remove unnecessary details. Share this document with your key stakeholders and your team. Arrange a few meetings to work on the document and challenge the key assumptions. Writing a document helps to refine your thoughts, while giving time for other people to think about it. Face-to-face meetings and conversations are typically much more productive when people have seen the document before and are given room and time to think and process key assumptions and suggestions. The famous writing culture of Amazon is a good example of such an approach (you can find one example describing it here: `https://justingarrison.com/blog/2021-03-15-the-document-culture-of-amazon/`).
- **Narrow down the scope and push back on excessive requirements**: Focus on evaluating the new technology, understanding its limitations and opportunities. For example, sometimes when people start with a proof of concept, they aim for everything: a high-quality solution, low latency, scalable and performant architecture, and low cost of ownership, all at the same time. Unfortunately, that typically only complicates things and increases the chances of failure. When you start to build with a new technology such as GenAI, your first goal should be to verify the business feasibility. When you've demonstrated that it solves some important problem, you can start working on reducing costs and improving throughput and scalability. Of course,

you should take some production requirements into account and not design prototypes that would never go to production, but don't become too constrained by such non-functional requirements. LLM inference costs have been declining almost 10x per year over the last few years (`https://a16z.com/llmflation-llm-inference-cost/`). At the same time, when you know what you need to improve, engineers can typically solve such a problem. Just decompose the original problem into pieces, split the development into different phases, and solve the original problem step by step.

- **Identify the most important problem, and focus on solving it first**: This is related to the preceding point, but it's important to emphasize it. Your users might face different problems, and all of them might be ideal to solve. Your challenge as a product or technical leader is to find the core problem, the so-called "user's pain point," something that is very critical and for which they'd be willing to pay for the problem to be solved. If you want to read more about capturing customers' needs to set your innovations for success, I'd suggest starting with the book *Jobs to Be Done: Theory to Practice* by Anthony Ulwick.
  Rule #1 from the famous *Rules of Machine Learning* paper (first published in 2017) by Martin Zinkevich is: "Don't be afraid to launch a product without machine learning." These days, we can rephrase it as follows: "Don't be afraid to launch without GenAI!"
- **Make it very clear what success looks like**: My favorite question to ask businesses is: "Let's imagine you had a magic black box that can do the desired predictions. How exactly would it change your life?" We will talk about various aspects of measuring success, such as A/B testing in a later chapter, but the crucial thing is to have an open conversation about how to define success and whether it's measurable, as well as estimating the potential business impact.
- **Don't forget about the data**: I'll mention this numerous times: data is crucial for any AI development, and GenAI is no exception. You need a dataset at least for the evaluation of your prototype. In *Chapter 2*, we'll talk about evaluation and data collection strategies. Be prepared to start with data collection and data cleaning and invest your resources in data cleaning and preparation.
- **Keep your stakeholders up to date on your progress and slowdowns**: This might sound banal and obvious. But I've often seen people trying very hard to solve the problem, becoming overwhelmed with the amount of work, and, despite their best intentions, not paying enough attention to keeping key stakeholders aligned. Sometimes they just don't have time for it, sometimes they forget, and sometimes they assume that senior leadership shouldn't be bothered.

> **Note**
>
> You cannot spend too much time with your users and stakeholders. Keep narrowing down the key problem you're solving and asking difficult questions about requirements.

I recommend starting with short status updates sent weekly by email (you can always add a note that recipients can inform you if they don't want to get these status updates). AI adoption is an interesting topic for many people, and you will make many important discoveries and learnings that might be beneficial for your colleagues. Hence, think about organizing knowledge sessions where you can share your findings and be very open about your difficulties. From my experience, such transparency helps to educate your leadership, and at the end of the day, it helps you to make them understand why your project might take longer than expected.

Starting a proof of concept as a start-up

You've realized that there's a window of opportunity, and you decide to start a start-up. Just to make it clear, I'm not talking about heavy-tech start-ups that invest deeply in research. A very famous example is Snowflake (a US company that developed a scalable and fast database for analytics at scale). The company was launched in July 2012, and they released their first version of the database in June 2015 (`https://en.wikipedia.org/wiki/Snowflake_Inc`). In other words, it took them three years of research, development, and experimentation to build the great product, but the founders came from Oracle (another well-established database company) and had a very good understanding of the market and the technology. My point is, when you launch a start-up because you see a window of opportunity and a shifting market landscape, your priority should be finding your users and achieving product-market fit. Focus on staying agile and experimenting quickly with the technology. Don't be afraid of using heuristics, even many *what-if* cycles, simple business rules, or regular expressions, and manual work behind the scenes in the early stages.

That means your early products will likely be rough around the edges, a bit hacky, with imperfect architectures that eventually break down. You will probably endure the painful process of rewriting your software as you grow. It is tough, no doubt, but it also means you have survived long enough to reach that stage, and, most importantly, you have found product-market fit.

The truth is, most tech start-ups in the consumer or B2B space don't have good datasets, and they don't have enough capital to conduct breakthrough research. Your goal is to take an existing new technology and be the first to find a way to apply it to a large-enough market. I've often seen founding engineers spending too much time discussing the best architectures for handling millions of users when they have zero or only a dozen users. Software design is all about trade-offs (as we will repeat multiple times across this book), and in many cases (especially in the early days of your start-up), you can't make good choices because you don't know your exact requirements yet. That's because you haven't found your users! Therefore, build fast, don't be afraid of quick hacks, and go find users who are so keen on a specific problem being solved that they are willing to pay you for even a not-polished solution.

Most of the things we've mentioned in this section apply to ML technologies, or any new technology in general. But what has actually changed in product development as a result of GenAI?

What GenAI has changed

Now, let's discuss what GenAI has changed so far in terms of engineering work and product development:

- **The time to market for developing a prototype has significantly decreased**: Many tasks (such as classification, entity extraction, image understanding, etc.) that required a separate ML model previously can now be solved with a single call to an LLM. In other words, many use cases that previously required developing a custom ML model can now be solved with a foundational model at the **state-of-the-art** (**SOTA**) level. In many cases, developing a GenAI agent is similar to developing an application. All you will be doing is integrating multiple APIs (with one key distinction regarding the need of extensive evaluation, which we will cover in *Chapter 2*). This means you can develop a prototype for a given use case within weeks, not months as before.
- **Infrastructure costs for developers of consumer-facing applications are significantly lower**: In most cases, you don't need to train or fine-tune your own LLMs. You will be stitching together a few APIs, and the initial infrastructure costs of developing such a prototype are very low since you don't need to invest in any hardware or buy any licenses. To a certain extent, model providers have already made huge upfront investments to train powerful models that can solve complex tasks.

> **Note**
>
> You might end up purchasing your own hardware and hosting your own models. But in most cases, try to start small and evaluate the potential of the technology. If the only use case you have found across your organization requires fine-tuning, hosting, or even training your own LLM, you might be overlooking some opportunities. Try to start small, gain some experience and expertise, get first wins, and scale afterward.

- **You can start with significantly smaller datasets than was previously possible**: Note that I am not saying that you *don't need any datasets*. We will talk more about this in *Chapter 2*, but looking ahead, you can start working on your use case with a validation dataset that contains only 40–50 examples (and in most cases, you won't need any training data).
- **You need a smaller team**: On top of GenAI decreasing the time to market to develop prototypes, there's a lot of evidence that GenAI boosts engineering productivity in general (`https://www.anthropic.com/research/labor-market-impacts`, `https://resources.anthropic.com/2026-agentic-coding-trends-report`, `https://www.bcg.com/publications/2026/how-ai-is-paying-off-in-the-tech-function`), and there are a lot of tools that make it easier to develop prototypes, such as Cursor and Claude Code. All of this together makes it easier to develop GenAI prototypes and bring them to production with a smaller engineering team than was required before.
- **The fear of missing out (FOMO) is huge**: Nobody can reliably predict what will happen in the coming years, but there are many predictions that some industries might be significantly disrupted. Gartner predicts that the global GDP "could drive a 7% (or almost $7 trillion) increase in global GDP and lift productivity growth by 1.5 percentage points over a 10-year period" (`https://www.goldmansachs.com/insights/articles/generative-ai-could-raise-global-gdp-by-7-percent`), and GenAI has already positively influenced labor productivity across many industries, such as software development, healthcare, and finance (`https://www.stlouisfed.org/on-the-economy/2025/nov/state-generative-ai-adoption-2025`). These predictions are based on an extrapolation of current progress.

There are several key factors behind the rapid progress of modern AI. We have witnessed a lot of great breakthroughs in the past few years, such as the following:

- More data and large models mean better models (`https://arxiv.org/abs/2211.04325`, `openai.com/index/scaling-laws-for-neural-language-models`)
- Emergent capabilities of LLMs that can solve tasks that they were not trained for (`https://arxiv.org/abs/2206.07682`, `https://blog.premai.io/emergence-capabilities-of-llms/`)
- Progress in specialized hardware, such as GPUs and custom chips (`https://blogs.nvidia.com/blog/ai-scaling-laws/`, `https://arxiv.org/abs/2409.03384`)
- Big progress in LLM reasoning based on reinforcement learning and synthetic data (`https://arxiv.org/abs/2501.12948`, `https://arxiv.org/abs/2406.14532`)

If progress continues at the current pace, we might see very powerful reasoning models in the coming years. That is what drives a lot of FOMO, since many companies and leaders have concerns about jumping too late into the race. These expectations extrapolate a trend over a relatively short period of time (3–4 years). An opposite view exists that represents skeptics about the rapid progress of GenAI. Yes, we have observed unexpected breakthroughs over the last few years, but does this guarantee that the progress will continue at the same scale? Opponents mention the limitations of Transformer architecture and the lack of additional data (almost all data available has already been consumed for training).

We've already observed some over-hyped predictions. For example, in 2017, comScore predicted that by 2020, half of all searches would be conducted via voice. In 2016, Gartner predicted that by 2020, the average person would have more conversations with bots than with their spouse.

> **Note**
>
> Many predictions around GenAI are based on the assumption that a relatively short trend of recent discoveries will continue over the coming years. Techno-optimists hope that's the case, but there are still a lot of challenges to be solved, and extrapolating short trends might easily lead to mistakes.

We don't know what predictions will come true. While it might be interesting to form your own opinion, it's not that important to estimate the probability of whether these predictions will come true. For readers familiar with Bayesian probability interpretation, it's either true or false; there's nothing in between. If these predictions are true, the consequences for your company or your market might be enormous. Clayton Christensen explains this very well in his book *The Innovator's Dilemma*.

> **Note**
>
> Clayton Christensen, in his book *The Innovator's Dilemma*, proposed the term *market disruption*, which has become highly popular. Market disruption happens when something (for example, a new technology) drastically changes how a particular industry operates. In such cases, often a smaller company with fewer resources can successfully challenge established, mature businesses because initially, the market for a new technology is small and ignored by large players (for example, the new tech might not be good enough for a broad market). But when the tech improves, suddenly new players who have focused on niche cases get a strong competitive advantage.

Hence, many corporate leaders have decided to invest in GenAI in case the disruption arrives, and your role as a technical leader is to assist them as best as you can. As scientists know very well, negative results are as good as positive outcomes since they provide valuable feedback that you can use for further research. Hence, even if you're skeptical, take it as a chance to learn and evaluate a new technology.

We have discussed how GenAI has changed product development, as well as attitudes toward the current hype. Now, let's look into some aspects of an ML model development life cycle and the importance of labeled data for any AI development.

We will discuss details that sometimes are misinterpreted by business leaders and create tension between them and engineering leaders. This should help the former to better understand the complexity of developing AI solutions.

The reality of developing AI products

I started my career in data analytics and forecasting in retail, analytics, and finance. After spending almost 10 years in these industries, I switched to tech and started to work on local search. I clearly remember my frustration with engineers not being able to fix "simple" bugs in search behavior, as well as the long iteration cycles that required the collection of data and running of online experiments. Since then, I've seen the same frustration shared by many business leaders who are dealing with AI-based products.

First, ML models are optimized for an average performance, and you can't guarantee their 100% accuracy. This means there would always be edge cases in which an ML model fails to give a correct answer. When we use ML solutions to automate business processes, we should evaluate the cost of error (or, in other words, the cost of an ML model giving a wrong prediction in a specific case) and keep humans in the loop for appeals. Let us look at a simple example. Imagine we're developing a GenAI assistant to help employees of an insurance company validate claims. To give you a heads-up, it's a binary classification problem, and we'll talk in more detail about how to measure a model's performance in such a case in *Chapter 2*. But let's see what can happen when an AI agent approves or denies the claim:

- **A GenAI agent approves the claim**: We expect the agent to be mostly correct (i.e., it approves valid claims along with a small number of claims that should not be approved). As long as the accuracy is high enough on average, it's OK, with one small caveat—we might want to add a human review for claims above a certain threshold (since 1% of approved claims might account for 10% or more payouts).
- **A GenAI agent denies the claim**: 1 out of 1,000 valid claims is denied payment; this can pose a problem in this case.

If an insured individual gets a payment they were not entitled to, that's an expense for the insurance company. Such expenses can be ignored as long as the average loss is small relative to the revenue. But when an insured individual is denied a payment that they were entitled to, it's a significant problem. When we design the automation, we should give customers an opportunity to easily appeal the case (and for it to be reviewed by a human) or introduce a human review (depending on the business requirements). AI cares about expected outcomes and tends to ignore edge cases as long as, on average, performance is high enough, but do not forget that there are real people behind these edge failures. We'll talk in more detail about AI fairness in *Chapter 7*.

Second, you'll experience obvious cases when your AI-based solution fails. In traditional software, we call such a situation a bug.

> **Note**
>
> There's no software without bugs. Failures and mistakes will always happen. Decreasing the rate of failures requires you to heavily invest in testing, development, and improving processes across your organization. Throughout this book, we'll be discussing this in more detail.
>
> But you should be prepared for bugs and failures. Even in such a critical industry as aviation, bugs occur. They happen rarely due to the high cost of developing this type of software. Your goal is not bug-free software, but to meet a reasonable level of acceptable failures and performance that helps your business thrive.

Typically, engineers can debug the software, find the reason for the problem, and fix it, and you'll never see the problem again (assuming you have good tests, of course). But when you have an ML model behind your product, it becomes almost impossible to fix one simple bug. We'll discuss some ways to add a backdoor for quick fixes for GenAI use cases in *Chapter 4*. But in general, if your model answers poorly to one specific question, despite it seeming obvious to fix, it requires a lot of effort.

The typical process of developing an AI-based solution looks like this:

1. Collect a labeled dataset—one that has examples of inputs and desired outputs.
2. Come up with hypotheses of how the model can be improved and implement them.
3. Run offline experiments and evaluations. Offline experiments entail running evaluations without testing on real users, but using a labeled dataset instead. We'll dive deeper into the topic of evaluation in *Chapter 2*.
4. Prepare for production implementation.
5. Deploy.
6. Test your solution with actual users (more about this in *Chapter 10*).

Each time you want to change the behavior of your model (if it's not a change in business logic that wraps the model's outputs), you need to go through the whole cycle, which might take up quite some time. More than that, it's not like you can instruct the model, "Do this in this specific case"; you will need to collect an updated dataset that represents the general issues you're experiencing, and only then re-train your model.

As you might have inferred from this discussion, a labeled dataset is crucial for the success of an AI-based solution. AI doesn't exist without the data, and you can't develop AI-based software without having a good labeled dataset.

> **Note**
>
> The **garbage in, garbage out** (**GIGO**) concept in AI (and computer science in general) refers to the fact that poor-quality input or data used to train a model results in the same poor-quality output (or model trained); see `https://en.wikipedia.org/wiki/Garbage_in,_garbage_out`.

In many cases, business leaders believe that they have good data since they've been investing in data warehouses, data collection, and things like that for at least a decade now. Unfortunately, that's very often not the case. Imagine you want to use GenAI to help your customer support engineers make decisions and even generate some clicks or invocations in internal systems. You might quickly realize that the data you have in the support case represents only the final resolution, but not the initial state order at the time the support engineer was looking at it and making a decision. Moreover, you don't collect data on which entities were clicked and user engagement, which were your success criteria initially; this means there's no data for a model to train on!

> **Note**
>
> In ML, the data used to train the model should be similar to the data available at prediction time. For example, temperature is a powerful predictor of ice cream sales, but we should not use the temperature on a given day as a predictor, but a weather forecast for that day available at the moment of forecasting. Read more at `https://www.evidentlyai.com/ml-in-production/data-drift`.

Last but not least, developing and deploying AI-based solutions requires a certain amount of investment into processes and tools for engineers. Sometimes you see a brilliant proof of concept and a demo, and you feel like deploying it immediately, but there's a long way until you have a production-ready application. We'll discuss the reasons for that in *Chapter 4*.

Let's summarize:

- ML models are optimized for average performance, and you need to take this into account when designing business processes. Always assume that in a particular case, you might get wrong predictions from the model.
- Development cycles in ML/AI might be longer than in classical B2C software development. Fixing a "bug" in performance is difficult, and it might require following the full cycle of re-training the model.
- Data is key, and most probably, additional investments in data labeling would be needed. Remember, "garbage in, garbage out."
- Engineers need to invest in the tooling and address the technical debt related to moving a shiny prototype to production.

We have discussed some aspects of ML model development, the importance of appropriate tooling, and investing in collecting, labeling, and cleaning the data. Now, let's look into some common misconceptions that businesses often have around AI development.

Misconceptions when developing AI products

Business leaders hear about AI being great from everywhere, and while it increases adoption, it also leads to certain misconceptions and mismatched expectations. This section should help business leaders to understand slightly better what they should expect, and at the same time, it should help engineers to better understand the business leaders' viewpoint. Once both sides are communicating openly about the issues, it helps to dramatically increase the success rate of any projects. Let's look at some common mistakes:

- **Assuming you don't need any labeled data anymore because foundational models are so powerful and can perform zero-shot learning**: As we will see in *Chapter 2*, you still need evaluation datasets, and it's a critical component before going to production.

  > **Note**
  >
  > GenAI allows you to build powerful AI-enabled applications with a smaller labeled dataset than before. But a clean and well-prepared dataset is still a prerequisite to almost any successful GenAI implementation.

- **Not investing in content creation and data cleaning**: This emphasizes the previous point. You might honestly believe that you have a clean dataset, but that's unlikely since, with GenAI, you will come across scenarios that you might not have considered. When planning your project, think about adding some **subject matter experts (SMEs)** to the team who will help with data labeling. Unfortunately, I've seen too often GenAI initiatives where millions of dollars and hundreds of days of engineering work were invested, but it was impossible to get an SME for a data-labeling task for a few weeks full-time.
- **Trusting an LLM blindly and not investing in evaluation**: I promise this is the last time I will talk about evaluation in this chapter! First, don't assume LLMs are good just because everybody is talking about them. I've seen LLMs struggle even with relatively simple classification problems. By struggle, I don't mean they ultimately failed at the task. The foundational model was able to solve the problem in general; it's just that it required a few attempts at prompting. Second, start your proof of concept with an evaluation pipeline. Rule #2 from Martin Zinkevich is: "First, design and implement metrics." Do this even before you have started with ML or GenAI! I've quite often seen project plans as follows:
  - **Weeks 1–6**: Developing a solution
  - **Week 7**: Evaluation
  - **Weeks 8–9**: Deploying to production

  I would recommend having the evaluation phase as early as possible; at least, start defining success metrics, develop an evaluation pipeline, and run it against your baseline. If you don't have an evaluation pipeline from the very beginning, you can't measure how well you're doing.

- **Thinking that a prototype is all it takes**: GenAI models demonstrate great performance on tasks such as "give me a summary of the document" or "rewrite this email." Sometimes it feels almost like magic, and it might create an illusion that it would work well on any task. The truth is, adopting a solution to your domain and your specifics still requires complex workflows and a lot of experimentation. An impressive prototype typically only opens the door to start adopting GenAI; it will take more effort to build a stable solution that can be safely deployed to your users.
- **Assuming GenAI is cheap**: LLMs cost a few dollars per million tokens. This may not sound like a lot, but just imagine how many emails you can generate for $100! But industrial use cases often require complex agentic workflows that go beyond a single text prompt sent to an LLM. We send more and more data, including multimodal inputs, to GenAI, and we start using more complex and expensive reasoning models, such as Gemini Pro or GPT-5. Agentic workflows might inflate the costs of a single request by 10 times or even more. In addition to the cost of querying an LLM, you need to prepare your data and structure and index it in the right way; this all requires running servers that store your indexes and serve your queries.
- **Assuming GenAI is expensive**: This might sound contradictory to the preceding statement, but as usual, it all depends on the context. Even if you believe that GenAI is expensive, it shouldn't stop you from trying it out! Keep in mind that the costs of serving LLMs are going down fast. Focus on the business value first, and once you've proven the business value, you can optimize the solution and drive the costs down. Plus, you can expect costs per token to go down further.
- **Not planning for the maintenance of an application**: This book is about how to move your application from sandbox to production. In many cases, it is hard. Don't become too overexcited by a brilliant demo; keep in mind that there's a long way to go before you can safely put this application in front of your users. At the same time, as usual, there's another side to the coin. Don't be afraid to run a quick test by putting an alpha version in front of a small number of users willing to test it, but be transparent from the very beginning about the risks and limitations related to it.
- **Leaning on "best practices" too much**: As an expert who has spent quite a few years in engineering consulting, I love it when people ask for best practices, since that's what I'm paid for. But software engineering is all about trade-offs. The biggest challenges my teams and I have faced have rarely been related to technical difficulties themselves. In most cases, the challenge was in gathering clear requirements.
- **Trying to automate processes as is and aiming for a perfect outcome**: Before automating any process, make sure it actually makes sense in its current form. If a process is messy, inconsistent, or overly complicated, automation will simply amplify

the existing problems instead of solving them. Focus on the areas where automation or GenAI can genuinely add value, especially for repetitive or high-impact tasks. Be ready to simplify or refine the process first; automation works best when things are clean and well defined. Also, not every problem needs a complex technical solution. Sometimes, a small change to the UX or workflow can achieve the same result much more easily than tweaking an AI model or backend system.

If I could summarize this section in one sentence, I'd say "keep it simple." We will talk about this more in *Chapter 4*, but for now, keep in mind that when you start building a new product, you should not overengineer, and you should start by establishing a simple baseline for future AI enhancements. Focus on business needs and go to market, and make sure that the business and engineering parts of your organization are well aligned, speak the same language, and understand each other's needs and challenges. Too often, the business and engineers are very skilled folks who just don't really get each other, and it leads to wrong incentives, misinterpreted requirements, and lost focus.

Summary

In this chapter, we began with a discussion on the importance of starting with an understanding of the problem to be solved before jumping into technical implementation, especially in the context of GenAI. Successful AI prototypes, whether in start-ups or large corporations, share similarities with starting a business: a focus on asking difficult questions and clearly defining the problem.

Then we looked into three key scenarios where AI would work well: in mature products with complex heuristics that are difficult to maintain, in products scaled to millions of users where even tiny improvements yield significant returns, and when new technology enables previously infeasible solutions, thereby changing the market landscape.

For large companies, we looked into the importance of understanding stakeholder needs, spending time with users, questioning assumptions, documenting preparation work, narrowing the scope, and focusing on the most important problem. We also stressed the importance of clear success metrics, data, and consistent stakeholder communication.

For start-ups, we discussed the importance of prioritizing finding users and product-market fit, being agile, and experimenting quickly with technology, even if it means starting with "hacky" solutions. GenAI has significantly decreased the time to market for prototypes, lowered infrastructure costs, reduced the need for large datasets, and enabled smaller teams.

Then we looked into common mistakes, such as assuming no labeled data is needed, neglecting content creation and data cleaning, blindly trusting LLMs without evaluation, believing a prototype is sufficient, and misjudging the cost of GenAI.

In sum, we emphasized that ML models are optimized for average performance, development cycles can be longer, data is crucial, and investment in tooling and processes is necessary for production-ready applications.

In the next chapter, we'll talk about the ML development life cycle, the importance of evaluation, and how to implement proper evaluation routines for your GenAI applications.

> **Note**
>
> The three key outcomes to remember are as follows:
>
> - Always start with business requirements and scope the problem you're solving. Getting requirements right is the biggest challenge in software engineering, not using the cool technology itself.
> - Do not overengineer, especially at the beginning. Focus on iterating quickly and validating users' needs and the feasibility of what you're building. Do not be afraid of using quick workarounds or hacks when developing the MVP.
> - GenAI has significantly decreased the time to market, but there's a long path from an impressive prototype to a production-ready solution since prototypes ignore edge cases and complex business requirements.

Further reading

- Cagan, M. *Inspired: How to Create Tech Products Customers Love.* John Wiley & Sons
- Thiel, P., Masters, B. *Zero to One: Notes on Startups, or How to Build the Future.* Crown Currency
- Fitzpatrick, R. *The Mom Test: How to Talk to Customers & Learn If Your Business is a Good Idea When Everyone is Lying to You.* Robfitz Ltd
- Ulwick, A. W. *Jobs to Be Done: Theory to Practice.* Idea Bite Press, 2016
- Zinkevich, M. *Rules of Machine Learning: In: Google for Developers.* `https://developers.google.com/machine-learning/guides/rules-of-ml`
- Christensen, C. *The Innovator's Dilemma: When New Technologies Cause Great Firms to Fail.* Harvard Business Review Press

2

Evaluation

Evaluation is often overlooked, both on the business and engineering sides of an organization, when developing and rolling out GenAI solutions. Evaluation helps you better understand the actual performance of your solution before you put it in front of users, prevents poor performance in production, and allows you to reliably improve the quality of an existing **machine learning** (**ML**) solution. Product development teams, however, tend to avoid investing effort in collecting labeled datasets (examples of input and expected outputs) and test only for a few randomly selected sample inputs.

Moreover, most of these systems generate open-ended outputs such as text, audio, and video. If we were to task the system to answer a multiple-choice question, it would only pick one option, which makes it easy to check the accuracy of the response. But if we task a system to write an email, summarize a text, or draw an image, many different outputs would be correct. This means it would be extremely difficult to compare the generated output with an expected one to reason about the quality.

In this chapter, we will discuss basic approaches to address evaluation challenges; we will also share some additional reading material at the end of this chapter. We will start with the basic challenge of ML called generalization, and see why evaluation is a core part of any ML development. We will explore some fundamental examples of evaluation metrics and how evaluation approaches have evolved in the GenAI era. We will conclude by looking at some examples of more complex evaluation scenarios, such as human-in-the-loop and evaluating RAG pipelines.

In this chapter, we'll be covering the following topics:

- Evaluating GenAI applications
- Metrics-based evaluation
- Comparing texts

- Using an LLM as a judge
- Human-in-the-loop
- More complex evaluation scenarios

Evaluating GenAI applications

Evaluation in ML and AI involves multiple dimensions, including:

- Collecting high-quality labeled datasets that are useful for training a model
- Predicting the model's performance on the new, unseen data
- Comparing expected and predicted outputs in complex scenarios and compressing such a comparison into a single numerical value

We'll start by discussing **generalization**, which is the key challenge in ML, then move on to why evaluation is a step of any ML development, and how the ML development lifecycle is different from "classical" application development.

Generalization in ML

The key idea behind ML is to collect a labeled dataset and use it to train a model that would perform well not only on that particular dataset, but on new, unseen data. The same is true for evaluation. When evaluating ML models, we don't want to compute how well our model performs on the evaluation dataset, but we need to estimate how well it would perform on new data – that is, get an unbiased estimate of how well our model will perform on new, real-world data it hasn't encountered during training. When evaluating ML models, the train-test split is a fundamental and critical procedure.

> **Note**
>
> Generalization is an ML model's ability to perform well on new, previously unseen data after being trained on a specific (labeled) dataset. The ultimate goal of building an ML model is to learn patterns from labeled data and apply them to new examples.

ML is an experimental field, and that's why it depends on evaluations so much. So, what does experimenting in ML look like? We iterate over different ML model architectures, or, in the case of GenAI, different prompts, agentic pipelines' architectures, and foundational models, and estimate their performance based on our test dataset using a selected metric. By running such experiments multiple times and adding more and more details to our model, we run the risk of **overfitting**: we start performing very well on our test dataset, but fail on unseen data.

> **Note**
>
> Overfitting in ML is a phenomenon where a model learns the training data too well, including its noise, outliers, and irrelevant details. This results in a model that performs exceptionally well on the data it was trained on but performs poorly on new, unseen data.

Two things happen when we overfit. First, we create a highly complex model that memorizes the test dataset and incorporates too many details from it instead of learning generalizable patterns. And second, our evaluation results don't represent the performance of the model on the new, unseen data (which is our ultimate goal). We may get good evaluation metrics, but when we release the model, it performs poorly.

Let's take a simple example. Imagine we're working on a question-answering assistant, and we have 20–30 examples in our evaluation dataset. We start evaluating the quality and perform an error analysis. If we see poor performance on these examples, we continue adding new hints to our prompts to mitigate these errors. If we continue such interactions for too long, we will incorporate, or *leak*, all the details from our training examples into the prompt (or, in other words, into the AI system we're evaluating). Let me exaggerate to an extreme. Imagine what happens if you have added all your 20 evaluation examples to the prompt as few-shot examples. You wouldn't do that, would you? But something similar happens when you keep iterating over the prompt and adding more and more nuanced instructions. You'll report high accuracy to the business, but once you deploy the assistant, users will start asking slightly different questions, and the pipeline will fail because there's too much noise and irrelevant instructions in our prompts.

One of the ways to prevent this is to randomly split our evaluation data into training, testing, and validation datasets, which is typically what we do in ML:

- Entities used to train a model go into the **training set**. In the GenAI context, entities used as few-shot examples in your prompts should be treated as a training set and be excluded from the validation set. Unfortunately, I've seen engineers ignoring this far too many times, and adding a few-shot examples directly from the validation set when working on pipeline improvements.
- A **validation set** is a part of your labeled dataset that you use to evaluate the performance of your model during hyperparameter tuning. What are **hyperparameters**? If you think about a classical ML model, it has model weights that are learned during the training process. You also choose a specific model's architecture (for example, a specific neural net architecture, or choose deep learning versus gradient

boosting) and other hyperparameters such as the number of layers, the number of epochs, or batch size, and so on. These parameters are under your control, and you can train many models and compare their performance while searching for the best combination of such hyperparameters. In the context of GenAI, you experiment with different prompts, prompting techniques, agentic architectures, and inference parameters such as `temperature` or `max_output_tokens`.

> **Note**
>
> **Hyperparameter tuning**, also known as **hyperparameter optimization**, is the process of finding the optimal set of hyperparameters for an ML model to achieve the best possible performance on a given task. Hyperparameters are external configuration variables that are set before the training process begins, unlike model parameters, which are learned during the training process.

- A **testing set** (or **holdout set**) contains examples reserved for the final, unbiased evaluation of the chosen model and its hyperparameters. It's like the final, untouched exam that helps you estimate the performance of the solution.

In classic ML, common split ratios (`training:validation:testing`) are 80:10:10, 80:15:5, and 90:5:5. In other words, a vast majority of labeled examples go to the training subset. In GenAI, it's quite different since we don't really train the model; hence, only a small subset (if any) of labeled examples would go into the training subset. Common splits would be 5:55:40, 5:45:45, and 5:60:35. One of the key lessons for you should be to keep a number of examples for the final evaluation of your solution before the release to estimate the performance. Otherwise, if you continue iterating and evaluating your system on a small dataset of examples, you might overfit it and experience poor performance in production.

> **Note**
>
> **Data leakage** occurs when information from outside the training dataset is inadvertently or improperly used to create or evaluate a model, leading to an overly optimistic and misleading assessment of the model's performance. One example of data leakage is **train/test contamination** when information from the testing set leaks into the training data and training process during preprocessing steps and the train/test split.

There is one thing we should always remember when implementing the train/test split: we mentioned that it should be performed randomly. This is true, but there is one caveat. We should prevent any data leakage when performing a split. As mentioned, data leakage happens when some information from the testing set makes it into the training dataset, and this can also happen during the train/test split step. For example, a medical ML model was trained on X-ray scans of a patient, but some patients had multiple scans, and this caused leakage since the dataset was split into training and testing pieces (read more at the systematic study: `https://www.nature.com/articles/s41467-024-46150-w`). Since the same scan from the same patients was both in the training dataset and the evaluation dataset, the model "saw" the actual diagnosis of a given patient during the training phase. It allowed it to memorize the right diagnosis for each patient instead of actually learning what patterns are related to which diagnosis. As a result, the researchers had a good performance during evaluation, but the model failed in production. Let's see what happens when you split a dataset randomly:

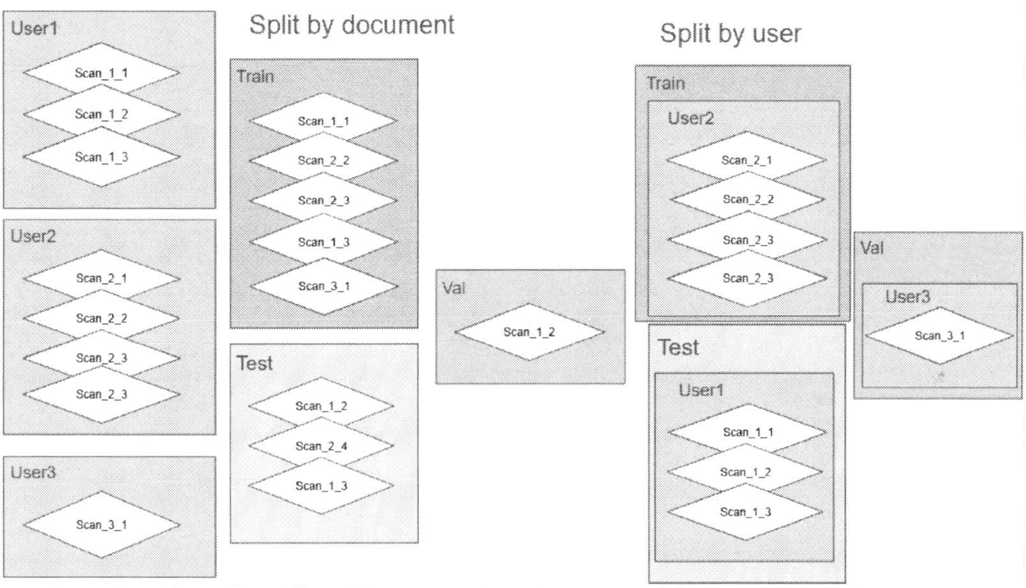

Figure 2.1 – Example of splitting the original training set into train-test-eval parts

Scans from one user might be included in the training set and the testing set, which means that the model will see labels for this user during training (the same that we'll evaluate later). That means, it might just memorize specific examples instead of learning actual patterns in the data. So, how should we split the dataset? It's illustrated in the right part of the diagram. We should perform a random split based on `user_id`, which means, in our specific examples, scans from one user are only in the training, testing, or validation sets (otherwise, a model).

Now, let's take a look at how we can incorporate constant evaluation in our development process.

ML development lifecycle

AI development is an iterative process that includes a lot of experimentation. You start by scoping a problem and collecting a labeled dataset. After that, you iterate over a few hypotheses and try different modeling algorithms to train various versions of the model in order to find a good-performing one. During these iterations, you evaluate the model's performance through offline experiments or on historical data using some metrics that are only a proxy for business objectives. Once you have a winning candidate (the model that achieves the desired offline performance or the one that performs better than the previous version), you prepare your model for deployment and run an online experiment.

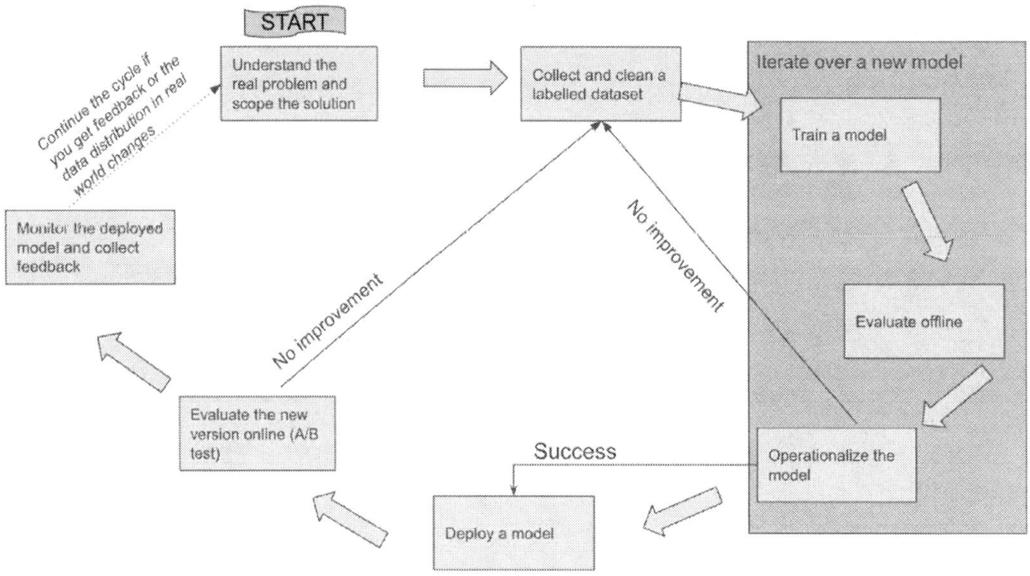

Figure 2.2 – ML development lifecycle

The preceding diagram illustrates two important distinctions of ML development. First, ML development is an iterative process that relies on many experiments, some of which fail. Second, you start your iterations on static data in a simulated and controlled environment (estimating performance on a test subset of your labeled dataset), and only after that, you continue with online experiments. Offline experiments are relatively cheap and fast to conduct, and they have a low associated risk since you don't put anything in front of the user. You need to carefully design how your experiment is set up, though: how your dataset looks, what your labels are, what metrics you choose, and how you perform a train/test split.

> **Note**
>
> **Offline experiments**, or **static evaluation**, in ML refers to evaluating a newly developed model on historical datasets using various metrics. After you've selected a winning candidate, you continue with **online experiments**, or **A/B testing**, by exposing your new version of the model to a subset of real users and measuring actual performance in real-time based on real users' interactions.

In this chapter, we'll focus on offline experiments, and in *Chapter 10*, we'll discuss online experiments or A/B testing. It's important to keep in mind, though, that when thinking about evaluation strategies, you need to think about both aspects. And in general, to improve any complex system or solution, you need to make your progress *measurable*, which means you need to invent a metric that you'll use to track your effort. That's why *scope* in *Figure 2.2* can mean *invent a metric and agree to use it as a baseline*. When you have a metric, you can iteratively improve, and you transform a problem into an engineering one. If you don't have a metric, it will be very difficult to begin with engineering work. And it's difficult to find an ideal fit-them-all metric. In practice, teams pick a metric based on business reasons, improve on it, and then switch to another metric. This means you need to change your labeled dataset and evaluation pipeline regularly. For example, let's look at a potential metric evolution for a team working on product recommendations at the checkout page for an e-commerce site:

1. First, you want clicks that lead to potential sales, so your business metric is click-through-rate, and you train an ML model that is an ML binary classifier with a focus on precision and recall (you predict a probability of a user clicking on an item).
2. Then, you realize that now it's time to focus on the relevancy of items displayed, so you want the top five items (that fit into the first screen without scrolling) to be highly relevant, and you train a ranking model with a focus on *precision@5* (we will introduce this metric in more detail in the next section).
3. As the business evolves, you start focusing on more sophisticated aspects such as trust and safety of your recommendations (for example, you don't recommend any SKUs that might offend a user), revenue per customer, or customers' lifetime value. And each time, you'll be inventing a proxy metric for the business metric, such as revenue, that can be used to evaluate the model.

Metrics-based evaluation

Before we start with the discussion on **metrics-based evaluation**, there are two important comments to be made. First, there is a clear difference between the business metrics and the metrics we use to optimize ML models. For example, the business is typically interested in metrics such as revenue per user, churn rate, and so on. In *Chapter 10*, we will see how we can run online experiments that are targeted more closely at such business metrics. However, we can't train an ML model using these metrics. Hence, we look for proxies such as precision and recall for classification tasks and **root mean square error** (**RMSE**) for regression tasks (there are many more complex metrics, though). In other words, in ML we build a model of the physical world (hence, the word ML model). By definition, such a model is a simplification of the world (and the given domain), and a chosen metric is part of it.

Second, sometimes teams try to mimic the complexity of the physical world by creating many different metrics. Of course, when you train a model, you optimize only for a single one (that has certain mathematical properties, depending on the ML algorithm you use). But when you compare multiple versions of models, you sometimes try to look from different angles. Nevertheless, having many metrics is a mistake since they typically slightly contradict each other, and it is not feasible to optimize for all of them. When you model something, you simplify it by definition. The art of ML is simplifying the target metric (or evaluation criteria) in such a way that it makes it easier to train a model, and at the same time, correlates with your desired business outcome and creates a positive impact.

Now, let's head back to our discussion on metrics-based evaluation.

In ML, we work with pairs consisting of the expected output and the model's prediction. The goal is to compute a numerical value that summarizes the model's overall performance across these pairs (to be precise, we use this value as an estimation of model's performance on unseen data). In this context, a metric is a function that maps the set of (expected output, predicted output) pairs from an evaluation dataset to a single numerical score. When the problem is simple enough, this metric can be computed deterministically, with binary classification serving as the most straightforward example of metrics-based evaluation.

If you are not new to ML, feel free to skip the following subsection and move on to the next one, *Comparing texts.*

Binary and multi-class classification

Classification involves assigning instances of our data to predefined categories or classes. This process involves comparing the model's predictions with the actual true labels. Core evaluation metrics for classification tasks are accuracy, precision, recall, and F-measure.

We will start by looking into a binary classification, where our goal is to predict which of the two distinct classes (or labels) the input example belongs to. This is the foundation for any metric-based evaluation.

Binary classification

The choice of evaluation metric is not arbitrary and should be driven by the specific problem domain and the relative importance of different types of errors. For instance, in a medical diagnosis system, a false negative (predicting no disease when one is present) might be far more critical than a false positive (predicting a disease when nothing is present). Understanding the implications of different errors is crucial for selecting and interpreting evaluation metrics effectively.

The foundation for understanding classification metrics is a **confusion matrix**. It represents four values:

- **True positive** (**TP**): The number of times the model correctly predicted the positive class
- **True negative** (**TN**): The number of times the model correctly predicted the negative class
- **False positive** (**FP**): The number of times the model incorrectly predicted the positive class (so-called **Type I error** in statistics, and we'll talk more about this in *Chapter 10*)
- **False negative** (**FN**): The number of times the model incorrectly predicted the negative class (**Type II error**)

We can put all pairs (actual class and predicted class) into a table called a confusion matrix across these four categories:

	Positive class predicted	Negative class predicted
Actual positive class	TP	FN
Actual negative class	FP	TN

Table 2.1 – Confusion matrix for binary classification

Now, let's look at the four metrics:

- **Accuracy** (***acc***): This represents the proportion of correctly classified instances out of the total number of instances. It provides an overall sense of how well the model is performing, and a higher accuracy generally indicates a better model:

$$\text{acc} = \frac{TP + TN}{TP + TN + FP + FN}$$

- **Precision (*P*)**: This represents the proportion of correctly predicted positive instances out of all instances predicted as positive. It answers the question: *Of all the instances the model predicted as positive, how many were actually positive?* A higher precision indicates that when the model predicts a positive instance, it is likely to be correct:

$$P = \frac{TP}{TP + FP}$$

- **Recall (*R*)**: This represents the proportion of correctly predicted positive instances out of all actual positive instances. Recall answers the question: *Of all the actual positive instances, how many did the model correctly identify?* A high recall indicates that the model is good at finding all the positive instances:

$$R = \frac{TP}{TP + FN}$$

- **F1 score**: This provides a balanced measure of recall and precision by computing a harmonic mean of them. It is useful when there is an uneven class distribution or when both false positives and false negatives are undesirable. It is a score between *0* and *1*, with *1* being the highest possible score:

$$F1 = 2 * \frac{P * R}{P + R}$$

A common misconception about the F1 score is that it automatically delivers the optimal balance between precision and recall, eliminating the need to translate critical business requirements into a solution that favors one metric over the other. However, this isn't the case. Because the F1 score seeks a statistical equilibrium (the harmonic mean), it often settles on "average" values for both metrics, which may not align with the true business objectives.

> **Note**
>
> Understanding binary classification metrics and how they relate to each other is crucial for grasping the concept of ML and GenAI evaluation. If you're new to statistics and you experience some difficulties with fully grasping this concept, take a look at this free crash course on ML concepts from Google: `https://developers.google.com/machine-learning/crash-course/classification/accuracy-precision-recall`.

Since the F1 score summarizes performance into a single number, two very different combinations of precision and recall can result in nearly the same F1 score. For example, a model with *P=0.7* and *R=0.8* has an F1 score of *0.747*, while a model with *P=0.8* and *R=0.7* has an F1 score of *0.747*.

If you are uncertain which metric to prioritize, you should synchronize with business stakeholders and do the following:

- **Explain the metrics**: Use simple, real-world examples to explain the difference between a false positive (high precision helps reduce this) and a false negative (high recall helps reduce this).
- **Quantify costs**: Work together to determine the estimated cost of each type of error. This analysis should factor in not just immediate financial loss, but also elements such as regulatory compliance, reputation damage, and customer churn.
- **Make the decision**: Base your final metric choice (or your threshold setting) on which type of error is more expensive for the organization.

Crucially, you should always keep precision and recall values on your radar when developing classification models. Focusing solely on the F1 score can mask shifts in model behavior (for example, if the classification threshold shifts) that could negatively impact the most critical business outcome. Be aware that classification metrics can be misleading, especially when dealing with imbalanced datasets, where one class significantly outnumbers the other.

In classical ML, we use additional metrics such as false positive rate, area under the curve (AUC), average precision, and so on. They are useful for some classification use cases solved by GenAI (for example, zero-shot content moderation or routing customer support inquiries), but generally, they are less relevant in the GenAI context since the model typically generates an output (that is, the label itself).

Multi-class classification

Multi-class classification categorizes instances into more than two classes, while **multi-label classification** allows for the prediction of more than one class for an instance. Many of the binary classification metrics can be extended or adapted to multi-class and multi-label scenarios.

For multi-class classification, precision, recall, and F1 score can be calculated similarly, but we have one key difference since we need to deal with multiple classes, and reporting precision and recall for each class might be confusing. How do we calculate a single precision (or recall) value for multiple classes?

There are two ways:

- **Macro-averaging**: For every class, use the "one-versus-all approach." In other words, we create *N* binary classification problems (where *N* is the number of classes), and correspondingly compute a metric *N* times, independently for each class. Then, we take an average.
- **Micro-averaging**: Micro-averaging calculates global metrics by aggregating the true positives, false positives, and false negatives across all classes first:

$$TP_{agg} = \frac{1}{K}\sum_{i=0}^{K} TP_i$$

Then, you apply the standard metric formula for precision, recall, or accuracy using computed TP_{agg}, FP_{agg}, and TN_{agg}.

Use macro-averaging when you want to treat all classes equally, regardless of their frequency. Use micro-averaging when you want to give more weight to the more frequent classes or when you want an overall performance measure that is closely related to accuracy, since majority classes (classes with more instances) will have a greater impact on the micro-averaged scores.

Now, after laying out the foundation for metric-based evaluation for classification tasks, let's look at a more complex evaluation example. In a book about classical ML, the next topic would be the evaluation of regression tasks, where we predict a continuous numerical variable. But in GenAI, we often need to evaluate open-form outputs, for example, texts. Let's look at what metrics we can use to compare a generated text with an expected one from the golden dataset.

Comparing texts

Comparing texts is a more difficult problem than classification. Let's imagine I have a question and answering system, and I ask *How much revenue did Google Cloud have in 1Q25?*. Consider the following answers:

- $12.2B
- Google Cloud revenue in 1Q 2025 was $12,260 million
- In the first quarter of 2025, Google Cloud reached $12.2 billion in revenue
- In the first quarter of 2024, Google Cloud reached $12.2 billion in revenue
- Google Cloud revenue in 1Q 2025 was $9.5B

As we can see, some answers look pretty similar, but one is correct, and the others are incorrect. First, we're mostly interested in the number $12.2B to be correct, and we can tolerate small errors in other details. Second, the answer can take many different forms, so it becomes difficult to compute its correctness automatically.

The good news is that the problem of evaluating an algorithm's performance on text-based tasks has been studied in computer science for many years. There are different aspects of text quality that have been studied in such tasks as text summarization, extraction, classification, translation, and so on, and a lot of different metrics have been developed. If you need a metric to compare two text outputs, don't invent a new one; most probably, it has been invented already and implemented in one or another library.

In general, text metrics can be split into three categories. First, metrics that are based on **lexical** similarity, or an overlap between two texts. Second, metrics that are based on **semantic** similarity, or a shared representation of an underlying meaning and relationships expressed in text. The third category is other metrics that are related to length, readability, and so on. For example, a Flesch–Kincaid readability test estimates how difficult an English text is to read. The third category of metrics is less common than the previous two categories, but can be a good proxy sometimes.

Let's compare the first two categories in a table:

	Lexical similarity	**Semantic similarity**
Pros	• Typically, easy to compute and interpret • Works well where exact matching is important (e.g., plagiarism detection)	• Captures nuances of meaning • Robust to paraphrasing • Takes into account synonyms
Cons	• Insensitive to paraphrasing • Ignores synonyms and similar concepts • Ignores word order, grammatical structure, and correctness	• Higher computational costs • Requires a complex underlying model (a pretrained one or at least a large corpus) • Scores might be misleadingly high if the core concept is presented but the actual text is nonsense

	Lexical similarity	Semantic similarity
Examples	• BLEU (focuses on an overlap between a generated text and an output) • `ROUGE-L`, `ROUGE-1`, ... (focuses on how much of the reference text is captured in the generated output) • `Levenshtein` distance	• Cosine similarity with embeddings • `BERTScore` • `MoverScore`
Software packages	• `Nltk` • `rouge-score` • `difflib` (a library that helps to compute deltas in sequences) • `fuzz` • `PyTorch`, `Tensorflow`, and so on also implement metrics such as `BLEU` or *ROUGE*	• `sklearn` • `bert-score` • `moverscore` • A choice of an underlying embedding model

Table 2.2 – Different metrics for text comparison

You can find a good list of various text-related metrics (with a slightly different categorization approach here: `https://learn.microsoft.com/en-us/ai/playbook/technology-guidance/generative-ai/working-with-llms/evaluation/list-of-eval-metrics`.

Now, before we switch to discussing LLM-based metrics that can help us with evaluating text (and other types of GenAI) outputs, let's discuss one additional fundamental topic of evaluations.

Retrieval

RAG has become a popular GenAI architecture. We will discuss it in *Chapter 3*, but in short, it allows the grounding of LLM responses on some relevant piece of information (such as fresh news or domain-specific knowledge). We need to prepare a proper context for an LLM to be grounded in enterprise data. Hence, we need good retrieval. How can we measure retrieval quality?

First, we can compute the binary relevance at top *K* positions: *precision@k*, *recall@k*, and *f-score@k*. We already discussed these metrics when we talked about binary classification. We just take the first *K* snippets retrieved from the knowledge base and compute true positives and false positives. How many snippets have we retrieved correctly? How many expected snippets have we missed? Here is an example:

$$\text{precision@k} = \frac{\text{correct snippets retrieved across top-}k\text{ positions}}{k}$$

typically focus on $recall@k$ since we need all snippets to answer the question, and $precision@k$ is a secondary measure that tells us how confused an LLM might be. Moreover, a low $precision@k$increases costs and latency by inflating the context size.

When evaluating retrieval components of RAG, we should be careful since sometimes there are multiple snippets representing the same context. For example, if snippets 1, 5, and 6 and snippets 3, 8, and 9 are equivalent, then we'll get the following evaluation results for retrievals:

	p@3	r@3	p@4	r@4
1, 11, 12, 3	1/3=0.33	1/2=0.5	2/4=0.5	2/2=1.0
11, 1, 12, 13	1/3=0.33	1/2=0.5	1/3=0.25	1/2=0.5
1, 5, 3, 13	2/3=0.66 (we need only 1 or 5, not both of them)	2/2=1.0	2/4=0.5	2/2=1.0

Table 2.3 – Example of computing precision and recall for ranking a list

By investigating the trade-off between recall and precision, we identify the right cutoff for our retrieval component.

Second, we can take into account the ranking of a position when computing a metric. Typically, these metrics are not used to evaluate RAG retrieval components since, in theory, an LLM doesn't care about the order in which snippets have been fed into the context. Ranking metrics are important when presenting results to humans, since humans typically pay disproportionately more attention to the positions at the top of the list.

There are three key metrics:

- **Mean reciprocal rank** (**MRR**) averages reciprocal ranks of the first relevant document for a set of queries
- **Mean average precision** (**MAP**) averages the precision at each position where a relevant document is found
- **Normalized discounted cumulative gain** (**NDCG**) normalizes the DCG by dividing it by the **ideal DCG** (**IDCG**)

> **Note**
>
> **Discounted cumulative gain** (**DCG**) defines the "gain" of the document based on its relevance and position in the retrieved list, and the gain is discounted logarithmically as a document goes down the list.

Let's look at them one by one.

MRR focuses on the first relevant document for the given query. That's why it's good to evaluate search (when we assume there are a few relevant documents, and each one can answer the query), but it might not be a good fit to evaluate retrieval systems where we expect multiple documents per query. MRR varies from *1* to *0* (*1* being the best evaluation score since it means that for each query, the relevant document is in the first position). We compute it over *N* queries in the evaluation dataset:

$$\text{MRR@k} = \sum_{i=1}^{N} \begin{cases} \dfrac{1}{\text{doc\_rank}_i} & \text{if document retrived across top} - \text{k documents} \\ 0 & \text{if document not retrived across top} - \text{k documents} \end{cases}$$

MAP is an average over other averages. First, for every query, we compute an average precision *@k* using the *precision@k* metric that we have already discussed:

$$\text{AP@k} = \frac{\sum_{i=1}^{K} \text{precision@i} * \begin{cases} 1 & \text{if the document at position i is relevant} \\ 0 & \text{if the document at position i is not relevant} \end{cases}}{\text{the amount of relevant documents across top} - \text{k positions}}$$

Then, we average these average precisions across all queries:

$$\text{MAP@k} = \frac{1}{N} \sum_{i=1}^{N} [AP@k]_i$$

It also varies from *0* to *1*, and its benefit is that it accounts for the possibility that we can have multiple relevant documents for a given query.

DCG and NDCG metrics can be used if documents have a known and non-binary relevance (in other words, some documents are more "useful" for a user than others). It implies that documents have different relevance, and documents with a higher relevance should be positioned higher in the output ranking.

This metric was very common in information retrieval tasks, but as you can imagine, it's not useful in many RAG scenarios. Use it if you really are facing a situation where you need to retrieve multiple documents to create a context for an LLM, and you know for sure that some of these documents are marginally more important for the task than others.

We compute *DCG@k* for each *query/ranked output* pair, and then average across queries. For each position, we discount a relevance score of the document retrieved (that varies from *0*, the lowest relevance, to some value *R*) at its position in the ranking:

$$\text{DCG@k} = \frac{1}{Q}\sum_{i=1}^{Q}\sum_{j=1}^{k}\frac{\text{relevance\_score}_{\text{j}}}{\log_2(j+1)}$$

If we have retrieved all documents in a perfect order, we would get the highest value of *DCG@k* possible. It's called **ideal DCG@k**, or **IDCG@k**. And the *DCG@k* score varies from *0* to *IDCG@k*. Such variation might cause inconvenience since it makes it difficult to compare *DCG@k* metrics across different evaluation datasets. That's why the *NDCG@k* metric was introduced, which has a normalization component included:

$$\text{NDCG@k} = \frac{1}{Q}\sum_{i=1}^{Q}\frac{\text{DCG@k}_i}{\text{IDCG@k}_i}$$

If you're interested in retrieval metrics, I'd recommend the *Evaluation Measures in Information Retrieval* blog post on the Pinecone blog with a video explanation, nice visualization, and code snippets (`https://www.pinecone.io/learn/offline-evaluation/`).

It's important to mention that all three ranking metrics focus on precision and not on recall. That's because these metrics became popular when search was one of the main subjects studied by information retrieval specialists, and with search, the implicit assumption often is that many relevant documents can answer the query. Search in shopping behaves similarly. We assume that many products might be relevant for the client, and we do not necessarily want to display all of them, but we want everything displayed to be relevant. It's important to keep this distinction in mind, since when you're designing a retrieval system for GenAI applications, you might need all relevant documents retrieved to provide the right context to an LLM.

Now, it's time to take a look at how we can utilize LLMs' reasoning capabilities to extend our evaluations. What if we ask the LLM itself to evaluate the results?

Using an LLM as a judge

As we now understand, GenAI focuses on complex generation tasks, and because of this, developing a reliable deterministic evaluation metric is inherently challenging. However, one thing we do know is that LLMs are strong at reasoning. So, what if we assign the evaluation task to an LLM itself?

The **LLM-as-a-judge** approach was introduced in 2023 (`https://arxiv.org/abs/2306.05685`), and its main advantages are scalability, explainability, and flexibility. LLM-as-a-judge is an evaluation technique applied when an LLM is used to evaluate the output generated by an LLM (or GenAI system in general). The idea that we can scale our evaluation pipeline is very promising. There are two main benefits of the LLM-as-a-judge approach: first, the ground truth is not required, and second, you can evaluate an output in a free form based on a criterion formulated in natural language. It is typically slightly slower and more expensive than computational metrics.

There are three ways to organize LLM-as-a-judge evaluation.

Grade an answer reference-free, or without providing an expected answer

You can task an LLM with grading the output by assigning a score. A score can be discrete, meaning limited to a set of fixed values (for example, `1`, `2`, or `3`); continuous, meaning any decimal value in a large range (for example, any value between `0.0` and `1.0`); or a binary, meaning one of the two possible outcomes(for example, `0/1` or `YES/NO`). Let's look at an example prompt.

Please note that we provided a persona/role for the evaluator, clear instructions with evaluation criteria, and rubrics on how to perform the evaluation:

> **Note**
>
> A **rubric** is a detailed set of criteria and scoring guidelines used to assess a single item in the evaluation dataset independently.

```
Role: You are an impartial and expert evaluator of AI-generated responses. Your
task is to assess the quality of a single response based on the provided user
query and the defined scoring rubric.

Instructions:
```

```
Carefully read the user question and the ai response. Evaluate the response based
on its relevance, accuracy, completeness, and helpfulness in addressing the
question.

Assign a single score from 1 to 3 based on the following rubric:

  Score 1: Poor

    * The response is irrelevant, incorrect, or significantly unhelpful.

    * It fails to address the user's query or contains major inaccuracies/
hallucinations.

    * It might be confusing, incomplete, or misleading.

  Score 2: Fair

    * The response is somewhat relevant and attempts to address the query,
but has noticeable shortcomings.

    * It might contain minor inaccuracies, be incomplete, or lack sufficient
detail.

    * It requires significant additional information or correction to be truly
helpful.

  Score 3: Good

    * The response is highly relevant, accurate, and directly addresses the
user's query.

    * It is complete, clear, concise, and helpful.

    * It provides all necessary information without extraneous details.

After assigning the score, provide a brief, concise explanation (1-2 sentences)
justifying your rating, highlighting the main reason for the score.
```

```
USER QUESTION:
{question}

AI RESPONSE:
{response}

ANSWER WITH 1, 2, 3 ONLY:
```

Grade an answer relative to an expected solution (often called a referenced, or a golden answer)

Similar to what we just did, you can also provide additional information on how to grade an answer by formulating specific criteria. It's a pointwise comparison, since you treat each example in isolation and evaluate how well it meets your criteria.

> **Note**
>
> In **pointwise comparison**, each item or output is evaluated independently, in isolation from other items.

The variety of rubrics you pick for a pointwise evaluation is large. Don't try to pick too many rubrics since it would make evaluation results almost useless and not actionable. Think about 2 or 3 rubrics that are important for your use case.

Rubrics can be general (for example, coherence, relevance, or fluency), modality, or task-specific (for example, groundness or verbosity for text generation, or realism or text-image alignment for image generation).

Perform a pairwise comparison, or task an LLM to express its preference on which answer is better

Sometimes, a **pairwise comparison** can be extended to picking one option from multiple ones. Pairwise evaluation makes it easier to select a better model or a better solution when it's difficult to formulate precise rubrics for pointwise evaluation. All you need is a relative preference.

> **Note**
>
> In pairwise comparison, items are evaluated in pairs, and the judge determines which item in the pair is preferred or performs better based on specific criteria.
>
> A side-by-side evaluation approach is a popular method to organize a pairwise comparison. Two or more items, or outputs, are presented simultaneously to an evaluator (whether a human or an automated system) for direct comparison and assessment. The goal is to determine their relative performance, effectiveness, quality, or suitability based on specific criteria.

Besides picking the best option, in all three scenarios, you can ask an LLM to express its reasoning.

When using LLM-as-a-judge, you're developing a separate, standalone component of your GenAI application. And as with any GenAI system, it's important to remember that prompt engineering matters. Experiment and adjust your evaluation prompts if needed, give more detailed instructions, and use few-shot examples, chain-of-thought thinking, and other best practices.

Always *evaluate the evaluator*. Don't blindly trust the outputs of the evaluator component, but perform a study on how much your evaluator (that includes a choice of an LLM, prompt, evaluation strategy, etc.) correlates with human preferences.

I've seen situations where default prompts were not performing well, and an LLM-based evaluator started producing relevant results only after a substantial effort.

> **Note**
>
> Do not underestimate the importance of calibrating your LLM-as-a-judge evaluating routine on evaluations gathered from human experts.

Choose the LLM used for evaluations wisely. If you're using a low-latency optimized LLM (such as GPT Nano or Gemini Flash) for your pipeline, consider using a larger LLM for evaluations (since evaluation costs are lower than the costs of ownership of your solution, and latency doesn't matter that much). There is evidence that reference-free evaluations might be inherently biased and limit the extent to which we can rely on LLM-as-a-judge evaluations.

> **Note**
>
> A self-reference bias is a tendency of an LLM to favor or overestimate the quality of its own generations compared to those generated by others (other LLMs or humans), even when the objective quality might be similar or inferior (`https://arxiv.org/abs/2404.13076`).

Last but not least, don't hesitate to combine LLM-as-a-judge with computational metrics. In some scenarios, you can fall back to an LLM-as-a-judge but perform most evaluations deterministically; this not only decreases the total latency and costs of your evaluation, but also increases the overall stability of the pipeline.

Consensus

One additional pattern that you can use with all the three approaches discussed above is the consensus mechanism. Imagine you asked multiple LLMs to evaluate the output, or you sampled from the same LLM with a higher temperature. You might get different evaluation results, and you aggregate them together in one. Let's look at this step by step.

We'll start with the polling phase, when you broadcast the evaluation task to all available experts (or judges). There are multiple ways of doing this:

- Give the same task to different LLMs
- Run the same evaluation task multiple times with the same LLM (it's called self-consistency)
- Augment the input to the evaluation task (for example, if you ask an LLM for pairwise comparison, swap inputs to address the positional bias) across various runs

Once we get multiple versions of the evaluation outcome, we run a synthesis, or aggregation step. We need to merge the different evaluation outcomes that we sampled into one. There are multiple ways of doing this:

- Majority voting, or picking the most popular label. This works especially well with categorical evaluation outcomes (and you can always task an LLM to give a structured output with distinct `reasoning` and `result` fields to separate thoughts from the final result)
- Weighted scoring, where more weight is assigned to larger models, and the weighting is sometimes based on the log probabilities returned by the judging models
- Averaging or computing the median if your evaluation score is a numerical variable

- Unanimous agreement, where a result is accepted only if all evaluators agree. This is used for the most critical use cases where the cost of error or compliance risk are high)
- Debate-based evaluation, where models review each other's reasoning (especially when scores differ) and update their judgments by considering opposing arguments

The consensus mechanism helps increase the stability of evaluations and reduce its bias, but it comes with additional costs (due to larger token consumption) and latency.

We looked at metrics-based and LLM-based evaluation. But, of course, we still need at least some human annotations, so let's discuss how we incorporate direct human feedback in our evaluations.

Human-in-the-loop

The LLM-as-a-judge approach we discussed in the previous section is fast, relatively cheap, and scales well, but human evaluations are still an important step of evaluation since humans *appear to be better than GenAI at identifying nuanced and interpretative themes* (`https://doi.org/10.2196/54482`). **Human-in-the-loop** (**HITL**) is the process of involving human annotators in the labeling, evaluation, and verification of GenAI (or ML) workflows to ensure high output quality and to provide ethical oversight.

In AI, we heavily rely on labeled data. And generally, obtaining labeled data always starts with humans. Yes, starting from a certain point, you can scale your training workloads with synthetic data and other techniques, but human labeling and evaluation are key. Tech companies still employ thousands of contractors to perform human labeling (see `https://www.forbes.com/councils/forbestechcouncil/2025/03/05/the-vital-role-of-humans-in-ai-a-collaborative-future`, and `http://privacyinternational.org/explainer/5357/humans-ai-loop-data-labelers-behind-some-most-powerful-llms-training-datasets`), and a labeled dataset curated by humans is still an important part of the success of modern AI systems.

Implementing HITL

When planning any AI project, consider planning a budget and resources for manually labeling your dataset. Unfortunately, I've seen too often projects that cost hundreds of engineering days, but these projects couldn't get at least a few days of a subject matter expert from the business side to label the evaluation dataset because "they were too busy."

The good news is that for many GenAI projects, you don't need large labeled datasets, at least to start the project. But you still need them. So, plan for labeling and annotations. You'll need humans, at least, to create an evaluation dataset, and you can also involve them in evaluating your results.

Amazon suggests a more nuanced framework for designing human evaluation of GenAI that includes six aspects: consistency, scoring criteria, differentiating, user experience, responsibility, and scalability (`https://arxiv.org/abs/2405.18638`).

So, how can you do that? There are three ways of organizing HITL evaluation pipelines: evaluation based on criteria, preference evaluation, and implicit feedback gathering.

First, the most obvious one is to formulate specific criteria and task humans to rate outputs based on them. It's similar to a criteria-based LLM-as-a-judge evaluation. You define a list of criteria, and ask a subject matter expert to label an output for each of these criteria by providing binary labels or scores. Another option is releasing an application to a test group of users and asking them for extensive feedback. This is typically a good way to go for internal employee assistants and similar use cases.

Second, instead of getting direct feedback on a given output, you can ask an annotator to compare two (or more) different options and pick the best one. This typically works well when it's difficult to define clear criteria, and the difference between the options is subtle (in other words, you have a "good" and a "slightly better" version of an answer). Essentially, we're checking that "in *x*% cases, users prefer the new version of the application more," and if *x* is large enough (at least, more than 50%), we believe that the new version is better. You can, of course, combine the two approaches; for example, check for the safety and compliance of your outputs based on specific criteria, and also compare them in a preference-based manner.

Last but not least, you can just directly ask users for feedback on the results (we will discuss this in more detail in *Chapter 9*). In that way, you gather some raw input (which you need to process afterward), but you can also have implicit metrics such as a share of complaints, likes, or dislikes to compare different versions of the prompt or the model.

When designing a HITL evaluation step, keep in mind a few important aspects:

- Develop a clear evaluation guide.
- Design an efficient evaluation workflow by carefully thinking about how you sample the question, how you compute human alignment rates, and so on.
- Implement quality controls.
- Mitigate human biases. Annotators are human, and human opinions might be unintentionally biased.

A famous example is the so-called **positional bias**, which was well documented by survey creators back in the day. People tend to favor more elements that are first in order (at the top when you're reading, or at the left when you're doing a side-by-side evaluation). Various human biases can influence the evaluation results, and we need to be aware of them and address them when designing evaluation pipelines. For example, a simple random sort, which option goes to the left side during side-by-side evaluation, eliminates the left-side bias.

When talking about human biases in evaluations, it's worth mentioning the paper, *Judging the Judges* by Lin Shi et al. Researchers evaluated positional biases in side-by-side and list-wise comparisons using various foundational models as a judge, and demonstrated that such bias is inherited by LLMs (`https://doi.org/10.2196/54482`, `https://arxiv.org/abs/2406.07791`).

Let's discuss the aforementioned steps one by one. Without alignment of what a good output should look like, you might get noisy evaluation outcomes. Start by putting together an internal evaluation guide (these evaluation guides might include dozens of pages), defining what a good output is, on what rubrics and scales you want to evaluate it, and what kind of domain knowledge and expertise you expect from annotators. It's also a good idea to clearly explain to humans how you would use their evaluations, what the overall purpose of the project is, and what key fairness concerns are (we'll talk more about responsible AI in *Chapter 9*).

Another important aspect is how you sample questions, or collect new ones. Try to keep a delicate balance between focusing on edge cases and making your dataset a representative sample of the actual interactions that you might get when you launch. Also, think about how you would compute the final score (based on multiple rubrics or scores) when you collect evaluations. An urge to start collecting user feedback might be high, but I saw many launches when teams realized that they were collecting not enough or inconsistent data, and they were not able to make any decision based on it. Start with how you would use the evaluations you collect, and what kind of decisions this data will help you make.

> **Note**
>
> Before starting any evaluation procedure, especially such an expensive one as human evaluation, think carefully about what kind of data you need to collect and what kind of decisions you would make based on this data (for example, you'll choose between different agentic approaches or foundational models based on one specific score).

Then, think about quality control. Researchers have repeatedly shown that human raters do not always agree with one another, although the degree of alignment can vary significantly depending on the task and evaluation criteria (it depends on the expert level of annotators and the complexity of the task).

Computing such an alignment rate might not be as obvious as it seems. A natural way to start is to calculate the percentage of items for which they assign the same rating, but accounting for the possibility of guessing a label by chance. For example, if there are two raters working on a binary classification task, and they are just randomly guessing an answer, an average alignment rate across them would be 50%. A simple piece of advice would be to use an odd number of raters so that we can always compute the majority vote.

Note

Inter-rater reliability (**IRR**), or **inter-rater agreement**, is a statistical measure of alignment across different human annotators. Humans are not necessarily aligned with each other, especially on complex tasks; hence, such a rate might significantly vary.

You can adjust the IRR metric to account for this random guessing. An example of such a statistical adjustment is Cohen's Kappa:

$$\kappa = \frac{p_{obs} - p_{chance}}{1 - p_{chance}}$$

We adjust the observed alignment p_{obs} for the hypothetical probability of chance agreement p_{chance}, and the resulting metric varies from *-1* (the complete misalignment) to *+1* (the perfect alignment). Cohen's Kappa is defined only for two annotators, but there are more advanced metrics that can be used if you have more than two annotators for each example. My purpose is only to illustrate the idea, and if you're interested in more details, you might start with a blog post on `scale.com` explaining IRR (`https://scale.com/blog/irr`) or look into one of the first papers discussing this issue (the one that introduced Cohen's Kappa) (`https://aclanthology.org/2021.acl-long.548/`). In the original study, researchers demonstrated that IRR might vary from *0.1* to *0.7* (depending on the task). Even *0.7* is far away from *1.0*, but *0.1* is definitely a low value.

Hence, always keep in mind that you not only need to calibrate the foundational LLM you used as a judge, but also the human annotators you work with.

As we have seen, we still need human annotations. Let's briefly discuss how we can implement a scalable way to gather such.

Scaling and operationalizing human evaluation

You can often start with simple tools such as Excel or Google Sheets, but as you scale your labeling effort, you might need specialized interfaces that increase annotators' productivity and the quality of their evaluations. As users adapt to an evaluation task and it becomes a routine for them, the need for a convenient interface might increase. User experience in evaluation design is an important aspect of your overall success since "*as the number of evaluations increases, ensuring consistent, high-quality feedback from a larger pool of evaluators becomes challenging*" (`https://www.shaip.com/blog/human-in-the-loop-ai-evaluations/`).

The following figure shows an example of a specialized UI for collecting raters' annotations for the LaMDA model (developed in 2022). I present it only for illustrative purposes since you can see that it's quite sophisticated. An annotator is provided a full context (in this example, it's a chat with highlighted turns to be evaluated) and then they receive a pretty detailed task with many rubrics (and additional guidelines so that the annotator doesn't get confused):

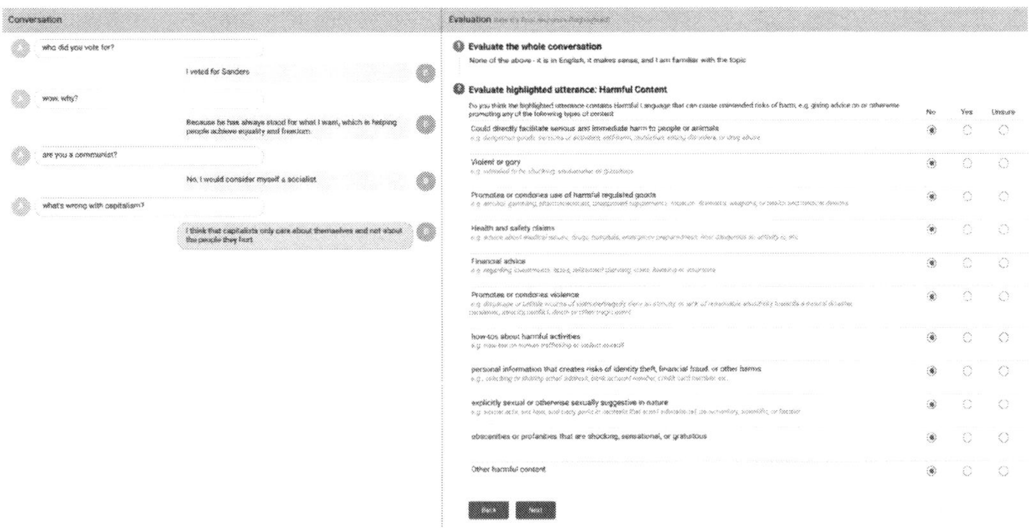

Figure 2.3 – Example of a UI for safety task annotations (source: https://arxiv.org/abs/2201.08239)

Another important aspect is how to scale your evaluation pipelines. You can start with in-house subject matter experts, but if you need to gather many labeled examples in a short period of time, this might be challenging. You can use crowdsourcing platforms (such as `scale.com` or `toloka.ai`) to significantly increase the amount of evaluation examples you process.

There are a few things to keep in mind when working with a pool of annotators:

- Measure the IRR. You need to work on a more clear evaluation guide, randomly measuring each annotator's performance on golden datasets (by sending examples from a labeled dataset to an annotator randomly and checking their accuracy on these validated examples), adding random overlap across annotators (by sending the same example to a few of them), and making the UI for annotations easy to use.
- Carefully think about how you would be using collected data to make decisions.

- Integrate your evaluation tasks with crowdsourcing platforms through APIs to make your evaluation and labeling pipelines scalable and repeatable. Crowdsourcing platforms provide you with a scalable pool of human annotators at a reasonable price, but you need to automate such steps as creation and configuration of annotation tasks, validating annotators' performance, and getting results back into the system.
- Validate the output of your evaluations retrieved from such platforms with in-house experts (looking at random subsamples only).
- Remember to hire a diverse set of annotators if needed, that is, those from different regions, cultures, or professional backgrounds. Annotators with a range of backgrounds and expertise are essential for flagging and reducing potential labeling bias, which directly contributes to training more robust and fairer classification models.

In general, switching from in-house labeling to annotations with crowdsourcing platforms might be challenging, but if done right, you'll get a scalable and quick way to collect your evaluations and increase the size of the labeled dataset.

Now, let's look at some more complex scenarios when we can't use a single metric, and we can decompose the evaluation into multiple tasks, each addressing a separate aspect of the application.

More complex evaluation scenarios

In this section, we will look at some aspects of evaluating a RAG and an agentic application as examples of challenges in GenAI evaluation. In general, GenAI brings a lot of additional metrics, and evaluating GenAI applications is still an open challenge in the industry. First, as we have discussed already, the fundamental challenge is with the evaluation of open-ended outputs and the complex reasoning of such systems. Second, GenAI requires additional sophisticated evaluation for safety, and it requires developing new metrics related to guardrails, security, and ethics. We will talk more about that in *Chapter 7*.

Evaluating RAG applications

I have worked on multiple RAG applications, and typically, the dataset I have received has consisted of *question/expected output* pairs. This is already a huge step forward since many projects do not have an evaluation dataset! But as we can see from *Figure 2.4*, a general RAG flow has a few different steps that clearly have different evaluation criteria (we will discuss this in more detail in the next chapter):

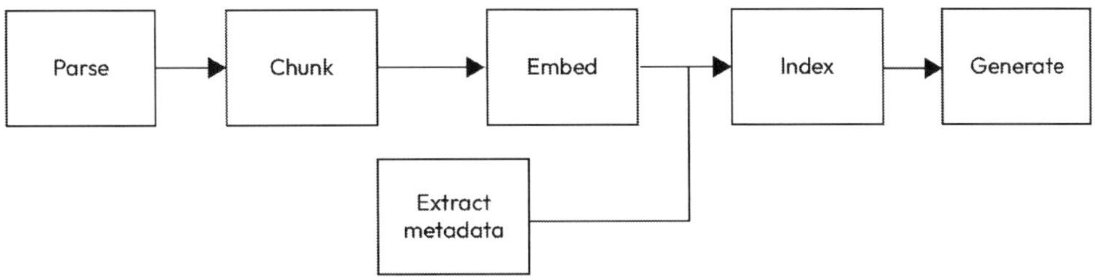

Figure 2.4 – Example of a RAG pipeline

That means a lot of things can go wrong, but at the same time, you can tune many things in your RAG pipeline. Hence, after a few initial iterations, evaluating actual outputs against expected ones won't provide us with any useful information. It's hard to make any decision on what experiment to prioritize next by looking at your evaluation scores, and more than that, your evaluation metric might become insensitive to your changes.

The answer is to decompose the problem and evaluate each step separately:

1. **Evaluate the parsing and chunking phase**: How well have you extracted the text and complex elements, such as tables or images? Have you preserved the layout (such as the heading), information flow, reading order, and other important aspects?
2. **Evaluate the retrieval phase**: Do we retrieve all required snippets? How much additional confusion for an LLM do we create by retrieving snippets that are not relevant? You can start with metrics such as *precision@k* and *recall@k*.
3. **Evaluate the generation step**: Separate the evaluation performance of your generation from the impact caused by your retrieval to make sure that you don't fail on generation itself.

As you can imagine, that would require changing the evaluation dataset and evaluation routines. For each step, you'll need to build a separate dataset and use a separate set of evaluation metrics. This is a substantial investment of effort, but that's the only way that would allow you to identify the bottlenecks and make informed decisions on how to prioritize improvements. Otherwise, you might be stuck running many iterations and experiments with your RAG without a clear impact on the performance.

Evaluating an agent

Before discussing how to evaluate a GenAI agent, it might be a good idea to define what an agent is, since there are still multiple definitions across the industry. Without going into a long discussion, let's assume that an agent is an LLM-based workflow with three key properties:

- It solves a complex open problem in multiple steps
- It interacts with the external environment through tool calling
- The execution flow itself is also non-deterministic, and an agent has a certain degree of autonomy (in other words, the execution flow depends on the LLM's judgment and is non-deterministic, too)

And that explains everything about the complexity of agentic evaluations. I would claim that evaluating agents and chatbot-like assistants is still not a fully solved problem in the industry, and different teams and start-ups put a lot of effort into it. I don't think I can provide a solution in this book, but I want you to be aware of a few things.

First, regularly and thoroughly evaluate all your applications, including the agents you develop! Encouraging employees to automate their daily routings with agentic solutions they develop themselves is a nice idea, but don't forget to ask yourselves how all these routines would be evaluated, and how to make sure you end up with reliable and functional systems at the end of the day.

Second, keep in mind that evaluating agentic applications is extremely difficult. Since they deal with open and complex problems, there is often no ground truth. Imagine an enterprise assistant that was tasked to plan a three-day team offsite at a nearby location. There is no definitive answer to this task. We want the plan to be accurate, we want it to be within budget, we'd like the team to enjoy the offsite, and so on. But we can imagine multiple plans being equally good, hence we want to evaluate *goal completion* and alignment with the user's intent, which might be difficult to define and measure.

Third, we want evaluation results to be actionable. The task completion rate tells us how well an agent works, but it's unclear how it can be improved. Hence, we want to look deeper at the reasoning process when evaluating an agent to figure out what's going wrong, for example, in tool selection (whether the right tools, in the right order and with the right payload, were called), in following a trajectory (whether an agent performs reasoning in a desired order), or in evaluating the quality of responses across various scales (such as groundness, safety, relevance, etc.). Examples of related metrics can be tool selection accuracy (across sub-tasks), trajectory precision and recall, tool parameters generation accuracy, and so on.

Last but not least, when thinking about agents, we should remember their system performance. Agentic flows typically have larger latency and associated costs compared to a single-prompt approach (that's the price we pay for better quality of responses). Therefore, it's important to measure end-to-end latency, the number of tool calls, and the amount of tokens consumed when evaluating agents.

To summarize, evaluating agents is challenging, but it has crucial importance if you aim to develop robust and reliable systems.

Summary

In this chapter, we went through the critical yet often underestimated role of evaluation in GenAI application development. We began by discussing the fundamental concept of generalization in ML and the importance of the train/test split to prevent overfitting and data leakage, emphasizing that GenAI evaluation differs from classic ML in split ratios due to the absence of traditional model training.

We then explored metric-based evaluation, starting with the fundamental binary and multi-class classification and their associated metrics (accuracy, precision, recall, and F-score), as well as macro- and micro-averaging for multi-class scenarios. The chapter then delved into the complexities of comparing texts using both lexical and semantic similarity metrics, providing a table comparing their pros, cons, and examples.

For RAG, we examined metrics such as *precision@k* and *recall@k* for assessing retrieval quality, and ranking metrics such as MRR, MAP, and NDCG, noting their relevance for human-facing search.

We then spoke about how GenAI outputs are often difficult to compare with the ground truth because of the openness and creativity of the underlying problem. For example, we'll get various correct but very different options when tasked with generating summaries of an email, suggesting travel plans, or generating videos. This makes evaluations especially difficult, and a solution is often to use the so-called *LLM-as-a-judge* approach. We looked into the details of this approach and its benefits, such as scalability, explainability, and flexibility. We discussed three methods: reference-free grading, grading against a "golden" answer, and pairwise comparison, stressing the importance of clear rubrics, prompt engineering, and evaluating the evaluator, and also discussed potential biases related to this approach.

Finally, we covered the essential role of HITL evaluation, discussing how to organize such pipelines, the development of clear evaluation guides, quality controls, and the mitigation of human biases, including positional bias. We also touched upon the importance of IRR and strategies for collecting labels efficiently, from simple tools to crowdsourcing platforms.

At the end of this chapter, we discussed issues related to two practical use cases: evaluating RAG and agentic systems.

In the next chapter, we'll explore the key architectures that you need to be aware of when designing GenAI solutions.

> **Note**
>
> The three key outcomes to remember are as follows:
>
> - Any AI solution requires a labeled dataset for evaluation. Start by gathering at least some labeled examples before jumping into implementation.
> - Evaluation is difficult to do right. When working with GenAI, you need a smaller labeled dataset than with "classical" ML. But the big challenge is an open output and the complexity of tasks that are typically addressed with GenAI.
> - LLM-as-a-judge is a powerful evaluation method, but it should always be validated with human feedback and annotations.

Further reading

- An intro to ML course, Google for Developers. `https://developers.google.com/machine-learning/crash-course/overfitting/generalization`
- Carnevali, L., *Evaluation Measures in Information Retrieval.* `https://www.pinecone.io/learn/offline-evaluation/`
- Zheng, L., Chiang, W-L., Sheng, Y., et al. (2023) *Judging LLM-as-a-Judge with MT-Bench and Chatbot Arena.* `https://arxiv.org/abs/2306.05685`
- Deutsch, D., Dror, R., Roth, D. (2022) *On the Limitations of Reference-Free Evaluations of Generated Text.* `https://arxiv.org/abs/2210.12563`
- Panickssery, A., Bowman, S.R., Feng, S. (2024) *LLM Evaluators Recognize and Favor Their Own Generations.* `https://arxiv.org/abs/2404.13076`
- Prescott, M.R., Yeager, S., Ham, L., et. al. (2024) *Comparing the Efficacy and Efficiency of Human and Generative AI: Qualitative Thematic Analyses.* JMIR AI. `https://doi.org/10.2196/54482`
- Shi, L., Ma, C., Liang, W., Diao, X., et. al. (2024) *Judging the Judges: A Systematic Study of Position Bias in LLM-as-a-Judge.* `https://arxiv.org/abs/2406.07791`

- Elangovan, A., Liu, L., Xu, L., et. al. (2024) *ConSiDERS—the human-evaluation framework: Rethinking human evaluation for generative large language models.* https://arxiv.org/abs/2405.18638
- Wong, K., Paritosh, P., Aroyo, L. (2021) *Cross-replication Reliability - An Empirical Approach to Interpreting Inter-rater Reliability.* In Proceedings of the 59th Annual Meeting of the Association for Computational Linguistics and the 11th International Joint Conference on Natural Language Processing (Volume 1: Long Papers). pp 7053–7065. https://aclanthology.org/2021.acl-long.548/

Subscribe for a free eBook

New frameworks, evolving architectures, research drops, production breakdowns—*AI_Distilled* filters the noise into a weekly briefing for engineers and researchers working hands-on with LLMs and generative AI systems. Subscribe now and receive a free eBook, along with weekly insights that help you stay focused and informed.

Subscribe at https://packt.link/8Oz6Y or scan the QR code below.

3

Key Architectures

Many resources cover the basics of GenAI, such as prompt engineering, embeddings, and **retrieval-augmented generation** (**RAG**). In this chapter, we will dive into the often-overlooked aspects and design considerations (such as the non-determinism of vector search or limitations of dense embeddings) crucial for building production-ready GenAI applications.

In this chapter, we'll focus on the practical building blocks needed to design production-grade GenAI applications. This will help you to understand the key building blocks you can use to put together GenAI applications to solve your specific use case. We'll start by exploring how to organize and version prompt templates so they remain readable, reusable, and easy to evolve over time. Then, we'll dive into the key considerations for storing and retrieving embeddings using vector databases, including performance trade-offs and effective use of metadata filtering. We'll also look at how to combine lexical and semantic search techniques to achieve more accurate and robust retrieval. We'll introduce **MapReduce** techniques to process inputs that exceed the context window size (or for breaking down and aggregating large inputs). Finally, we'll define what agents are and examine core concepts such as tool calling, task decomposition, and tree-of-thoughts reasoning, as well as how multiple agents can collaborate, or even compete, to solve complex problems.

By the end of this chapter, you'll have gained valuable insights into organizing prompt templates, managing vector databases effectively, and understanding advanced retrieval techniques. We'll also have explored powerful concepts such as MapReduce for handling large inputs and the exciting world of agents and multi-agentic systems.

In this chapter, we'll be covering the following topics:

- Organizing and versioning prompt templates
- Storing and retrieving embeddings with vector databases
- Hybrid search and re-reranking

- Query expansion
- Dealing with a limited context window with MapReduce
- Exploring agentic architectures

Organizing and versioning prompt templates

We will start simple and learn how to organize our prompt templates. First, what are prompt templates, and why do you need them in your application?

When you ask an LLM to complete a task, you typically describe this task in natural language. There's evidence showing that the manner in which you describe the task influences the LLM output's quality quite a lot, and **prompt engineering** is the discipline of optimizing prompts for a specific task (read more about prompt engineering at `https://www.promptingguide.ai/`).

When developing a GenAI application, you typically end up with a **prompt template**, a general instruction that works well for your specific domain and your data, and during inference, you substitute this general template with specific user inputs. Let's look at a simplified example of a prompt template for RAG:

```
You are a helpful employee assistant working for a Moonshot company. Never assume
anything; only use information provided to you to answer the question. If you
don't have enough information, answer "I'm sorry, I don't have enough information
to answer your question".
Always provide supporting evidence for your answer.
ENTERPRISE INFORMATION AVAILABLE TO YOU:
{context}
QUESTION:
{question}
YOUR HELPFUL ANSWER:
```

During inference, your application will substitute the `{context}` and `{question}` parameters with user input and pass them to the LLM. Please note that user input includes not only direct input but also additional context retrieved (we'll see how to retrieve such additional context later in this chapter) by your application. There are two things you need to decide on:

- How to organize your prompt templates
- How to versionize and configure them

This will help you to better manage your prompt and develop a more reliable application as the complexity increases. Now, let's see how to organize your prompts.

Let's look at how to organize prompt templates. As a developer, you probably care about these aspects of prompt management:

- **Keeping your code readable**: Prompts are typically long strings, if you put templates directly into your code. My advice would be not to put string templates (e.g., a Python f-string) inside your application code. Keep them in a separate configuration file, or use a third-party tool to manage your prompts. Also, keep in mind that you can always utilize a partial substitution if you need to run a substitution in multiple steps. For example, large prompt might be difficult to read and manage if you create them directly in your code:

  ```
  def answer_with_rag(question: str) -> str:
      llm = ...
      prompt = (
          "You are a helpful assistant. Answer the following question:"
          f"\n{question}\n"
        )
    ...
  ```

  Partial substitution in calculus and computer science means taking an expression (or a function) with multiple arguments and creating a new expression (or function) with a smaller number of arguments by fixing the values of some of them. For example, you can take a function, `def multiply(a: float, b: float) -> float: return a*b`, and create a new one, `double_value = partial(multiply, 2)`. A call to `double_value(x)` will call `multiply(x, 2)`. This helps with code reusability and also allows deferring execution if needed.

- **Enable easy review of prompts**: That sounds like a tiny little detail, but let's compare two ways of organizing prompts in Python.
  In one way, we use long lines without formatting (we break to the new line only when there's a line break):

  ```
  PROMPT_RAG = """A VERY LONG LINE UNTIL PARAGRAPH BREAKS...
      ANOTHER VERY LONG LINE
      OTHER LINES"""
  ```

  An alternative way is using a string composition pattern:

  ```
  PROMPT_RAG = (
      "A VERY LONG LINE "
  ```

```
        "UNTIL PARAGRAPH BREAKS...\n"
        "ANOTHER ONE"
    )
```

In the second case, a linter will complain about long lines, and you'll need to format them. But imagine if you've changed a word in the middle of a long line; it will be difficult to review or track such a change on GitHub. As you can see, the second version is a better way of organizing your prompts from a readability point of view, so I personally prefer that one.

Let's summarize key best practices around prompt management:

- Keep your prompts versionized and make these versions part of the configuration. Consider using tools such as LangSmith or LangFuse, which are essentially key-value storage with permission management. You can reference each prompt by its name and version, and use different version labels, such as `default` or `dev`, on top of version numbers.
- Make prompts composable and make pieces of your prompts reusable across different applications or prompts. As your application grows, your prompt will grow too, and you should split large prompt templates into smaller parts that are easier to manage.
- Keep prompt parameters consistent. For example, pick one name for a user input variable. The variable name `question` is no better than `input`, `query`, `user_question`, or anything else, but the main thing is to stick to a single name. Otherwise, it increases the risk of errors in your code.

Now that we have discussed how to organize prompt storage in the code base, let's look into aspects of storing and retrieving embeddings, or vectors.

Storing and retrieving embeddings with vector databases

Vector search is behind many GenAI architectures. You may recall that we can represent texts with dense embeddings, or vectors. When we need to find text that is semantically similar to a specific one, we transform the search query into an embedding, use vector search by searching for the nearest vectors to the query, and map found vectors back to the original chunks. This is a classical retrieval phase that is part of RAG applications.

There are a few things you need to understand about the vector search technique. First, vector search is a computationally expensive operation, and performing a brute-force search on a large dataset is almost unfeasible for production purposes. That being said, if you have only 1,000–2,000 vectors, a brute-force search would most likely do the job, and you don't need all the complexity that comes with using a vector database. Many real-world use cases fall into this category, so you can just use a brute-force search and should not overengineer your solution without necessity.

Second, any vector database most likely uses **approximate nearest neighbor** (**ANN**) as a search mechanism. It is designed to prioritize latency over precision. That means that results might not be consistent across runs (for many reasons, including the algorithmic randomness included by design), and it complicates evaluation. Another consequence is that you're not guaranteed to find all matching entries (or all the neighbors). Also, there is no guarantee that ANN will return the best match. If you have such a requirement, consider re-architecting your application and using a different approach.

Different vector databases use different ANN techniques, and you can configure which specific algorithm and distance measure to use when you create an index. Therefore, there are additional hyperparameters of your workflow that you need to tune during development (which, in turn, means that you need to collect an evaluation dataset and run offline experiments, as we discussed in the previous chapter). Support for various ANN algorithms varies across vector databases, so this might influence your choice of vendor.

ANN has other limitations that we will explore next. When designing your GenAI solution (and this is generally true for any data solution), think carefully about your read and write patterns, in particular, the following:

- How often do you want to add new vectors, and what latency do you expect?
- How often do you want to update existing vectors, and what latency do you expect?
- Do you expect to store any metadata and filter by it?
- Do you need to delete vectors, and how often?
- How are you going to promote a new index from staging to production, and what should the process look like?

Answering these questions might help you choose the best vector databases across the many frameworks available.

Now, let's consider the limitations. ANN-based search might not perform well for your use case. If you chunk the knowledge base and represent the resulting chunks as embeddings, you may expect the resulting vectors to be separable based on the semantic meaning of the incoming query (or task). But it's very important to keep in mind that *this doesn't always work well for any use case*. In other words, while you would expect semantically relevant chunks to cluster close to the query in vector space, this is not always the case. Sometimes it works quite well, but in many cases it doesn't, and being aware of this limitation is critical when deciding whether vector search is the right retrieval strategy. That's why we discussed the importance of evaluating the retrieval part of the RAG in the previous chapter. If you discover that a simple out-of-the-box approach doesn't fulfill your needs, try more advanced architectures (which could include trying different hyperparameters, such as a chunking approach, experimenting with hybrid search, re-ranking, agentic RAG, etc.).

In enterprise use cases, there's often a need for additional metadata-based filtering. Almost any vector database allows attaching certain key-value metadata pairs to every vector. This metadata can be retrieved together with embeddings, and you often need to filter it based on certain metadata keys. Let's consider a very simple example, where we have documents that are each associated with a department. When performing a search, we want to search for a given user, and we want to scan through documents only from the IT and product departments. We can do this with either pre-filtering or post-filtering (*Figure 3.1*).

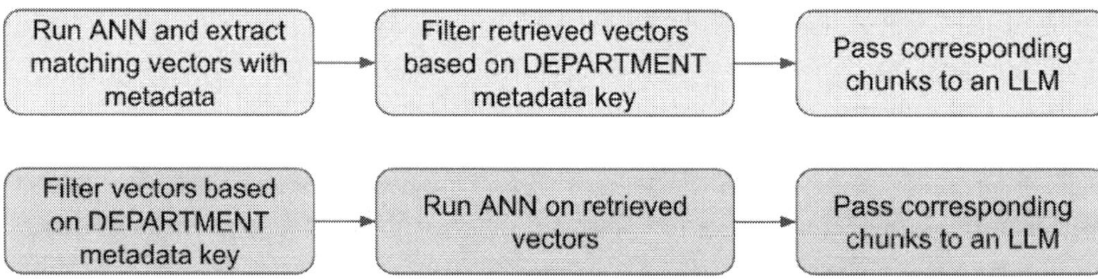

Figure 3.1 – Post-filtering (top) versus pre-filtering (bottom) with ANN

With pre-filtering, we first filter vectors based on metadata, and then we run ANN on an extracted subset of vectors. With post-filtering, we first extract a subset of vectors with ANN, and then we apply an additional filtering step based on metadata. An often-overlooked issue with ANN and metadata filtering is that almost any modern vector database offers only post-filtering (you can read more about how ANN works at `https://research.google/blog/soar-new-algorithms-for-even-faster-vector-search-with-scann/`).

Sometimes it's an advanced post-filtering, for example, a vector database dynamically expands the search if too many results are filtered out based on the metadata filters. Carefully read the documentation of the vector database you're using and be aware that most likely, post-filtering is applied. In most cases, it doesn't influence the retrieval performance too much, but in some cases, it does. The key takeaway is that filtering with vector databases doesn't work in the same straightforward way you're used to when working with relational databases. Applying filters might drastically influence not only latency but also the recall for the given query, and you need to investigate the distribution of your data, the details of the ANN algorithm you're using, and the cardinality of your filters.

If you're interested, take a look at the advanced approach to metadata filtering that Qdrant (a company that develops high-performance, open source vector similarity search databases) uses. They introduce a filterable index, a special way to add additional connections to clusters of vectors to increase the recall when filters are applied (`https://qdrant.tech/articles/vector-search-filtering/#qdrants-approach-to-filtering`).

Going back to the previous example, imagine there are multiple departments and many similar documents across every department. In this case, if we create a separate ANN index per department and search through this index, we might get different results if we search through a unified index with post-filtering. Why is that? In the case of post-filtering, ANN will return a lot of similar documents, but most of them would be filtered out by the metadata filter. This is one additional reason to highlight the crucial importance of a thorough evaluation of the retrieval method using your specific documents and retrieval patterns.

Therefore, when using vector search in your applications, keep in mind the following things:

- Measure the performance of your vector search using recall and latency. Use your domain dataset (that is, data that is close to texts you'll see in production, and queries, including filters, that are close to real ones).
- If you're using metadata-based filtering, analyze your data and remember that if you use metadata filtering, then post-filtering, rather than pre-filtering, is likely being applied.
- Experiment and benchmark! There are multiple hyperparameters that you can tweak during your experiments that might influence overall recall and latency.
- Try hybrid search and re-ranking (more about that in the next section), or more complex techniques, such as query expansion or agentic retrieval.

Now that we've discussed the basics of vector search, let's look at how hybrid approaches can help to overcome the limitations of semantic search we've discussed.

Hybrid search and re-reranking

In the previous section, we discussed some limitations of semantic search, particularly its potential for poor performance when filtering or working with certain types of data. How can these challenges be addressed using hybrid search, and what exactly is hybrid search? To answer that, let's begin by exploring the other search algorithms that are available.

We were able to perform text search before we got good text embeddings. A very basic approach to a text search would be to split a query into separate words, search for documents containing those words, and then combine the results. We can also carry out advanced preprocessing and text normalization techniques such as lemmatization or stemming. Human language is very complex, and text normalization aims to reduce this variability to make it easier to understand for computers when searching. For example, we split texts into words, remove punctuation and very common but "unmeaningful" words, such as *a*, remove suffixes, lowercase words, and so on.

> **Note**
>
> Text normalization is a common preprocessing step when working with text that reduces some noise and complexity from the text and makes it easier for a machine to understand. Examples of text normalization include lowercasing, punctuation removal, stemming, and lemmatization. Stemming is the process of removing a prefix or suffix from a word by converting it to its stem (***studies -> studi, finally -> final***). Lemmatization is a more complex transformation that aims to reduce a word to its lemma, or dictionary form (***studies -> study, finally -> finally***).

Now, let's discuss how we implemented text search before the LLM era (that brought us high-quality embeddings for large texts) and how it can help with RAG development. We will see that vector search can be combined with other search techniques, an approach known as hybrid search.

Inverted index

At the core of a full-text search is an inverted index that maps every word to a list of documents that contain this word.

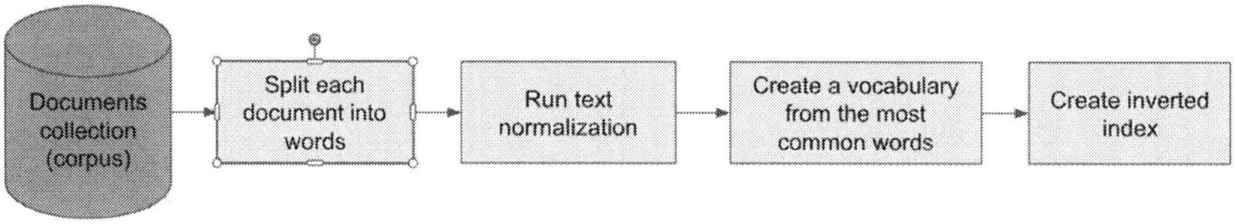

Figure 3.2 – Example pipeline for creating an inverted index for a full-text search

So what do we do when we want to build an inverted index? First, we start with creating an index from a corpus (a collection of documents we're searching across), which includes creating a vocabulary, or a limited list of words that we use for our search. We then transform every piece of text into a finite list of such words. Essentially, we transform the text into a very long vector of 0s and 1s (where a position in a vector represents the ID of the word in the vocabulary list). In other words, we embed our text into vectors, but this time we used *dense* embeddings.

> **Note**
>
> **Dense embeddings** represent text as relatively short (or low-dimensional) vectors (if normalized, then each value is from 0 to 1) that capture semantic representations (i.e., texts with a similar meaning have a similar vector representation). They're called dense because most of their values are non-zero. A **semantic search** is based on dense embeddings and utilizes ANN vector search.
>
> Sparse embeddings represent text as long (or high-dimensional) vectors where most of the values are zero, and dimensions often correspond to specific words in the vocabulary. Sparse embeddings are easily interpretable, and they capture a lexical overlap between a query and a text (by matching exact keywords). We use spare embeddings to build a lexical search using an inverted index.

Now we can split a query into words and retrieve a list of passing documents for every word that is part of the query. This retrieval happens very fast since we keep an inverted index (which maps an ID of a word in the vocabulary to a list of document IDs) in memory. After that, we just merge the documents. We use an inverted index for that. A simplified version of it is shown in *Figure 3.3*, but you can read about more advanced ways of creating indexes for full-text search in the wonderful book *Introduction to Information Retrieval* by Manning et al. (it is available online for free at `www-nlp.stanford.edu/IR-book/`).

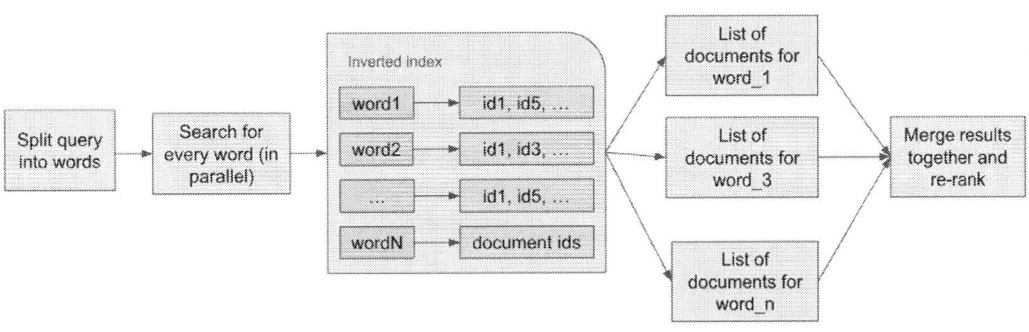

Figure 3.3 – Running a full-text search with an inverted index

Re-ranking and merging results

But how do we merge the resulting lists? A very simple solution would be to just combine all of them, but ideally, we would like to rank the results so that more relevant documents are higher in the list. Algorithms such as **term frequency-inverse document frequency** (**TF-IDF**) enable reflecting how important a word is to a document in a corpus during retrieval. The core idea behind TF-IDF is achieving a balance between how often a word appears in a specific document and how common that word is across all documents in a collection. Words that appear frequently in a single document but are rare in the overall collection are considered more significant and are given a higher ranking score. There exist different variations and extensions of TF-IDF algorithms (for example, BM25), and Elasticsearch, one of the most popular open source engines, based on Apache Lucene, allows the definition of custom similarity functions to perform a fast document search (`https://www.elastic.co/docs/reference/elasticsearch/index-settings/similarity`).

Of course, more advanced techniques exist, and the science of retrieving and ranking text documents is called information retrieval. The book I recommended previously is a great introduction to this topic.

> **Note**
>
> One quick note on language. Many popular embedding or stemming models work well for English (and some other popular languages). But if you're working with non-English languages, double-check the performance of a model of your choice (if it's not sufficient, you might consider other alternatives or even think about training your own embedding model). A funny example that I came across is that a job search platform found out that a popular embedding model didn't perform well for their use case. Why was that? Apparently, a large proportion of its training data was media articles, many of which included clickbait, and that created unexpected associations between some of the job posts. As we will see, sometimes we need to go beyond vector search based on dense embeddings.

But how is full-text search and re-ranking relevant to RAG and GenAI applications? We have a powerful vector search technique based on LLM embeddings (which are dense embeddings), so why do we need to know some old-fashioned way of doing things? First, as our application becomes more sophisticated, we will need to measure the retrieval and re-ranking quality. This has been one of the major topics studied in information retrieval, so we can learn a lot. Second, the hard truth is that this simple schema of *embed -> search based on cosine similarity* doesn't necessarily work well. In some cases (we'll look at an example shortly), we need more sophisticated retrieval approaches, including lexical search. When a user is looking for a specific term, name, or product code, a lexical search typically outperforms a semantic one. Examples of such knowledge bases are legal and academic research, product search (when a user searches for a specific **stock-keeping unit** (**SKU**) and the product code appears in the description), or searching for specific error codes or code snippets in a code base.

We have discussed the possibility of alternative search techniques being beneficial. But what if we want to utilize several of them? For example, say you're working on a chatbot for a retailer and you'd like to add context to specific **SKUs** from the knowledge base to an LLM. From the point of view of dense embeddings, "iPhone 14" and "iPhone 15" are very similar terms, when in reality, some advice for iPhone 14 doesn't apply to iPhone 15. Another example is an enterprise assistant. Imagine you're looking for a rare term, such as "Project DeltaS001" or other internal terms or niche jargon. Dense embeddings won't catch it, while a lexical search would catch exactly the rare term you need.

Let's imagine we run the same query through a lexical and semantic search. Now we need to merge the resulting lists and, ideally, have a meaningful ranking. There are two ways that we can approach this task.

The first one is to merge documents from both lists based on their scores and ranks in the original list. This is called the *fusion* approach. Multiple ways exist, and you can balance how many results you want to include from each list (for example, in practice, we tend to take more items from a semantic search than from a lexical one). Ideally, you should evaluate your retrieval and tune your hyperparameters (such as threshold for semantic or lexical search, maximum number of items from both searches, a specific version of the fusion algorithm, etc.).

To give you a brief idea of how fusion works, let's look at a very simple algorithm called **reciprocal rank fusion** (**RRF**). It takes into account only positions (or ranks) of elements in two (or more) lists. For each element in every list, we first transform the rank to make it smoother (where k is a hyperparameter, for example, $k = 50$):

$$new\_rank_i = \frac{1}{old\_rank_i + k}$$

Then, we summarize all the ranks for a given element across all lists. This is a new score that we use to re-rank all the elements in the final list.

The second way is to use a specialized re-ranking ML model (many of them are based on cross-encoder architectures that are, in fact, transformer ones, as is the case for most of the foundational LLMs) that takes the original query and the list of resulting documents and efficiently re-ranks them. There are some open source re-ranking models (including ones based on the BERT family), as well as proprietary ones from Cohere, Google, and other vendors. You can consider fine-tuning your own re-ranking model when you collect a large enough dataset of examples.

> **Note**
>
> There are two widely used approaches to merging two or more lists resulting from a hybrid search. One is fusion, which represents a function to compute a new score for each element based on its ranks and scores in the resulting lists. Another uses a specialized re-ranking ML model that takes the original query and lists of documents and produces the final ordered list.
>
> Choosing and tuning any of these methods requires a thorough evaluation of your retrieval quality.

Let's look at additional ways to increase the recall of our retrieval phase.

Query expansion

We can even take this a step further. What if we ask an LLM to produce multiple additional queries that might capture different nuances from the original query, search for all of those queries, and then combine the results?

Let's look at a specific example of an advanced RAG pipeline shown in *Figure 3.4*.

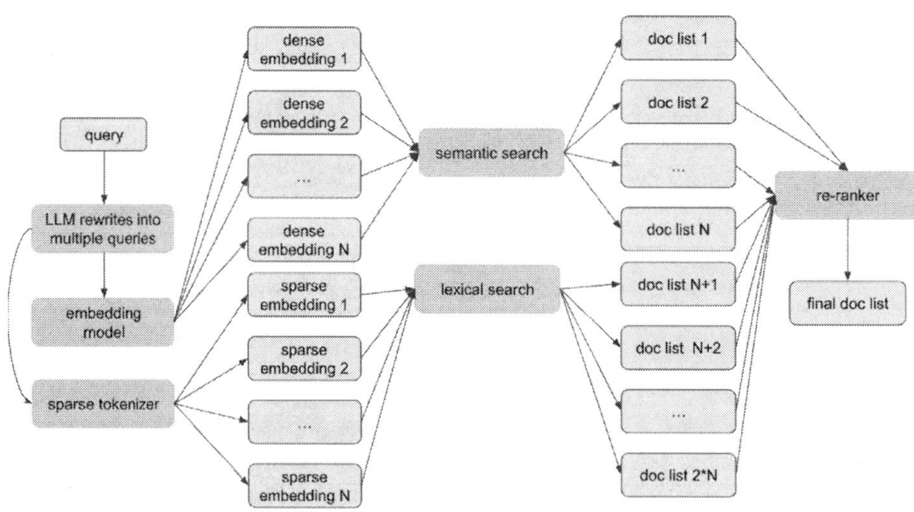

Figure 3.4 – A complex RAG pipeline that utilizes both dense and sparse embeddings

We start with query expansion, and then we run each query through an LLM to get its embeddings, and we tokenize them for lexical search. We perform semantic and lexical search and retrieve corresponding documents for each type of search for each query. Finally, we apply re-ranking to the combined results and return a final list of retrieved documents to the user.

Please note that the final results will be de-duplicated, and we can throw away items with low scores to prevent the final list from being too large (otherwise, we might introduce too much noise to the context passed to an LLM).

We have learned the details of hybrid search and how we can use it for RAG pipelines. Now, let's see another well-known computer science algorithm that is useful in the context of GenAI applications.

Dealing with a limited context window with MapReduce

In GenAI, we need to deal with the issue of a limited context window. This is where MapReduce comes in. We can apply the MapReduce algorithm to GenAI tasks to overcome the limitations of an input context window. MapReduce is a framework for distributed computations that became very popular in the 2010s. It allows data processing to be significantly scaled and has made it possible to develop practical algorithms (such as search, recommendations, transaction analysis, etc.) based on massive amounts of data. Today, many data-processing tools and frameworks use advanced versions of MapReduce where the details of the algorithm are fully abstracted away. Let us take a quick look at the key components of this approach and how we can apply it to GenAI applications.

MapReduce consists of two primary functions: *Map* and *Reduce*. The input data that we need to process is split into multiple chunks that are processed independently and in parallel by a *mapper* that takes each part of the data and transforms it into key-value pairs. After that, a *reducer* applies a reduce function that gets all outputs of the previous step grouped by key as input, and produces an output. The *Reduce* step can also be run in parallel, but to a limited extent, since we need to reshuffle our data so that each worker gets their own key partition.

Let's assume that we want to perform a summarization task on a large text. We have two options. One is to apply the MapReduce paradigm. We split the original text into chunks and summarize each of them in parallel. As a next step, we combine all the sub-summaries into a single input and task an LLM with generating the final summary based on it. Of course, the final quality depends on many factors, including our prompts, how we split the text into chunks, and whether we want these chunks to overlap. This is a fast (since the first sub-summaries can be generated in parallel) and cost-effective process.

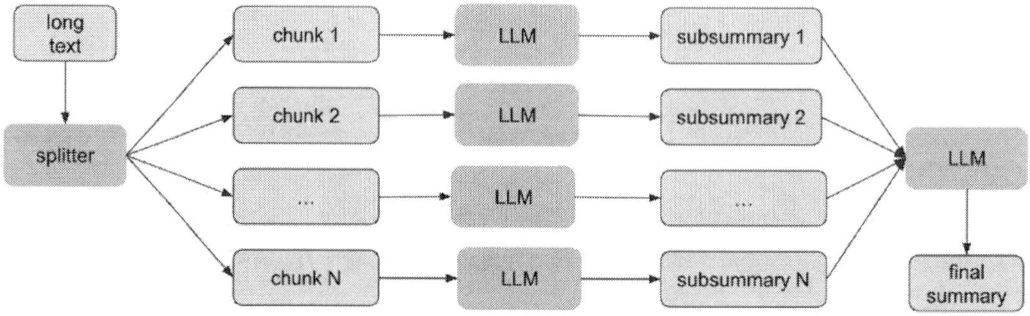

Figure 3.5 – Summarizing a long document in a MapReduce manner by producing multiple sub-summaries in parallel

An alternative way of generating summaries is through consecutive summary generation. We do *N* turns sequentially, and on each turn, we pass to an LLM a new chunk and the previous summary. Of course, it takes $N/2$ more times to generate the final summary, although token consumption is approximately the same, but on certain tasks, the summarization quality might be better with this approach.

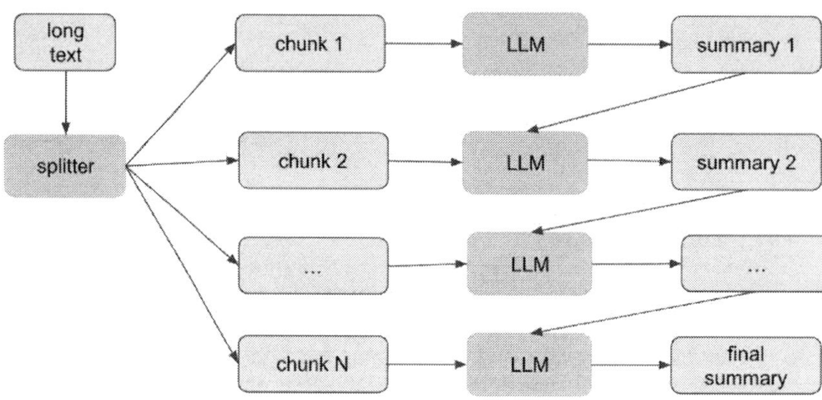

Figure 3.6 – Summarizing a long document in a MapReduce manner by producing sequential sub-summaries

You might ask a reasonable question: why is this relevant? Modern LLMs have very long context windows (up to 1M tokens), and it seems like these approaches were very useful in the early days of GenAI when we were dealing with relatively short context windows. However, knowing such design patterns might still help us design GenAI workflows. First, we sometimes deal with very large inputs that keep growing and exceed even the current context window (as they say, *appetite comes with eating*). Second, we're dealing more and more with multimodal data input (audio, video, images, PDFs, etc.), and the context windows for such data are still limited. Imagine you need to summarize a very long YouTube video or podcast; you would definitely need to take the approach we discussed in this section!

Finally, it's time to talk about one of the hottest topics in GenAI. Let's dive into agents and agentic architectures!

Exploring agentic architectures

In January 2025, at CES in the US, Jensen Huang, the CEO of NVIDIA, said that 2025 would be the year of agents (`https://www.barrons.com/articles/nvidia-stock-ceo-ai-agents-8c20ddfb`). Indeed, we have seen more and more agentic workflows being deployed across enterprises. Let's talk about various aspects of agentic architectures, starting with the definition of an agent.

We briefly discussed what an agent is in the previous chapter, when we talked about evaluating one. There are a lot of definitions of what an agent, or an agentic workflow, is, and it doesn't look like the industry has fully aligned on a single definition. In my book with Ben Auffarth, *Generative AI with LangChain*, we provided an alternative definition of an agent by describing all of its attributes (similar to duck typing). One of the key distinctions of an agent is that it is an orchestrator that wraps an LLM and gives it the capability to interact with an external environment.

Another interesting attribute of an agent (and what is a key distinction between an agent and a workflow) is the degree of freedom that we give to an LLM on how the problem is supposed to be solved. For example, earlier in this chapter, we discussed a MapReduce summarization pattern. We utilize LLMs' in-context learning capabilities; the output of our workflow is non-deterministic, but the execution follows a very specific path. Exact prompts passed to an LLM might change, but they still follow a certain template, and we have determined execution steps. An agent, on the contrary, utilizes an LLM to create the final execution plan. In the next section, we will explore tool calling. We start the execution of a program, and the LLM decides which tools, in which order, and with which input to call. So, an execution flow becomes non-deterministic too. However, we as developers still keep a certain level of control over it; for example, we control the recursion depth (or the maximum number of tool calls an agent is allowed to make before being forced to generate a final answer), which specific tools to use, and so on.

You can imagine additional attributes that characterize an agent (besides interacting with an external environment and letting an LLM partially decide on the execution flow). For example, you may say that an agent typically solves a complex task without a predetermined algorithm to find a solution. Or you may say that an agent is an entity that is helpful to a human.

Now that we have defined what an agent is, let's discuss one of the key paradigms behind agentic AI.

Tool calling

Tool calling is a powerful design pattern for building GenAI applications, enabling LLMs to interact with the external world. While an LLM fundamentally generates tokens based on an input prompt, it has proven to be particularly effective at several subtasks involved in tool integration. Specifically, LLMs are good at the following:

- Generating tokens that represent a valid tool choice
- Generating tokens that represent a relevant payload that can be sent to this tool
- Generating tokens that represent a valid response given intermediate tool calling results

Let's discuss a classic example. We want to ask an LLM questions about the weather forecast. By default, an LLM doesn't know the weather forecast in a given city for the next day. Of course, it can guess, and it can generate tokens that represent the statistically most probable weather forecast for that city (assuming it has seen a lot of weather forecasts in the training data). But we call this a hallucination, since it's most likely not true. What other options do we have? Of course, we can retrain or fine-tune an LLM daily to incorporate all the recent weather forecasts. But that would be a very expensive and complicated process. Luckily, we have another option, which we call the **Reason-Act** (**ReACT**) pattern. Let's give an LLM access to two tools: a weather API and a search engine. But what does "giving access" really mean? We wrap the LLM with an orchestrator, and we add a special instruction to our prompt, something such as this (this is a very simplified example):

```
You have access to a search engine and a weather API. If you're asked about the
weather, you can query the weather API by replying with "WEATHER: " and then
adding a valid JSON that has the date in ISO format and the city name.
```

An orchestrator parses the response, and if the LLM has decided to query the weather API, it does so, and then it adds the initial query and the response back to the prompt that is sent to the model. You can have multiple cycles like this, invoking multiple tools one by one or in parallel, until the LLM replies to the user.

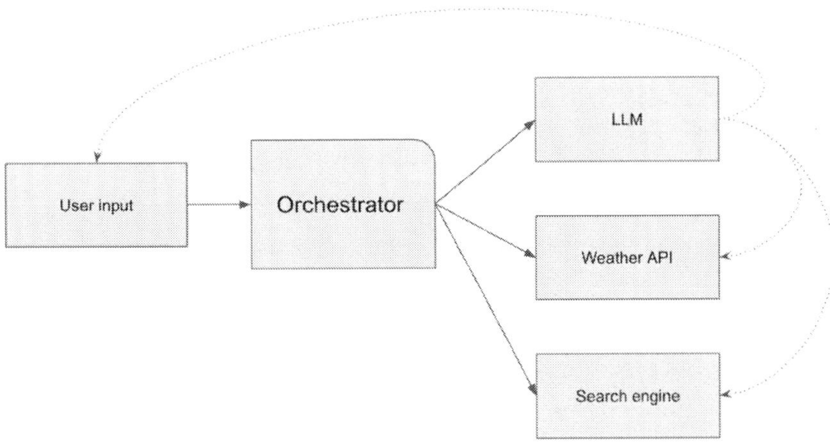

Figure 3.7 – ReACT agent with access to tools such as a weather API and a search engine

In practice, you don't need to do prompting and parsing yourself. Almost any foundational LLM (at least, if we're not talking about small open sourced ones) has an API that allows you just to define tools as special objects, and you get a special formatted `tool_call` object (the name might be different, depending on the LLM provider you're using) as a response from the model's API (if it decides to call a tool). You still need to add orchestration logic on your side that would call a tool, and resend the request (the original request, the LLM's response, and a specially constructed tool response) to the model's API. But composing it all into a final prompt would happen on the provider's side.

So, what are tools? Tools are external APIs or other callables that have a structured input and a description, and when called, they provide an output that an LLM can interpret. Note that the terms *tool* and *function*, or *tool calling* and *function calling*, are used interchangeably in the industry.

There are three important things to keep in mind.

- First, an LLM expects an OpenAPI-compatible specification of a tool's input. The OpenAPI specification is pretty rich, and your tool might have a complicated input schema that has nested fields or references to other schemas, allows for union, or keywords such as `optional` or `oneOf` (if you are new to this specification, you can explore `https://swagger.io/docs/specification/v3_0/data-models/oneof-anyof-allof-not/`). If you're using such a complex schema, a good idea would be to double-check that the foundational model that you're using supports all these definitions, and how the SDK converts your tool schema to the actual schema that is sent to the model. Sometimes you may need to manually adjust the input schema so that it's understood by the model.

- Second, names and descriptions of tools and their variables are often crucial for the performance of your application. Think about defining your tools as a continuation of the prompt-engineering exercises that we're all accustomed to; pay attention to this aspect and continue experimenting. For example, if you have the API `open-meteo.com`, it might be a good idea to rename it `weather_api` and add the description `This API provides a weather forecast for the next 30 days for the given location.` Then, you can tweak the description if you observe that an LLM fails to call this tool when appropriate. In an agentic flow, an LLM can fail on multiple fronts:
    - It can miss calling a tool that it should call
    - It can call a tool that it shouldn't call
    - It can call a tool with an invalid schema (for example, forget about required arguments)
    - It can call a tool with a valid schema but wrong values (for example, you ask for the weather in Munich, but the agent calls a weather API for the weather in London)

  If you spot such issues during debugging and evaluation, an immediate way to fix them is to tweak the description of your tools. In the preceding example, I might change the description to something such as `Call this API when you need a weather forecast for the next 30 days for the given location. Always pass a location that is a three-letter code for the city.`

  An LLM doesn't have access to your tool and its actual implementation; all it knows is the information you provided to it in the description. So, treat it as another part of the prompt engineering exercise.

- Last but not least, tool calling is a more powerful paradigm than connecting an LLM to an external environment (although this alone opens up plenty of possibilities). You can use a tool-calling paradigm for controlled generation. Let's imagine we want an LLM to define a plan of action that is actually a list of strings (or it might be a more complex object). Instead of carefully instructing the LLM and parsing its output, we can define a data class or a Pydantic (or another schema definition language) model. It's an easy and abstract way to define a data structure. Let's take a look at an example of how we define a `Plan` object with Pydantic using type hints and a `Field` object to provide arguments' descriptions:

```
from pydantic import BaseModel, Field

class Plan(BaseModel):
    """A high-level plan to accomplish a task."""

    steps: list[str] = Field(description="A concise description of a step.
Focus on WHAT should be achieved and provide additional guidance on HOW to
do that.")
```

Most modern SDKs and GenAI frameworks can auto-convert such a structure into a tool, since it has a name and a description (a docstring), and each argument has a docstring too (we need to create one, though).

You can generalize it to other use cases besides controlled generation. Let's take a look at another example.

Task decomposition and tree of thoughts

When we talk about agents, there are two crucial patterns that we need to know about. The first is task decomposition. To phrase it simply, *"LLMs have demonstrated ability to solve complex tasks when the tasks are broken into simpler subtasks"* (`https://arxiv.org/abs/2308.08155`). An LLM's performance on a complex task can be improved if it is wrapped by an external program that goes through the planning and execution phases. During the planning phase, the LLM itself prepares a step-by-step plan, and during the execution phase, it works on each part of this plan (taking into account outcomes from the previous steps). This idea seems very simple, but it works incredibly well. If you're interested in learning more, I recommend taking a look at the original paper *Plan-and-Solve Prompting: Improving Zero-Shot Chain-of-Thought Reasoning by Large Language Models*, the link to which can be found in the *Further reading* section at the end of the chapter.

> **Note**
>
> The decomposition, or plan-and-solve, design pattern illustrates many other design patterns in agentic AI. Instead of having one large complex prompt with multiple instructions and conditions inside, try to guide an LLM on how to solve the task by giving a reasoning flow to it. Keep in mind that we give the LLM a lot of freedom: it builds the plan and it executes this plan itself. But we still give it a certain framework of how the execution flow should look.

We can take it a step further. Let's remember that LLMs are non-deterministic, which means we can generate not just a single plan but multiple plans. Or at each step, when we're adjusting the next step based on previous results, we might generate multiple candidates (or maybe execute a specific step in a slightly different way with varying outcomes), as shown in *Figure 3.8*. In other words, we're building a tree of actions (such a paradigm is called tree of thoughts), and this tree grows very fast.

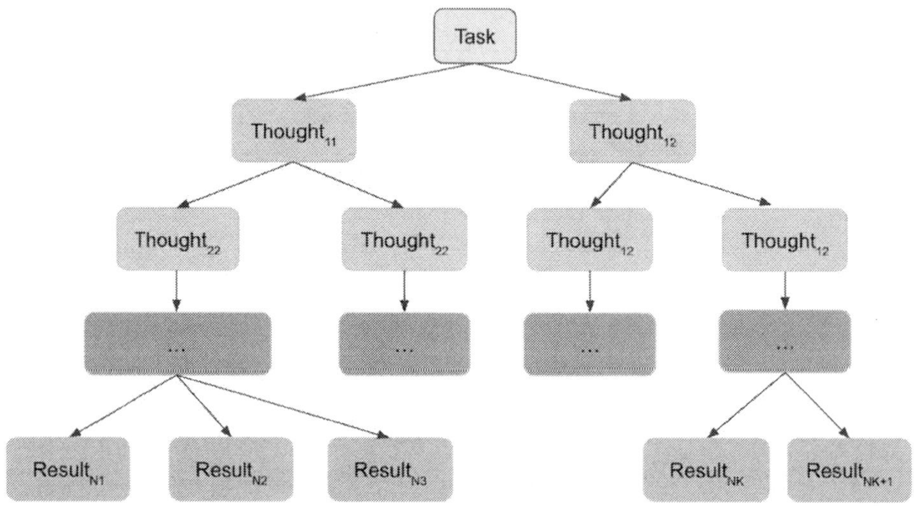

Figure 3.8 – A tree-of-thoughts agent

Let's forget for a moment the polynomial expansion of this tree and explore this tree to the final nodes. We have simulated different outcomes for the problem. How do we pick the best one to return to the user? We can use an external simulator to evaluate the quality of the solution (if we have one), or we can use the LLM-as-a-judge approach that we learned about in *Chapter 2*. Anyway, we generate multiple solutions for the problem, and we find a way to pick the best one to present to the user. We have seen that such an approach improves the problem-solving abilities of LLMs on many kinds of non-trivial tasks. Of course, since we are exploring many options, our costs increase significantly, but for complex tasks, that might be worth it.

Now, let's get back to the problem of the tree expanding very fast. We can use various heuristics to trim it early and drop the paths that are definitely not worth exploring. If you're interested in learning more about that, take a look at the paper *Language Agent Tree Search Unifies Reasoning Acting and Planning in Language Models*, linked in the *Further reading* section, to get started.

Such approaches that balance exploration and exploitation remind us of reinforcement learning techniques. If there is a way to get feedback from the environment on how good the solution you have found so far is, you can explore more promising branches of the tree.

Allowing GenAI to run multiple experiments when interacting with the external environment is a powerful pattern that is behind the famous AlphaEvolve, a coding agent for designing advanced algorithms presented by Google in May 2025 (`https://deepmind.google/discover/blog/alphaevolve-a-gemini-powered-coding-agent-for-designing-advanced-algorithms/`). A simple version of this agent called FunSearch was the first to make discoveries in open problems in mathematical sciences using LLMs; you can study its detailed design in the original paper and the open sourced code that was behind this agent at `https://github.com/google-deepmind/funsearch`.

The task decomposition and tree-of-thoughts patterns have a significant implication on how we think about GenAI products. We're used to thinking that we want to give users interactivity and real-time performance when they interact with assistants, and that's how we design our products. But pause for a moment and imagine that you're using an AI assistant that helps you prepare a slide deck. What would you prefer—a rough presentation that is created almost immediately after you've asked for it, or a perfect presentation that takes an AI tool 10 minutes to prepare? It probably depends. If you need to present in five minutes, you would probably prefer the first option. But I can very much imagine a lot of situations where the second option would be preferable (at the end of the day, we all like to let AI work while we sip a coffee, from time to time). Hence, we need to redesign the interaction with such systems and let them work asynchronously, exploring and simulating multiple options while finding the best one to present to the user.

Multi-agentic systems

In the previous section, we discussed how splitting a complex problem into subtasks might improve its performance on complex tasks. Some of these tasks might be performed in parallel, so let's go a step further and imagine a multi-agent system where different sub-agents have access to different subsets of tools, and they work on different subtasks. Sub-agents can vary from each other in the following ways:

- By having access to different subsets of tools (it has been demonstrated that if we have many tools available and an LLM has access to all of them simultaneously, its performance degrades)
- By utilizing different prompting strategies and hyperparameters specific to specific classes of tasks
- A sub-agent might have different underlying flows and configurations that result from tuning its performance on specific classes of tasks (for example, we can have a very specialized deep research agent that the upstream agent involves when needed)

How do sub-agents communicate with each other? There are two polarities. First, we task each sub-agent with the same task as shown in *Figure 3.9* and then choose the best outcome (in other words, we make them compete). We choose to use the same consensus mechanisms we discussed in *Chapter 2* that use LLM-as-a-judge, majority voting, or similar approaches.

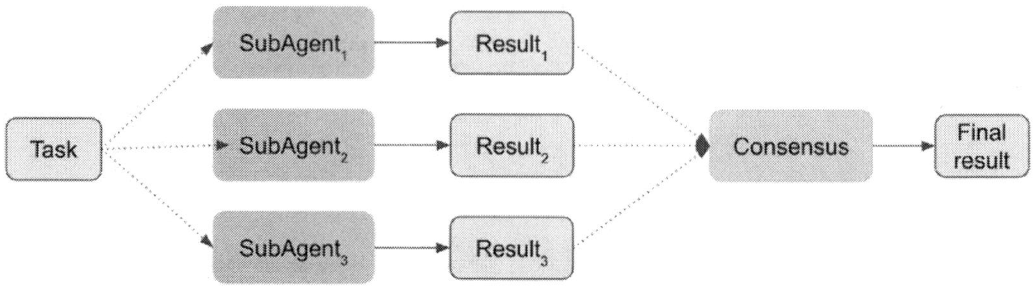

Figure 3. 9 – A multi-agentic system that parallelizes the task execution and reaches a consensus afterward

On the other hand, as shown in *Figure 3.10*, we can orchestrate sub-agents by the upstream agent that breaks down the task into subtasks and assigns subtasks to specific sub-agents.

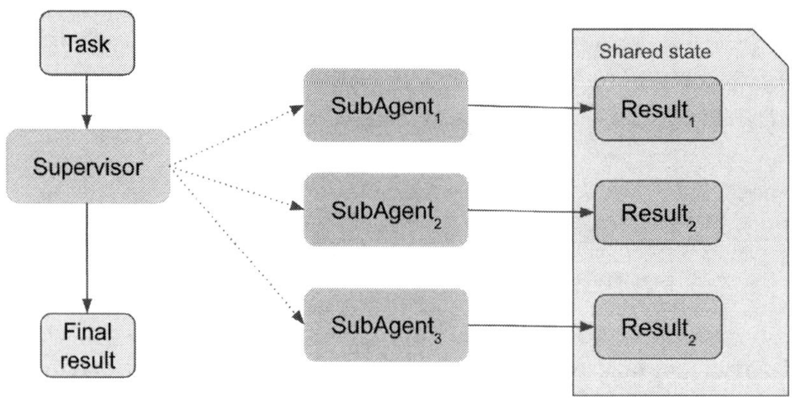

Figure 3.10 – A multi-agentic system with a supervisor that schedules tasks to sub-agents and reuses their results

And, of course, we can design our system somewhere in between: let sub-agents communicate with each other and work on solving a task collaboratively (either directly in a one-by-one manner, or in an all-to-all manner). A very simple example of such a pattern (it looks more complicated when you have a larger number of agents) is a reflection pattern where you ask another instance of an LLM to review the result of the previous step (that has a different system prompt, instruction, and hyperparameters such as temperature).

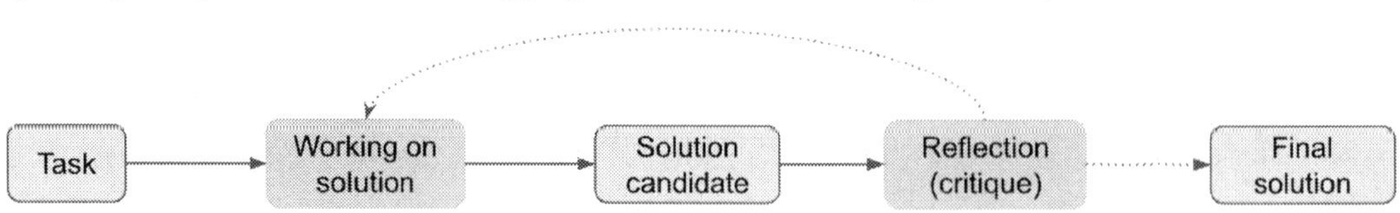

Figure 3.11 – An agent that uses a reflection pattern

Your workflows might even benefit from blending different foundational models: both models of different providers or different families. For example, you might use a cheaper and faster model family (such as Gemini Flash) to solve most of the easy subtasks, but use a larger reasoning model (such as Gemini Pro) for planning and evaluation steps. If you're interested in learning more, check out the *Further reading* section at the end of this chapter.

An important design choice remains around a shared context. Should all sub-agents have access to the same shared state, or should we give them only a very specific task and the information needed for this task? If we do the former, we're at risk of our context increasing and becoming noisy for a sub-agent (we might try to address this by using context-compressing techniques that summarize it or extract important aspects). If we do the latter, we're at risk of the sub-agent missing some details because they don't have access to the full context. That's why the design choice always depends on the details of the specific task. A good blog post from Congition.ai, *Don't Build Multi-Agents*, discusses this design choice in more detail (`https://cognition.ai/blog/dont-build-multi-agents/`).

As we discussed in *Chapter 1*, always start simple. Multi-agentic systems are associated with higher costs and higher latency (which might not fit well with users' expectations). And, of course, as we already know, the evaluation of multi-agentic systems gets more complicated, and the accuracy of the end-to-end workflow might drop unexpectedly. Let's do a simple math exercise. Imagine that each LLM-based step has an accuracy of 95%, and all steps are independent. Then, if you have two steps in the workflow, the end-to-end accuracy will be $0.95^2 = 90\%$. But if there are 10 steps in the workflow, the end-to-end accuracy will be $0.95^{10} = 60\%$.

External orchestrator

As discussed in the previous section, an LLM has only partial control over the execution flow. That gives us an answer to a potential question you might ask: why do we need a specialized framework to build agents? From my point of view, the answer is simple (although there is always more nuance). Many orchestration frameworks (such as Airflow and Dagster) do not allow cycles, and they don't provide a good enough developer experience to encode partial control over the execution flow. To account for that, we need to use frameworks such as LangGraph or write our custom mini-frameworks.

Another rationale behind a specialized orchestration framework is that many agentic executions are long-running operations. Either a lot of time lapses as an agent needs to run multiple simulations until it finds the best solution (as we saw in the *Task decomposition and tree of thoughts* section), or just planning, exploring, and executing the task takes a long time. By "a long time," I mean a length of time that makes it impractical to maintain the connection (and the frontend waiting for the result). Also, you are left hoping that the workflow runs without errors or exceptions. The more tools the agent calls while working on a task, the more likely it is to fail and need a restart from the last successful state (it's like trying to pass a level in a computer game; you might need to save and restore multiple times).

If you're interested in learning more about this topic and seeing a comparison of various frameworks, take a look at the blog post from Harrison Chase, the CEO and co-founder of LangChain (*Why do I need LangGraph Platform for agent deployment?*, `https://blog.langchain.com/why-langgraph-platform/`).

Operationalizing the tool-calling pattern

When thinking about bringing our applications to production and scaling the number of agents and the number of tools they use, we need to keep in mind a lot of additional aspects that we will cover in later chapters, such as modularizing our tools and creating a tool registry, authentication, managing permissions, and creating secure environments for tool execution.

I often see, in teams developing GenAI applications, an urge to start using an MCP server. My advice would be to think twice before deciding to use an MCP server. Let's first discuss what **MCP**, or **Model Context Protocol**, is. It is an "*open standard that enables developers to build secure, two-way connections between their data sources and AI-powered tools*" (`https://www.anthropic.com/news/model-context-protocol`) introduced by Anthropic in November 2024. MCP operates based on a client-server architecture. Note that you can have multiple MCP servers to connect with since different providers might have different MCP servers implementing their integration, but they expose the same API, and you can use these MCP servers in the same way. A good starting list of available integrations can be found here: `github.com/modelcontextprotocol/servers`.

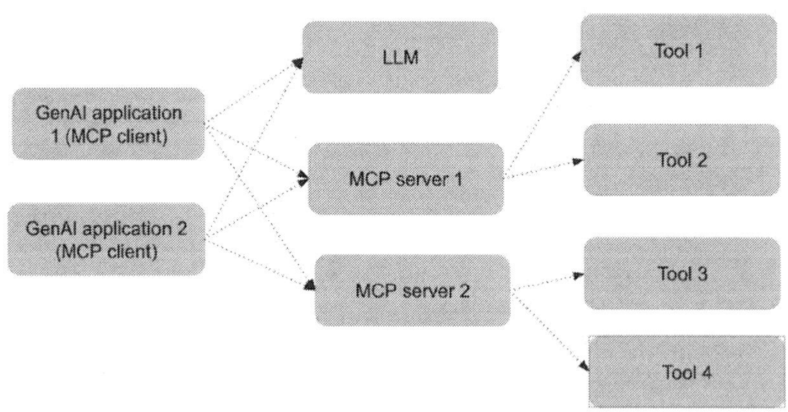

Figure 3.12 – GenAI applications accessing tools through an MCP server

An MCP server exposes a list of available prompt templates, tools, resources, and, of course, an API to call exposed tools. We have talked a lot about tools, so let's now quickly touch on resources. Resources are a way for an MCP server to expose any type of content to its users (for example, database entries, drafts of emails composed by a corresponding tool, files, etc.). The website `modelcontextprotocol.io/introduction` is a good starting point if you want to learn more about MCP.

Nonetheless, remember that you're developing a relatively simple and self-contained application that uses a fixed amount of integrations and internal tools; you most probably do not need the complexity that MCP brings with it. But if you want to expose your agent to customers who are going to connect it with their own tools and data sources, then MCP might be a good thing to try.

Agentic memory

Agents need external memory for two reasons. First, as agents become increasingly complex, and one execution takes more iterations, the probability of a failure increases. Secondly, this is further compounded by the fact that agents interact with external systems and invoke tools. Since tool calls often rely on LLM-generated payloads, failures can occur at various stages. We need to recover from such failures and continue execution from where we failed, not from scratch. Hence, we need short-term memory. The ability of an agent to memorize the current dialogue also falls under the short-term memory definition.

> **Note**
>
> Short-term memory has a limited capacity and duration, and it typically covers one session with the user. Important aspects of short-term memory are trimming the history (if needed) and the ability to serialize and deserialize an agent at every stage in order to recover from failures efficiently.

When talking about short-term memory (or, in other words, the ability of an agent to preserve context within a session), we need to discuss two aspects.

One is that at each sub-iteration, an agent's state should be serializable. In other words, we should be able to dump it into a file and restore an agent so that it can continue its work on a task exactly from the same state. If that's the case, then we can easily dump an agent's state to a file after each step and restore it if needed. Frameworks such as LangGraph do this under the hood, and they allow for keeping so-called snapshots in a filesystem or in a database. And, of course, we need to delete (or garbage collect) older stale snapshots that are not needed anymore.

Another important aspect when working with short-term memory is trimming the dialogue history. In general, we can trim the history in three ways:

- Delete older messages when the total length/number of messages (based on the number of messages or tokens consumed) exceeds a certain threshold.
- Summarize all the history into one summary that will be added to the LLM's context. Modern frameworks allow performing this summarization asynchronously (as a background task) in order not to influence the end user's latency.
- Combine both approaches (keep part of the history below a certain threshold as is and compress the rest with summarization).

Again, as the context window of modern LLMs increases, these trimming techniques become less important. On the other hand, users continue passing more and more complex input to the document (such as video, audio, and long PDFs) that might still exceed the context length.

Another type of agentic memory is long-term memory. Many researchers and practitioners have highlighted the importance of lifelong agents' memory in long-term, multi-session interactions, "*where agents ought to constantly keep track of both old and newly introduced information shared with users throughout their service lives and converse accordingly*" (`https://arxiv.org/abs/2406.10996`). In other words, long-term memory is the ability of an agent to preserve important information across a session. For example, if you've implemented a shopping assistant, a user would expect it to memorize the preferences and details of the user (once they have mentioned it in the conversation), such as whether they have kids, drive a car, play sports, or prefer healthy food, and not ask this question each time. An assistant should extract this information, store it, and add it to the context, but in a smart way (if it just put everything it has learned in the context each time, this would inflate costs and might decrease the quality as it would add noise to the input).

When we talk about long-term memory, we need to store information efficiently and retrieve only relevant context from memory to add to the current prompt, as shown in *Figure 3.13*. One approach is to utilize existing components that we know LLMs excel at: attribute extraction from text, retrieval, re-ranking, and so on. We extract facts or snippets from previous conversations and store entries in a memory bank, and we run a classical retrieval process on top of the memory bank.

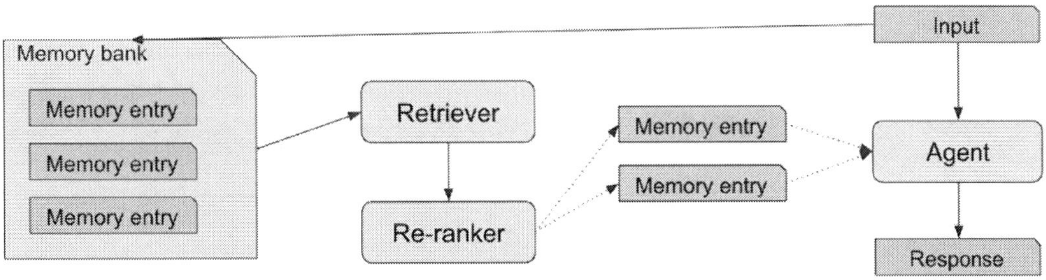

Figure 3.13 – Using long-term memory

To learn more about memory banks, the paper *In Prospect and Retrospect: Reflective Memory Management for Long-term Personalized Dialogue Agents*, which you can find linked in the *Further reading* section, is a good starting point.

Summary

In this chapter, we looked into key architectural patterns and design considerations crucial for building production-ready GenAI applications. We began by exploring how to organize and version prompt templates. Then we discussed vector databases, a key aspect of developing RAG applications. We examined the nuances of vector search, the trade-offs of ANN algorithms, and the critical role of metadata filtering in enterprise use cases. We then expanded our understanding of retrieval techniques by discussing hybrid search and re-ranking, contrasting dense and sparse embeddings, and highlighting situations where lexical search can outperform semantic search. We also explored fusion approaches and the use of specialized re-ranking models.

Next, we introduced the MapReduce paradigm, demonstrating how this distributed computation framework can be applied to GenAI tasks such as summarizing large texts, especially when dealing with limited context windows or multimodal data.

Finally, we ventured into the world of agents, defining their attributes and examining powerful design patterns such as tool calling, task decomposition, and tree of thoughts. We discussed how these patterns empower LLMs to interact with external environments, plan complex tasks, and even explore multiple solutions asynchronously. We also touched upon multi-agentic systems, exploring different communication and orchestration strategies and the importance of external orchestrators and memory (both short-term and long-term) for robust agentic applications. In the next chapter, we will talk about issues related to scaling your application from a prototype to production, and how to overcome them.

Note

The three key outcomes to remember are as follows:

- Vector databases typically use ANN search, which doesn't guarantee that the closest vector will be returned, and metadata filtering is often post-filtering rather than pre-filtering. Hence, always consider running a separate retrieval quality evaluation when developing a RAG solution, and explore various hybrid search approaches (sparse embeddings might work better than you expect!).
- Multi-agent systems typically come with a higher latency and are complex to evaluate. Consider starting simple, and keep in mind that each additional step in your workflow might lower the overall accuracy due to compounding errors. If a single step has 95% accuracy, then a workflow that has 10 independent steps will have only 60% accuracy.
- The tool-calling paradigm is a very powerful approach that allows LLM to interact with the environment and get domain knowledge. But the LLM doesn't have access to the tool implementation itself. Hence, it's important to treat tool description (including its schema and description of each field) as a part of the prompt-engineering exercise, and iterate on various descriptions to increase the performance.

Further reading

- *Prompt Engineering Guide*. `https://www.promptingguide.ai/`
- Auffarth, B. and Kuligin, L. (2025) *Generative AI with LangChain: Build production-ready LLM applications and advanced agents using Python, LangChain, and LangGraph*, Packt Publishing
- Wu, Q., Bansal, G., Zhang, J., et al. (2023) *AutoGen: Enabling Next-Gen LLM Applications via Multi-Agent Conversation*. `https://arxiv.org/abs/2308.08155`
- Wang, L., Xu, W., Lan, Y., et al. (2023) *Plan-and-Solve Prompting: Improving Zero-Shot Chain-of-Thought Reasoning by Large Language Models*. `https://arxiv.org/abs/2305.04091`
- Yao, S., Yu, D., Zhao, J., et al. (2023) *Tree of Thoughts: Deliberate Problem Solving with Large Language Models*. `https://arxiv.org/pdf/2305.10601`

- Zhou, A., Yan, K., Shlapentokh-Rothman, M., et al. (2023) *Language Agent Tree Search Unifies Reasoning Acting and Planning in Language Models.* `https://arxiv.org/abs/2310.04406`
- Romera-Paredes, B., Barekatain, M., Novikov, A. et al. (2024) *Mathematical Discoveries from Program Search with Large Language Models.* Nature 625, 468–475. `https://doi.org/10.1038/s41586-023-06924-6`
- *Building effective agents.* `https://www.anthropic.com/engineering/building-effective-agents`
- Multi-agent systems. `https://docs.langchain.com/oss/python/langchain/multi-agent`
- Ong, K.T.-I., Kim, N., Gwak, M., et al. (2024) *Towards Lifelong Dialogue Agents via Timeline-based Memory Management.* `https://arxiv.org/abs/2406.10996`
- Tan, Z., Yan, J., Hsu, I.-H., et al. (2025) *In Prospect and Retrospect: Reflective Memory Management for Long-term Personalized Dialogue Agents.* `https://arxiv.org/abs/2503.08026`

4

From Prototype to Production

You've done the hard part: you have a working proof of concept that demonstrates that your idea is technically feasible and brings real value to the business. This moment of success, however, is often where teams make their first critical mistake: not realizing that a prototype is *very* different from a production application. We will understand what this "very" entails in this chapter. Your initial focus was on the "happy path" and impressing stakeholders; now, you need to shift focus to delivering reliable value at scale.

As we already briefly learned in *Chapter 1*, teams often underestimate the effort required to make a prototype production-ready. The real engineering and architectural work begins with the transition from a successful experiment to a system your users can truly depend on, and simultaneously preparing for the chaotic reality of real-world systems, where malformed data and third-party failures are the norm rather than the exception.

This chapter serves as your practical blueprint for making your GenAI application production-ready. We will move beyond the high-level concerns to examine the specific changes needed in your code, architecture, and team processes to guarantee stability, robustness, and ease of extension. You will learn the fundamental differences between prototypes and production applications, as well as learning about core engineering best practices for version control systems, code readability, and principles such as the **Single Responsibility Principle** (**SRP**) and **Don't Repeat Yourself** (**DRY**). We'll then discuss a comprehensive testing strategy for GenAI, including unit, integration, and load testing.

Finally, we will discuss the balance between engineering quality and the speed of product delivery, how to keep a backdoor for quick fixes in your AI product, and how to onboard new users when expanding the user base.

By the end of this chapter, you will have learned how to implement essential code quality standards, and, most importantly, design a testing strategy that accounts for the non-deterministic and external dependencies inherent to GenAI. In this chapter, we will be covering the following topics:

- Why operationalization matters
- Code readability
- Testing
- Keeping it simple
- Taking the quick-fix path
- Onboarding users

Why operationalization matters

You might have heard about "operationalization" or "productionization" of an ML model or a prototype. However, when you already have a perfectly working prototype, why should you bother at all with operationalization? In fact, what is operationalization? It is the process of converting a prototype to a production-ready system. In this section, we'll discuss what additional qualities such a system should have.

When you're developing a prototype, your main goal is to evaluate the business feasibility of your idea. You want to see clear evidence that GenAI is useful, and that it can solve some problems that exist in your organization or across your customers in a new, unprecedented way. Your focus is on the happy path, and you want to see clear evidence that the core idea is useful and can solve a problem in a new way. You want to iterate fast since you need to run a lot of experiments before you end up with a well-working model, and all you care about is impressing stakeholders.

What changes when you go into production? Now you take responsibility for delivering *reliable* value at *scale*. You now have an implicit contract with your users that you will always (or, to be precise, *almost always*, but we will talk more about reliability in *Chapter 8*) provide a certain level of quality and user experience. This shift in responsibility forces you to think about a new set of priorities. While your prototype focused on the happy path and a wow effect, when you go to production, the team needs to balance multiple aspects of your application, such as the following:

- **Stability**: Stability, or reliability, in software engineering corresponds to the ability of an application to function as intended for a long period of time. We will learn more about this in *Chapter 8*.
- **Generalization and robustness**: This entails checking that your application works for all users and their use cases, not just for a curated happy path.

- **Cost and performance**: This includes the implications of high latency and the cost of infrastructure.
- **Cost of maintenance**: This includes ease of improving the system, fixing bugs, and adding new features.

We will talk more about stability in *Chapter 8*, and about improving cost and performance in other chapters. For now, let's discuss the importance of generalization, and then we will talk about the cost of maintenance and what a production-ready application really means (in the *Code readability* and *Testing* sections).

When you develop a prototype, you curate some common scenarios, prepare clean examples of input and outputs, and demonstrate that the idea works. When you move to production, you need to face the chaotic reality of real-world systems.

The first of these realities is that your production application will, at some point, receive malformed, inconsistent, or unexpected data and inputs (different encodings, varying quality of data you depend on, etc.), which might lead to a failure, or even worse, bad output. For example, if you're building a RAG application, you probably used a few curated examples of documents to ground responses on. A real knowledge base might contain malformed PDFs, scans that are of poor quality, or PDFs that are thousands of pages long. I once had my chunking pipeline fail because one of the thousands of provided PDFs had a size of more than 100 gigabytes and contained thousands of malformed pages.

Second, your GenAI application most likely depends on some third-party APIs or services. It calls an external vendor API (such as Google or Anthropic), a vector database, or internal microservices. What happens when one of those services fails or times out? A prototype might simply crash and you need to restart it, but a production application should handle failures gracefully with retries, fallbacks, and user-friendly error messages.

Third, you will need to deal with different edge cases and nuanced business requirements. You might need to manage different input or output languages or maintain some obscure business logic.

Last but not least, you will need to deal with non-functional requirements, such as security, guardrails against adversarial attacks, compliance, and fairness.

And dealing with these new requirements (functional and not-functional) that will keep popping up will require you to change and evolve your application. Constant changes and unclear requirements that do not allow us to choose the most appropriate architecture is the fate of almost any software engineering project. Hence, let's see how to make your application ready for such an evolution. Let us look at how to use version control systems that help you manage your code evolution and what changes you should make when transitioning from a proof of concept to a production-ready application. Later, in *Chapter 5*, we will provide a more general perspective of automation engineering processes, and we will discuss DevOps and its philosophy.

You may think that version control systems are universally known now. However, while software engineers might be familiar with them, for some data scientists, they might be a new way of working that they haven't fully adopted.

> **Note**
>
> **Git** is the most popular version control system, and many platforms, such as GitHub, GitLab, and Bitbucket, use it.

Even if you're familiar with version control systems, you may benefit from the following recommendations while using them:

- Store all project artifacts in GitHub, including Jupyter notebooks. Keep notebooks in a dedicated experiments folder and commit them as-is. Engineers sometimes clear cell outputs before committing, either to make future diffs easier to review or to reduce diff size. However, this practice can make notebooks harder to read and understand, especially when important outputs are removed.
- Add code reviews even for Jupyter notebooks. Getting a second opinion always helps, and teams often underestimate the importance of reviewing analytical, data exploration, and ML prototyping results. Reviewing Jupyter notebooks in the GitHub UI might be difficult; hence, consider using libraries such as `nbdime` or `reviewnb`. But it's still very important to introduce a review phase for Jupyter notebooks, too.
- Switch to writing reusable code early in the process. It speeds up development, makes your code more reusable and readable, and decreases time to market.
- Keep track of the dependencies from the very beginning. Sometimes installing a library and making it work requires quite a few steps. For instance, running a `pip install` command may be simple, but installing OpenCV or another library that requires binary packages to be installed on your OS can be complex.
- Be careful with introducing too many dependencies. Of course, you don't need to re-invent the wheel, but too many dependencies can make your applications heavy, increase the risk of vulnerabilities, and so on. If you introduce a new open source library, it's also a good idea to check how well it is maintained. It might be a good idea to check the frequency of releases, how active the community is and its size, and so on. And, of course, as you move to production, try to remove unnecessary dependencies

from the runtime application. It's typically a good idea to have separate lock files for production, development, and test environments.

- Track binary (and non-binary, such as large CSV or JSON files that, for example, contain data) artifacts larger than a few kilobytes outside of Git. Use blob storage (such as GCS, S3, etc.) or Git LFS to store Excel files, PDFs, and other artifacts. Otherwise, large binary files will pollute the Git log since it will grow too large in size. Sometimes, data scientists use Excel files as configs, but I would advise against this; since the size of a binary is large, it pollutes the Git diff, and the diff is not displayed properly over iterations. Use JSON, YAML, or any other text-only format.
- Do not forget to maintain Git hygiene. Implement a branching strategy such as branch protection rules (which don't allow pushing to the `main` branch directly or merging unreviewed pull requests), connect your GitHub to your project management system, unify pull request descriptions and branch names, and use commit and branch naming conventions.
- Master Git command-line commands and learn how to rebase, switch between branches, squash commits, move files to and from staging, and so on. Being familiar with Git will speed up your development. Commit locally more frequently in small chunks, which will help you to experiment faster and roll back failing attempts. Often, while you're working on a feature and you've made some progress, you mistakenly perform some code changes or refactoring. If you haven't committed your previous successful state, it becomes difficult to undo everything and start again from the checkpoint. So, the proper use of Git with intermediate commits (which you can squash together when creating a final merge request) can save you as an engineer a lot of effort.

If you're new to Git, a great free website to learn Git commands is `https://githowto.com/en/setup`.

Next, let's talk about another aspect of working with production code.

Code readability

When you're prototyping, you often start with Jupyter notebooks. It's a convenient way for a data scientist or an ML engineer to run quick experiments. But as you can imagine, it's not recommended to go to production with such notebooks since it would be very difficult to guarantee reliability (for multiple reasons such as issues with testability, reproducibility, ease of change, etc.).

As I've already mentioned in *Chapter 1* and *Chapter 3*, there are very few universal best practices in software engineering. You should always consider your current context and business requirements. For example, let's say you need to run a batch job, which is not crucial for a business process, every week, and you expect it to just be a temporary solution. In this case, simply scheduling a Jupyter notebook to run weekly might be the best way to achieve your goals. But the situation changes completely when you have dozens of batch jobs, you serve thousands or millions of users, and your applications are business-critical.

Production-ready code has four important properties:

- **Ready to read and understand for everybody**: It's likely that in six months, you will forget what you're doing now because you will have other important tasks. Coming back to code that you wrote a while ago might be a difficult task even for you as the author. Pretty often, you need a quick answer to the question, "Why does the system behave this way?" You should be able to get an answer by quickly scanning the code base.
- **Easy to maintain for everybody**: Typical maintenance tasks involve small changes (fixing a bug or adding a new tiny feature) or extending the functionality. A sign of good, production-ready code is that your colleagues are able to extend it quickly and feel confident doing so. Clear business logic and good test coverage decrease the probability of unintentionally breaking things by adding a small change (more about this in the next section).
- **Easy to extend**: While this might sound similar to the previous point, it's slightly different. How often have you experienced a situation where a relatively small change in business logic required a large refactoring of the code base? While you can't completely avoid such situations, you can reduce their frequency by using the right design patterns. We will dive deeper into this later in the chapter.
- **Efficient**: You shouldn't aim for ultimate efficiency, but when you go from a prototype to production, you might start caring about latency, compute resources consumed, and other such details. That means you might need to rewrite your code.

In Google, there's a specific notion of "code readability." As Brian Lee, an ex-Googler and a tech blogger, describes in their blog post (`https://www.moderndescartes.com/essays/readability/`), "*having readability means that you know the language's ins and outs, design patterns, ecosystem of libraries, and idiomatic usage at Google, and are thereby trusted to catch any issues in language usage.*"

> **Note**
>
> Readable code means that any of your colleagues, even those who are new to a particular part of the code base, can easily understand and modify the code without risking unintended changes to the business logic.

Code readability becomes especially important as your engineering team grows. The more engineers you have on the team, the more applications they need to maintain, and they need to be able to navigate multiple code bases fast and efficiently. The size of your engineering team might be a constraint for the scalability of your application. If you work at an organization with many engineers or your start-up grows fast, you need to adjust your processes accordingly, including investing in the readability of your code.

Making your code easy to read in Python

Code is easy to read if it follows a certain code style and uses unified patterns. Almost every programming language has a few different code styles. I'm not recommending that you specifically pick any specific code style; just pick the one code style and use it across the company!

> **Note**
>
> You can find Google's code style for various languages at `google.github.io/styleguide/`.

If you select Python, here are a few recommendations:

- Use a unified code style, code formatters, and linting libraries such as `ruff`, `pylint`, or `flake8`. Take some time to master how to configure the general code style imposed by any of these linters to your corporate one.

  > **Note**
  >
  > A linter is a static code analysis tool used by developers to "*analyze source code for potential errors, bugs, stylistic issues, and suspicious constructs*" (`https://en.wikipedia.org/wiki/Lint_(software)`).

- Use type hints and type checkers such as `mypy`. While Python is a strongly typed language, it's also a dynamically typed one. That means each variable has a type, but types are checked only during execution (and not at the compilation stage). Mypy might save you a lot of time since it helps to catch errors with incompatible types before running the code and tests.

> **Note**
>
> A **type checker** is another static tool for code analysis with a focus on verifying that the types of variables, function arguments, and return values are used consistently throughout your code (`https://realpython.com/python-code-quality`).

- Separate private methods and variables from public ones clearly, use names that are easy to understand, and follow other best practices (I recommend a few good books that detail best practices in the *Further reading* section).
- Start writing your code early. Jupyter notebooks are great for prototyping and interactive development, but I'd highly recommend setting up a proper IDE with support for notebooks (you can connect a local IDE to a remote instance if that's your setup) and start using the `autoreload` magic. The following cell in a Jupyter notebook will force the underlying Python kernel to re-import any module when it's changed on disk (which means you can write your functions in Python files and interactively run them in a Jupyter notebook without the need to relaunch the kernel):

```
%load_ext autoreload
%autoreload 2
```

There are many wonderful books and blog posts on code readability. If you're interested, I'd recommend *Fluent Python*, a wonderful book written by Luciano Ramalho, or the online tutorial available at `realpython.com/python-code-quality/`.

Making your code easy to extend

We mentioned the cost of maintenance earlier. It is related to the fact that adding changes to existing code is tricky for two reasons:

- You can break things unintentionally
- The existing solution might require a lot of refactoring

If you're a data scientist, you're the master of training and fine-tuning ML models, but in the era of GenAI, in many cases, you do not develop models from scratch, but you build applications on top of existing foundational models (of course, that might include steps such as fine-tuning). Hence, your job might start looking more and more like the job of an application developer.

Now, let's take a look at a few simple but very powerful design patterns that might be very beneficial for you (of course, there are many more to learn as you progress).

Single Responsibility Principle

SRP advocates for designing narrow-focused software components that have a single responsibility. That makes the code easier to read and maintain and reduces the probability of failures that happen when a developer is changing something and unintentionally breaks another functionality that the same object was responsible for.

> **Note**
>
> SRP states that any object (class, function, or method) should have only a single reason to change since it is responsible for only one well-defined aspect of the overall system's functionality.

Sometimes SRP is interpreted as "each object should have only one task", but this simplification is not entirely correct. A single reason to change means that only one stakeholder (or actor) can initiate a change. You can learn more about this in Robert Martin's book *Clean Code: A Handbook of Agile Software Craftsmanship*. For now, let's take a simple example. Let's imagine that we have a LangGraph node (if you're unfamiliar with LangGraph, a node represents a single step in a GenAI workflow).

This is a function that fetches a web page, summarizes its content with an LLM, and returns its summary to the agentic workflow:

```
async def summarize_webpage(state):
    llm = ChatOpenAI(...)
    req = urllib.request.Request(state["web_page"])
    with urllib.request.urlopen(req) as response:
       page_content = response.read()
    prompt = ("Your task is ...")
    chain = PromptTemplate.from_template(prompt) | llm | ...
    summary = await chain.ainvoke({"page_content": page_content})
    return {"page_summary": summary}
```

Now, let's take a look at a simpler way of doing the same. If you look at this function, you will probably understand what's going on in seconds:

```
async def summarize_webpage(state):
    web_page_content = _fetch_webpage(url=state["web_page"])
```

```
    summary = await _summarize_text(web_page_content)
    return {"page_summary": summary}
```

Not only is this version easier to read, but we have also split the responsibilities. The only reason to change the `summarize_webpage` function is when the business wants to change the logic. Fetching the web page and summarizing a text are separated into different objects, and if a technical or networking team wants to adjust the technical implementation, they would make the changes in the corresponding functions. Moreover, you can write one unit test for fetching a web page and another for summarizing its text.

Don't Repeat Yourself

The name of this principle speaks for itself. During the prototyping phase, you might end up copy-pasting small snippets of code here and there. Production-ready code means that you try to avoid code duplication as much as possible. It improves the readability and the ease of making a change since complexity rises with the number of lines, and navigating through a large code base is difficult.

One practical aspect of applying the DRY principle to ML code is separating the constants from your code base. For example, think about how much the following or a similar line might be repeated over your code base:

```
llm = ChatVertexAI(model="gemini-2.0-flash-001", project="...", temperature=0.1)
```

What if you needed to change the model name and migrate to the new generation of the Gemini model? You would need to apply dozens or more changes across your code base. Maybe this would be slightly better:

```
from constants import GEMINI_MODEL_NAME
...
llm = ChatVertexAI(model=GEMINI_MODEL_NAME, project="...", temperature=0.1)
```

Or even better: you can implement a factory method to get an LLM and use it across your application:

```
llm = get_llm_low_temp(provider="google")
```

As we'll see in the next section on testing, the DRY principle is relevant not only to your application code but also to your tests.

Loose coupling

When you use a higher level of abstraction, you decouple parts of your application from each other.

> **Note**
>
> Coupling describes the degree to which two separate components of a system are interconnected and reliant upon one another. In simpler terms, it informs you how much changing one component forces you to change the other. In software engineering, we often aim for loose coupling, which means that components interact in such a way that they need very little knowledge about each other, and it allows us to change one of them without affecting the other.

In a GenAI application, loose coupling becomes even more essential due to the dependency on external vendor-provided components such as LLMs or vector databases. As we saw in the *Don't Repeat Yourself* section, defining a factory method to retrieve an LLM is the first practical step toward reducing tight coupling. By abstracting the core components behind well-defined interfaces, you ensure that the main application logic is not hardwired to a specific vendor or implementation. This allows you to easily substitute one component for another, such as migrating from a third-party foundational model provider to a self-hosted custom model, or swapping a managed vector search solution for an open source one, with minimal impact on the rest of your code base. Note that this is one of the core ideas behind the open sourced LangChain framework. If you're interested, feel free to see how they define interfaces and implement integrations with vendors (`https://github.com/langchain-ai/langchain`).

Furthermore, loose coupling is essential to developing effective testing. As we will discuss in the next section, unit tests must be performed in isolation from external dependencies, especially non-deterministic ones such as foundational models. When your LLM interaction is encapsulated in a small, well-defined function or class method, you can easily mock the external call. This allows you to simulate specific responses (for example, malformed outputs or API timeouts, which are crucial edge cases to test) without making an actual, expensive, and unpredictable network request. This approach ensures your tests are fast, stable, and focused only on validating your application's logic, rather than the external service's behavior.

Your goal is to design your system such that one developer (say, a data scientist) can change the underlying model, while another (a software engineer) can modify the data ingestion pipeline, without accidentally breaking each other's functionality. A highly decoupled system minimizes the "blast radius" of any change, increases the team's confidence to refactor, and is key to achieving the robust stability and ease of extension that a production-ready application demands.

Now, let's talk about testing, a very important aspect of software engineering. Tests increase reliability and decrease the cost of maintaining our code.

Testing

These days, there's a common understanding that we need automated testing for production-ready software. Tests are essential to creating production-ready software for three reasons:

- **Quality**: Having tests doesn't guarantee that you'll always ship software without bugs. However, they drastically improve the quality of the software by checking that the main scenarios are working as intended before deployment.
- **Consistency**: They help keep a consistent behavior for edge cases. For example, if you've added a complicated use case implied by your business logic, you or another developer might forget about this in a few months and break the intended behavior. A small test that checks for this edge case would help enormously to keep things consistent over a long period of time.
- **Versatility**: If done right, writing tests encourages an engineer to think deeper about requirements and account for various edge cases.

Software engineers sometimes perceive writing tests as a boring and time-consuming part of the job. I remember multiple occasions when I spent an hour fixing a bug and half a day writing tests (trying to figure out how to properly mock dependencies, or solve some other seemingly unrelated challenge). So, while I can empathize with this feeling, I strongly disagree with the perception of boredom! If done properly, tests do enhance engineering productivity since they allow you to catch errors early and debug better.

Before we go further, let me make a short note on using coding assistants. They're great in writing tests (especially unit tests), but keep in mind that thinking about how you test your program is part of the architectural work itself. While using a coding assistant, keep the focus on the readability and usefulness of your tests, and give clear instructions to your coding agent on what exactly you want to test (and, of course, you can ask it to suggest new scenarios and use cases, but always take them with a grain of salt and double-check for a common sense).

There are multiple types of tests. The most important ones are unit and integration, and we'll discuss them both in more detail. We'll also look into load tests since they might be important if you want to use custom GenAI models or other parts of the GenAI stack, such as open sourced vector databases. But you might also encounter terms such as **acceptance tests** (when you cut a release, you check that performance and other system requirements are met) and **regression tests** (verifying that your change has not decreased the quality of the system relative to the previous release). Many good books on software engineering discuss testing strategies in detail, and if you are new to production engineering, I highly encourage you to read a few such books (I have recommended a few in the *Further reading* section).

Unit testing

Unit tests test the smallest standalone parts of your applications, such as functions, classes and their methods, and other objects. You use unit tests to check that these parts behave as expected, and you perform testing in isolation from external dependencies, such as other parts of your application, third-party libraries, and databases. This isolation makes unit tests fast to execute and stable since they don't depend on any changes and aren't affected by failures of third-party systems.

> **Note**
>
> A *unit* is the smallest testable part of the software application, and it's tested in *isolation* from any external dependencies.

Unit tests improve code quality and readability and serve as a good source of documentation. They also help with refactoring since good unit test coverage gives a developer more confidence that they haven't broken anything when refactoring the code. Of course, unit tests should be readable.

Here are a few practical recommendations and cautions for anybody who is writing unit tests (meaning, everybody who develops software):

- Give unit tests meaningful names so that if your build fails, you can quickly understand what's going on just by looking at the name of the failed test from the build report.
- Focus on specific scenarios that you want to test. A smaller number of well-designed tests is more valuable than many tests that appear random or are difficult to understand. Avoid writing excessive unit tests; think carefully about which scenarios you'd like to test. This is particularly important in the era of **vibe coding**. Coding assistants are very good at generating unit tests, but from my experience, they often produce too many. When using a coding assistant, provide clear guidance about not only which function should be tested but also which exact scenarios the tests should cover.
- Don't test for too many things within the same test for the same reason; a failing test should clearly indicate what's going on. You should quickly understand what is failing by looking at the test report itself, meaning test names and assertions should be meaningful.

- Don't aim for 100% test coverage since, like any KPI, it might force developers to start playing with the system. Some functions are just not worth adding a unit test to, and if you have too many non-meaningful unit tests, they become complex to read and hamper the readability of your code instead of improving it. Still, I believe using tools such as Coverage.py is useful since a decline in your coverage might signal that developers are under pressure and they could sacrifice code quality to push more features. Always check how the tool you're using defines test coverage. Most automatic tools measure the percentage of lines (or functions) executed during running tests, but they can't estimate the percentage of actual business requirements that are covered by tests.
- Yes, writing tests takes time! But it's part of the software development process, and if you're not writing tests, you're sacrificing the long-term code quality and introducing technical debt. Modern coding assistants are very good at writing unit tests, but use them wisely. Unfortunately, I've started to see a lot of code bases with plenty of unit tests that are difficult to read since they are clearly produced by AI assistants. In the classical test-driven approach, you start with developing test cases when thinking about requirements! Of course, in real life, developers often do not do that, but at least think about testing strategies and test cases. Make sure you use the same testing strategy across all your tests (e.g., the same approach for mocking dependencies, using fixtures, setting up test environments, etc.). You can document your chosen approach in an `.md` file that you include in the context for the coding assistant. When tasking an AI assistant with writing unit tests, be very clear in the prompt what test cases you want it to cover (yes, you might use a separate AI step to suggest test cases, but it still depends a lot on the details in your input prompt and you reviewing the outcomes carefully, as well as providing meaningful feedback to the AI assistant). In other words, writing tests with a coding assistant is an iterative process and not a one-shot experience. Perform it step by step and don't just ask an assistant to write multiple tests in one bulk request.

Note

Test coverage is a metric that estimates the share of your code that is executed when your tests run. It can be measured in multiple ways, for example, you can count the number of lines, or the number of unique objects, such as methods or functions. A popular Python package called coverage computes the line coverage.

Unit testing in Python

If you're new to unit testing in Python, you need to master a few things to quickly start writing powerful unit tests yourself:

- **Mock dependencies**: Learn how to mock dependencies with the `unittest.mock` library (read the tutorial and understand how `patch` and `MagicMock` work). These two tutorials provide a great starting point: *Understanding the Python Mock Object Library* by Real Python (`https://realpython.com/python-mock-library/`) and *Pytest with Eric* by E. de Andrade (`https://pytest-with-eric.com/`).
- **Create fixtures**: Depending on whether you're using `pytest` or `unittest` to write your tests, look at how to create `pytest` fixtures or master the `setUp` methods of a `unittest.TestCase` class. This would help you to mock some complex dependencies in an easier way. Start with the documentation, and use the two tutorials I cited in the previous point, too.
- **Compare dictionaries**: Keep in mind the nuances of comparison dictionaries and lists in Python. First, lists are sorted objects, but often the order should be ignored during comparison (the `unittest` library has a `TestCase.assertCountEqual` method for that). Comparing nested objects is not always straightforward (take a look at the `TestCase.assertDictEqual` method).

Now that we have discussed some aspects of unit testing and understand what a unit test is, let's look into the nuances of testing GenAI applications.

Unit testing GenAI applications

Unit testing your GenAI applications might be challenging since they typically depend on many internal integrations: foundational models, embeddings, vector databases, and so on. Many of these integrations are non-deterministic. But remember that with unit tests, we test our code, not an LLM or a third-party API. A few recommendations that might help you when thinking about how to test a GenAI application are as follows:

- **Test the code flow, branching, and processing**: Pay attention to testing your prompt construction and substitution logic and how you handle an interaction with foundational models (including managing parameters and dealing with potential errors such as timeouts and denial of service). Note that having a unit test that tests the final construction of a prompt (by asserting the expected prompt value with the one after all substitutions) also improves the readability of the code (since anybody can quickly grasp what kind of prompt is sent to an LLM). It might sound excessive for a prompt with a simple substitution, but as your application grows, your prompts become more complex and constructed from multiple pieces that depend on the user input and the context of your application. I once saw an application with a prompt that was more than 20-pages long with dozens of nested instructions and `if-else` conditions. It felt like a large business requirements document rather than a task for an LLM.

- **Test your workflows for edge cases**: These cases may include malformed outputs from an LLM, empty strings, extreme numerical values, or default return values for errors.
- **Test your preprocessing and ingestion steps**: In ML (and GenAI is no exception), there are a lot of cleaning steps that are required when handling the data. Typically, these data-processing parts are tested interactively and manually in a Jupyter notebook, but following a proper test-driven approach helps you to think about test cases. From my practical experience, almost every time I've started writing unit tests for my data pipelines, I've spotted errors. One good practical guide is this one published by Sam Zamany on Medium: `https://medium.com/@samzamany/unit-testing-in-data-engineering-a-practical-guide-91196afdf32a`.

> **Note**
>
> Approximately 9/10 times, when I start writing unit tests for my data processing and data analysis steps (components that typically are not tested at all), I spot errors and mistakes.

- **Test your evaluation pipelines**: As we discussed in *Chapter 2*, evaluation is critical, so remember to write tests for your evaluation pipelines, too.
- **Maximize using LLMs**: LLMs are great at suggesting unit tests for your applications, so start using them. But remember that an LLM only "*helps humans, doesn't replace them!*" (Alshahwan et al. 2024). If you're interested in this topic, check out the paper *Automated Unit Test Improvement using Large Language Models at Meta* by N. Alshahwan et al. on their experiments with using an LLM to improve test coverage.

GenAI applications depend a lot on external APIs, such as LLMs and tools. There are two ways of testing in such a setup:

- Mock all external dependencies, such as a foundation model, and check only that the corresponding API has been invoked with appropriate parameters
- Use a factory method and pass a `pytest.fixture` object when initiating the class or calling a function that you want to test

Integration testing

Integration testing tests different components together. Unit tests mock dependencies, and they test the logic of each small part of the code (a unit) independently. But we need to make sure that everything works from end to end, and integration testing helps us with that. In classical software engineering, we run an integration test and check that we get the expected output (including that we save the correct results to the database). GenAI applications are a little different. First, we need to check that they run from end to end and produce the expected results (that is, authentication works; all parts are talking to each other without errors; and we can invoke databases, LLM APIs, tools, etc.). Another aspect is the correctness of the outputs, which is difficult to check because of the inherent non-determinism of such applications; we discussed this problem in detail in *Chapter 2*. That's why when it comes to GenAI, we need both integration tests and evaluation pipelines. I sometimes observe developers confusing these two aspects, which leads to flaky tests that are hard to interpret.

An integration test suite should not be focused on evaluating the correctness of the outputs, but should just check that the application runs successfully from end to end and provides meaningful outputs. For example, a check could look like the following:

```
assert isinstance(rag_output, str)
assert len(rag_output) > 100
```

Note that we do not verify the linguistic correctness of `rag_output` (this is the job of the evaluation pipeline). We just check whether it's generated, and the assertion should remain focused on technical success, such as verifying the output format (e.g., correct JSON structure), the absence of critical error messages, or the proper handling of structured output parsing. The goal is simply to confirm that the full data flow pipeline has executed, and a meaningful (i.e., non-error) response has been generated.

While the purpose of integration tests is to verify that the entire system works together, in a GenAI application, we must be pragmatic about how we define the scope for testing. Making live calls to a foundational model or a vector database in a development loop is both time-consuming and expensive. Also, keep in mind that the output would be non-deterministic, which makes it difficult to actually test the system.

Typically, integration tests are run frequently (on every commit), while evaluation pipelines (since they're slower and more expensive to run) are invoked only on demand. You typically run an evaluation pipeline on a schedule (for example, once a week), or when you make major changes to the prompts. Therefore, we should view integration tests not as a comprehensive correctness check but as a crucial "connectivity and flow" check. They exist to ensure that all the separate modules (remember, they are loosely coupled and unit tested!) can successfully interact with one another.

Load testing

Load testing is an important part of performance testing. Not every application needs to be load tested. With GenAI, you might need a load test in two cases:

- When you use custom models or vector search solutions and you want to understand their performance from cost, latency, and throughput perspectives
- When you expect a large number of concurrent users and you want to make sure that you can handle them well

> **Note**
>
> In software engineering, load testing is a kind of testing where you put a system under a simulated workload and check how it performs. You typically look at the overall stability of the system and check metrics such as throughput, latency, resource utilization, and error rates under a given load (`grafana.com/load-testing`).

What can go wrong with our applications under load, what do we want to understand during load testing, and what do we want to validate during testing to avoid potential failures?

- **GPU workloads**: If your application relies on GPU-based workloads, they usually require careful load testing and tuning. For example, if you are serving a custom model (such as a foundational model or a re-ranking model), you want to make sure it can be served efficiently; you need to ensure it can be served efficiently under load. A key optimization is **continuous batching**, which improves GPU utilization by processing multiple requests together (see: `https://huggingface.co/blog/continuous_batching`). Note that not all models from Hugging Face support continuous batching, and serving such models on GPUs under heavy load can become very expensive. If you're serving a custom model
- **Performance of data stores**: Pay particular attention to the performance of your data stores, especially vector databases. In many practical scenarios, GenAI systems rely on grounding responses in enterprise data (with some exceptions such as summarization, entity extraction, or document understanding tasks). This means your system must store and retrieve data efficiently, often using vector search. Since these retrieval patterns are still relatively new in many organizations, it is important to test them properly. If you are using new index types or database providers, evaluate them not

only on small evaluation datasets but also on large datasets, possibly synthetic ones that approximate the size of production data, and under realistic load conditions.

- **Scalability of cloud infrastructure**: Evaluate how your cloud infrastructure behaves under peak load, including any third-party APIs (such as foundational models, MCP servers, etc.) your system depends on. Many GenAI applications rely heavily on external APIs, and in some cases foundation models themselves are consumed as APIs. Test how your system behaves under load and ensure you can handle failures caused by rate limits, quota exhaustion, service outages, or other API-related errors.

As before, let's take a look at what additional aspects we need to take into account when load testing GenAI applications:

- Since we are interested in additional metrics such as token consumption, we need to adjust the existing load-testing infrastructure (if it exists) to collect them
- Response time becomes longer in general and more volatile; hence, we need to look at latency distribution more carefully and increase the load-testing duration
- We face more complex dependencies and larger computational demand, which increases the complexity of load tests

On the bright side, don't forget that GenAI can help you to create and implement these tests! Now let's look at some practical aspects of running load tests with Python.

When using Python, you should probably take a look at Locust, a Python-based open source load-testing tool (`https://locust.io/`). It allows you to write your own testing workloads, run distributed testing workloads, simulate complex user behavior, and create realistic load patterns. It comes with both a UI (which you can run locally or easily deploy on a Kubernetes cluster) and a CLI.

I've put together a list of suggestions that might be helpful when planning the load testing of your application:

- Start with simple and isolated load tests, but don't hesitate to simulate actual user behavior (which might consist of querying multiple APIs one by one). Sometimes, you might catch some flaws in integration or unexpected correlation across different services. For example, if service A can handle a peak load up to *X* QPS (queries per seconds) and service B can handle a peak load of *Y* QPS, they together can't handle a peak load *X+Y*. If a user is using them together, that becomes a problem.
- Learn how to collect additional data to add to your load-testing reports. You not only need to collect the distribution of latencies and error rates, but you also need to analyze them across prompt length, generation output length, and maybe some other variables. With Locust, you most probably need to use the `EventHook.fire` method

(`https://docs.locust.io/en/stable/api.html#eventhook-class`) for those purposes. Implement asynchronous clients, and test for streaming performance since it's a common pattern of interacting with GenAI applications such as chat. If you use streaming, implement metrics such as time to first token.

- GenAI applications might be sensitive to your input dataset (for example, the length of input prompts or the complexity of tasks). Try to gather a representative dataset of users' prompts and sample from this dataset to generate a realistic load. Do not load test with a single input request; that is a common practice in application load testing.
- Carefully study how to interpret the results of the load-testing tool you're using. For example, Locust has the notion of a `User` that is a single running load-testing task. When you define a target load (QPS), you essentially define the rate of requests per second per user (your target QPS divided by the number of users spawned). The trick is that a user sends a new request only after they receive the answer to the previous one.
- Keep an eye on the CPU consumption of Locust workers. You might need to schedule the number of workers (and properly deploy them across a cluster); otherwise, the load that you generate might be bound by the load generators themselves, and you'll get biased results.
- Don't focus on just average latency; analyze tail latencies, for example, P90, P95, and P99 percentiles.
- Don't span all users simultaneously; use a realistic hatch rate (for example, add 20 new users at a time).

In GenAI, an increased load initially leads not to a spike in error rates but to an increase in latency (because of continuous batching, retries, and timeouts on the model provider side). This effect is way stronger than in classical applications, where a spike in traffic also leads to a spike in latency because databases and other downstream services start working slowly. But typically, you still observe an immediate spike in error rates, and that means Locust can continue sending more and more requests. With Locust, you observe increased latency, but you might never reach your target QPS at all (because your requests are eventually fulfilled, and all load-testing tasks are busy waiting for the result of these long-running requests). Hence, if you just automatically launch a load test with a target QPS of *X* QPS, look at error rates, and report a success, you might be misinterpreting the results. As a result, you ignored an increased latency. More than that, you have never actually tested your application for the desired throughput, which was your goal. This is an example of how misleading load-testing frameworks might be if you don't look at their internals and understand how they generate the load and report the results.

We discussed some of architectural practices (and there are many more you might learn if you take a look at the *Further reading* section!). But let me point out one important point. Do not overengineer, and keep it simple. Let's discuss what I mean by that.

Keeping it simple!

We've talked a lot about engineering best practices so far, and we'll continue this conversation throughout the book. While all of this (and many more recommendations even outside of this book) will help you to make your applications production-ready, it's important to always keep in mind that production quality is not a goal by itself. We don't need production-ready code; we need to solve business problems, and production-ready code, in most cases, helps us to solve these problems better and more efficiently. But the key secret in building efficient engineering teams is finding the right balance between the size of the technical debt and the speed of product delivery.

The trick to "keeping it simple" is to manage this debt strategically, never letting it become so crippling that you cannot ship new features or fix bugs. On the one hand, the higher the technical debt is, the more it will cost you in the future to maintain and improve the product. However, if you focus on implementing all the engineering best practices in one go, you might lose time that you could have spent on searching for product-market fit.

When resources are scarce and time is of the essence, your highest priority must be to validate the business idea, not to achieve architectural perfection. Start with onboarding a few core best practices, such as version control, logical code separation, and minimal testing (do not aim for a high test coverage!). Such a minimalistic approach creates the minimum viable production setup. It is the baseline against which you need to deliver value and iterate quickly, while preventing your technical debt from turning into a complete architectural block. As your application gains traction and your team grows, you can, and must, invest time into incrementally paying down this debt by introducing the full suite of best practices we've discussed.

You can even take it a step further. In most cases, you don't need to start building your product by developing an ML model or a complex agentic pipeline. For example, Sam Udotong, a co-founder of Fireflies.ai (a start-up that transcribes and analyzes conference calls), describes their first steps in his LinkedIn post at `https://www.linkedin.com/posts/sudotong_we-charged-100month-for-an-ai-that-was-activity-7393690382884044800-9X8J`.

They had an idea of a product that takes meeting notes of video calls and makes them searchable. But instead of building complex tech first, the founders sold a service that promised an AI bot would join calls and send transcripts. When their first customers invited the bot to the meeting, one of the founders manually dialed in, sat silently on the call, and typed out detailed notes by hand to email them to the customer about 10 minutes after the meeting ended. Only after they had validated the idea and gathered specific product requirements did they start building the product, and now the company has a few billion dollars in valuation.

This example reflects the famous mantra of the start-up world, "fake it until you make it." However, you should take into account ethical, privacy, and other concerns when following this path. A discussion on LinkedIn in the post's *Comments* section mentioned such concerns in the context of this example. Nevertheless, it's often a good idea to start developing an AI product by validating the user pain and implementing the baseline: a simple rule-based (or heuristic-based) solution and metrics that capture how well this solution performs. Then, you build more complex tech on top of this foundation.

Now, let's look into an additional very practical architecture example that can help us with managing production applications.

Taking the quick-fix path

Once, I helped a large corporation develop an internal enterprise assistant in the form of a chatbot. This assistant was grounded on internal data and was working fine. As a funny coincidence, during the last testing phase, a new CEO was appointed. Since it was the first GenAI project within the company, the board wanted to see the presentation. A few days before this demo, we got an urgent call from one of the top managers. Somebody had asked the chatbot, "*Who is the CEO of company X?*" and the chatbot replied with the old CEO's name, not the new one's name. As you can imagine, it was treated as clear evidence that a chatbot wouldn't be useful to employees since it couldn't answer a basic internal question correctly. We needed to fix it immediately. The demo to the board was postponed, and the rollout to employees was blocked because of that.

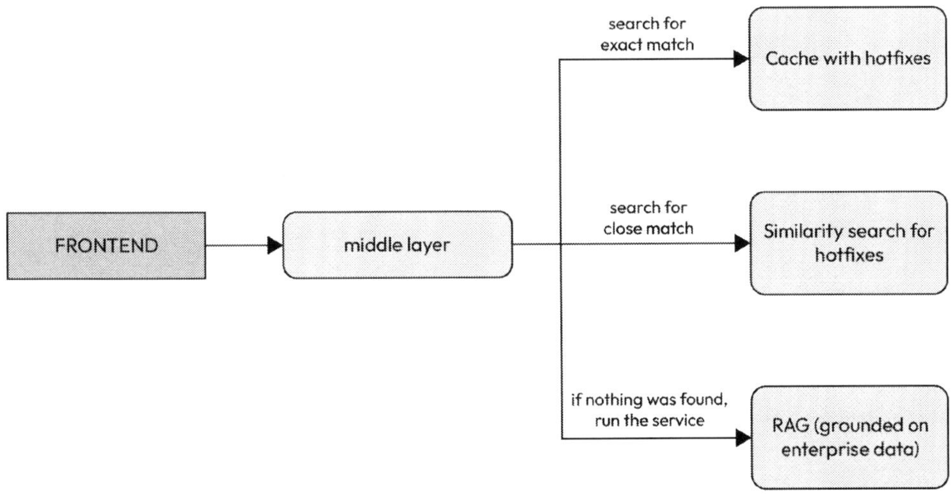

Figure 4.1 – Example of a middle layer that checks for hotfixes if a user request is similar to a list of manually curated examples

Lucky for us, we had considered such a scenario when designing our architecture. We had a simple middle layer that allowed us to add hardcoded hotfixes in cases like this. We were able to add a question-answer pair, and before going the complex route, the solution always checked for exact or similar matches. Of course, it's important to mention that by no means has this method replaced proper development. You need to narrow down the problem, gather evaluation datasets, iterate on development, fix the problem reliably, and then roll out a new version of a model or a solution. But this takes time, and having a shortcut can help a lot to maintain your application in production (although, as with any shortcut, be responsible and don't overuse it!).

Now, before we conclude this chapter, let's briefly discuss how we can educate users and onboard them to our application. All our hard work will be in vain if we fail to deliver value to our users.

Onboarding users

When going to production, you need to keep in mind how different users will use your application, and some might be new to GenAI as a technology. For example, it's very clear to everybody who works with GenAI that an LLM might hallucinate, and we shouldn't take every answer it generates at face value. This might not be obvious for every employee of a large organization who gets access to an LLM-enabled enterprise assistant. You should also consider how to inform your users about hallucinations, as well as ethical and other risks related to GenAI.

> **Note**
>
> Managing expectations and educating your users is an important part of the rollout process.

You might consider using different strategies to inform users about these risks, such as the following:

- Thinking through the business process and identifying critical touchpoints to educate your users on additional features or considerations (for example, remind them that human oversight is required to validate AI-generated outputs)
- Introducing training that a user should take before being allowed to use your application or its advanced features (of course, this only works in an enterprise setup)
- Adding disclosures and popups to the UI that clearly inform users about potential performance gaps, risks, and misuses related to GenAI
- Adding additional checks that evaluate whether prompts submitted to the application are compliant with the usage policy

Another important aspect is capacity planning for a launch. It might be difficult to understand user demand, especially when you launch for external users (but even launching an enterprise assistant for 15K employees might become tricky). You don't know in advance how many requests users will send to your service daily, how many of them will use the service overall, what the distribution of input and output lengths looks like, and other such important considerations. We'll talk more about reliability in *Chapter 8*, but for now, I'll give two simple recommendations:

- Consider testing first on a small group of production users—for example, an invite-only launch, a dark launch, or rolling out to a subset of users (e.g., on a country level).

  > **Note**
  >
  > Dark launch is a software deployment strategy when a new product or feature is made available to a limited set of users only, without making those users explicitly aware of the new functionality.

- Clearly mark your launch as beta. It is a simple psychological technique, but it works. The reason is that many things in product engineering and business in general are about managing expectations. Once you have clearly communicated to your users that your service is in beta phase, they understand that it's something new and it might be unstable, and they become much more tolerant of errors or failures.

Summary

In this chapter, we learned that transitioning a GenAI prototype to a production application requires a significant shift in focus. We discussed critical priorities, such as stability, generalization, and robustness across all users and use cases; performance; and ease of maintenance and extension.

We also learned about adopting version control systems such as Git from the start, focusing on code readability by utilizing unified code styles, linters, and type checkers, and ensuring code is easy to extend by adhering to principles such as SRP and DRY. Furthermore, we delved into the importance of a robust testing strategy, differentiating between unit tests (isolating small components), integration tests (checking the end-to-end flow and meaningful output), and load tests. For GenAI, we specifically noted that unit tests should focus on the application logic, such as prompt construction and error handling, rather than the LLM's non-deterministic output. We also examined load testing for custom models, vector databases, and cloud infrastructure, stressing the need to analyze metrics such as tail latencies and time to first token. Finally, we touched upon practical aspects such as having a mechanism for quick, hardcoded fixes in emergencies and the necessity of managing user expectations and educating them about the technology's limitations, such as hallucinations, during the rollout process.

In the next chapter, we'll talk about automation of routine and repeatable aspects of the engineering work (including code delivery processes), and, in particular, about LLMOps.

> **Note**
>
> The three key outcomes to remember are as follows:
>
> - A successful prototype aims to impress stakeholders and convince them of the feasibility of the proposed solution. A product solution needs to meet functional requirements (provide user value and cover edge cases) and non-functional requirements (stability, performance, and maintainability).
> - Testing is an essential part of software development. Tests help you improve the quality of your code and increase the ease of maintenance. Good tests also increase the readability of your code since they serve as part of the documentation. Make sure you have both integration and unit tests in your application, and use other types of tests (such as load tests) if appropriate.
> - Code readability is an important quality of a production-ready code. Make sure all your workflows are reproducible and versionized. Write code that is easy to read and extend for your colleagues by following principles such as loose coupling and DRY.

Further reading

- Online Git tutorial:`https://githowto.com/en/setup`
- *Readability: Google's Temple to Engineering Excellence*: `https://www.moderndescartes.com/essays/readability/`
- *Python Code Quality: Best Practices and Tools*: `https://realpython.com/python-code-quality/`
- Ramalho, L. *Fluent Python*, O'Reilly Media, Inc.
- Zamany, S., *Unit Testing in Data Engineering: A Practical Guide*: `https://medium.com/@samzamany/unit-testing-in-data-engineering-a-practical-guide-91196afdf32a`
- Alshahwan, N., Chheda, J., Finegenova, A., et al. (2024) *Automated Unit Test Improvement using Large Language Models at Meta*: `https://arxiv.org/abs/2402.09171`

- Ejsmont, A. *Web Scalability for Startup Engineers: Tips & Techniques for Scaling Your Web Application*, McGraw Hill
- Martin, R., *Clean Code: A Handbook of Agile Software Craftsmanship*, Prentice Hall

Subscribe for a free eBook

New frameworks, evolving architectures, research drops, production breakdowns—*AI_Distilled* filters the noise into a weekly briefing for engineers and researchers working hands-on with LLMs and generative AI systems. Subscribe now and receive a free eBook, along with weekly insights that help you stay focused and informed.

Subscribe at `https://packt.link/8Oz6Y` or scan the QR code below.

5

Moving from DevOps and MLOps to LLMOps

In *Chapter 4*, we briefly touched on the importance of automating code delivery and other operations to make your application easily maintainable. Now, we will dive deeper into the operational practices that transform a good piece of code or an exciting machine learning prototype into a reliable, scalable, and evolving product running in production.

We will start with the foundational concepts of DevOps, introduce terms such as **continuous integration/continuous delivery** (**CI/CD**), and then discuss what specific challenges related to machine learning systems stand behind the separate subdiscipline of **MLOps**. We will continue this line of thinking by looking into the specialized needs of **LLMOps** in the GenAI world. We will learn that the term *Ops* (or *operations*) is not a fleeting trend but a critical set of practices, tools, and a cultural philosophy necessary to succeed in modern software and AI development.

Throughout this chapter, we will discuss the core pillars of DevOps and the automation provided by CI/CD. We will explore how MLOps builds upon this to solve unique challenges for ML models, such as ensuring reproducibility and managing model degradation over time due to data and concept drift. Most importantly, we will focus on why the rise of GenAI demands yet another layer of operational maturity, as LLM-based applications introduce new difficulties in evaluation, cost management, and the tight coupling of code and data.

By the end of this chapter, you will understand DevOps and its two core pillars: **culture** and **automation** (CI/CD); the evolution from DevOps to MLOps and ML pipelines; and the role of continuous training in addressing data and concept drift. You will also explore metrics for measuring MLOps impact and the unique challenges that drive the need for LLMOps (GenOps/AgentOps).

In this chapter, we'll be covering the following topics:

- DevOps
- MLOps
- LLMOps

DevOps

In many organizations, software engineers are responsible for writing code, and other teams take responsibility for running applications in production and maintaining servers, the network, and other infrastructure. These teams are IT, Ops, ITOps, **SRE** (which stands for **site reliability engineering**), and many other names. By the way, for some of our readers (who have started their career in engineering only a few years ago), the preceding statement might sound strange, since, in recent years, many engineering teams follow the principle of "*You build it, you run it.*"

To make it easier to deliver and maintain software products, since the 2010s, a set of DevOps practices has been introduced (`https://devops.com/the-origins-of-devops-whats-in-a-name/`). Atlassian, a company that develops tools such as Jira and BitBucket to enhance developers' productivity, defined DevOps as a "*set of practices, tools, and a cultural philosophy that automate and integrate the processes between software development and IT teams*" (`https://www.atlassian.com/devops`). It is based on two pillars: a culture of **shared responsibility** that boosts collaboration and communication across different teams, and **automation** of deployment and code delivery processes.

The cultural aspect of DevOps emphasizes a shared responsibility with a focus on results. While many teams might be involved in the development of your applications, this sometimes creates silos across different teams, and nobody feels responsible at the end. We will discuss this in more detail in *Chapter 8* when we'll talk about reliability. Here, we focus on the automation of the code delivery and deployment process.

Automation of code delivery processes

Software development has a lot of manual repetitive tasks that can be automated for the benefit of speed of releases, scalability of the development process, and reducing the number of errors. Such tasks include the following:

- Creating environments to run the software
- Building software
- Running tests

- Deploying software to production
- Monitoring the software that is already running

In *Chapter 4*, we discussed how the focus of the team changes when the application is deployed to production, and what changes to code, strategy, and architecture you need to take. One important aspect of all of these changes is automation. If you need to maintain your production application (which means supporting it over the long term by fixing bugs and vulnerabilities, adapting to changes in user behavior, and adding new features), you want three things.

First, everything should be reproducible, which means we need automation. In the next chapter, we'll discuss how it becomes even more important for ML development. Second, we want to deliver value to our users faster, which means we need to increase release speed and frequency, and automation helps with that. And finally, repetitive tasks should be automated to decrease the cost of maintenance and the probability of a manual error. You want to avoid mistakes and human errors during releases, which means you need to manage testing, environment variables, and everything else automatically. That's how Terraform and Bash scripts come into your team's life when you become a production engineer. And yes, it's probably time to hire a DevOps engineer! But the good news is that in today's world, cloud providers and developer platforms such as GitHub offer you a great set of tools for automation.

This kind of automation is called CI/CD. Let's see what that is.

What is CI/CD?

CI, or **continuous integration**, allows you to quickly *integrate* any new change into a shared code base automatically by testing it. A common choice to run CI tasks is GitHub Actions (or GitLab Pipelines).

> **Note**
>
> GitLab defines continuous integration as a "*practice of integrating all your code changes into the main branch of a shared source code repository early and often, automatically testing each change when you commit or merge them, and automatically kicking off a build*" (`https://about.gitlab.com/topics/ci-cd`).

We still have the second component of our abbreviation, and **CD** stands for **continuous delivery** (sometimes it's referred to as **continuous deployment**).

> **Note**
>
> Continuous deployment "*automatically releases the updates into the production environment*" (`https://www.redhat.com/en/topics/devops/what-is-ci-cd`).

The idea behind CI/CD automation is simple. First, you want to integrate changes from your developers (not a single person!) frequently, multiple times a day. It fosters collaboration since engineers can work independently on smaller pieces of work and integrate them frequently. It might sound strange, but 10 years ago, software engineers worked completely differently, and releases happened rarely (for example, once a month). Engineers delivered larger chunks of code, and other engineers took care of deployments and maintaining servers that were running production code. Second, you want to detect bugs earlier, reduce the probability of manual errors, and reduce the amount of manual work.

For example, let's take a look at CI/CD jobs at the public `langchain-google` repository (libraries with GenAI integrations of Google products into LangChain). It's not the only way of doing things; it's just a good example, and you can take a look at the source code and actual jobs since it's a public repository. This is how the release process of a library looks:

1. Use `codespell` to check for spelling errors.
2. Analyze formatting and linting with `ruff` and `mypy`. It runs formatting (or type checking) for changed files, and if any differences or alerts are sent to `stdout`, the job fails.
3. Run unit tests. We run them in different environments (from Python 3.9 to Python 3.12).
4. Compile integration tests. The compilation step checks for different errors (including wrong dependencies), but it doesn't run tests themselves because of a lack of authentication.

   > **Note**
   >
   > You can run *steps 1–4* locally or as GitHub actions once you advance your automations (you need to set up GitHub action runners and a corresponding GitHub workflow for that), and they don't require any API keys since a unit test shouldn't depend on any third-party APIs.

5. Run integration tests. GitHub triggers an execution in an isolated environment on Google Cloud, where all the needed testing infrastructure (for example, vector indices or open source models deployed) is provided through Terraform.

> **Note**
>
> *Steps 1–5* are executed on every PR (pull request), and merging to the main branch is blocked if any of these steps fail. It is an automated CI job that doesn't require any manual intervention. There's also a CD job triggered manually that is responsible for releasing the new library, and it includes *steps 6–10*.

6. Build a library as a packaged artifact with all dependencies. Make sure you keep your production containers slim and do not bring unnecessary dependencies (such as those used for testing or data preprocessing). If you use dependency management tools such as `poetry` or `uv`, you can have separate groups for testing, data processing, and so on.
7. Upload the library to the `test-pypi` repository.
8. Install the library from the `test-pypi` repository in a clean environment, and run unit and a limited set of integration tests.
9. Publish the new package to the `PyPI` repository.
10. Combine and publish release notes.

This is only an example that you can use as a reference. You can find all Terraform, GitHub Actions configuration, and corresponding Bash scripts in the open-sourced repositories: `https://github.com/langchain-ai/langchain-google/tree/main/.github` and `https://github.com/langchain-ai/langchain-google/tree/main/terraform`. And, of course, not all applications should be built and published as a standalone Python library. *Steps 6–10* can be replaced with a different logic, for example, with pushing a Docker image to a private image repository and then redeploying a container on Kubernetes or another container orchestration service.

Now, let's take a look at the next step of the software delivery evolution that happened between 2015 and 2020, when more and more ML models were deployed to production.

MLOps

With the rise of ML, many engineering teams started to look for good ways of maintaining ML systems in production, and that's how DevOps evolved into **MLOps** (or **machine learning operations**). MLOps helps organizations move from ad hoc ML experimentation to systematic, reliable, and scalable ML operations. And as you can imagine, that's exactly what we want for our GenAI journey. That's why I'm going to give you a brief overview of MLOps before we jump to what came on top of MLOps. As you can guess, it would be LLMOps, or GenOps.

> **Note**
>
> Databricks defines MLOps as "*a core function of Machine Learning engineering, focused on streamlining the process of taking machine learning models to production, and then maintaining and monitoring them.*" They also highlight MLOps being a "*collaborative function, often comprising data scientists, DevOps engineers, and IT*" (`https://www.databricks.com/glossary/mlops`).

As discussed in *Chapters 1* and *4*, the tech community quickly recognized a significant gap between building a strong ML model and successfully deploying and maintaining it in production. *Figure 5.1* illustrates various building blocks beyond the ML model itself that are sometimes overseen when moving an ML prototype to production.

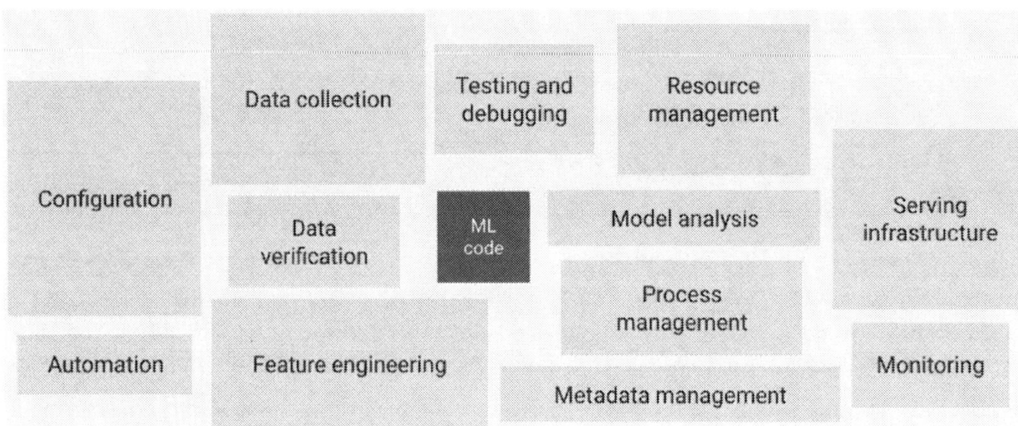

Figure 5.1 – Elements of ML systems (source: https://cloud.google.com/architecture/mlops-continuous-delivery-and-automation-pipelines-in-machine-learning)

MLOps builds on existing DevOps principles and focuses on automation, CI/CD, increasing reliability, scalability, and compliance of ML systems. One of the most important aspects of automation is ensuring the *reproducibility* of ML models. You want any other developer (including yourself three months later!) to be able to reproduce your model, and this starts with the data preparation. That means, CI is no longer only about validating the code itself; it includes validating the data and data schemas. That's why MLOps evolves on top of DevOps.

and it covers an additional set of tools and practices required to develop reliable, scalable, and maintainable ML systems, not only software in general. This set of tools includes the following:

- Tools for experiment tracking to allow better collaboration across ML engineers when choosing the best-performing architecture or hyperparameters
- Tools for deploying the model to production
- Tools for monitoring the model, since, as we remember, ML models can degrade in performance if the outside world changes and the training data is not representative anymore
- Tools for continuous retraining of the model on new collected data to improve its performance

You can already see that similar things would happen with the rise of GenAI applications, and there will be a lot of commonalities between MLOps and LLMOps. We'll talk about LLMOps in a minute, but now let's discuss ML pipelines, which are an important aspect of MLOps.

ML pipelines

What is an ML pipeline? There are many steps you need to take to train a modern ML model. You start with cleaning and preprocessing your data, then you train your model (this stage might include such steps as architecture search or hyperparameter tuning), and you end up with extensive validation. At every stage, you might be dealing with large distributed datasets that don't fit into a single machine's memory, and the artifacts you produce might also be large datasets or binaries (for example, you encode your text data as a vocabulary).

> **Note**
>
> An ML pipeline is a way to organize steps that are required to build and deploy your model as code and automate them. An ML pipeline either trains a new model or runs inference (prepares a prediction). Read more at `https://www.databricks.com/glossary/what-are-ml-pipelines`.

Figure 5.2 illustrates the different steps involved in an ML pipeline: from gathering and preprocessing data to training a model, validating it, and promoting the best-performing model to production for inference.

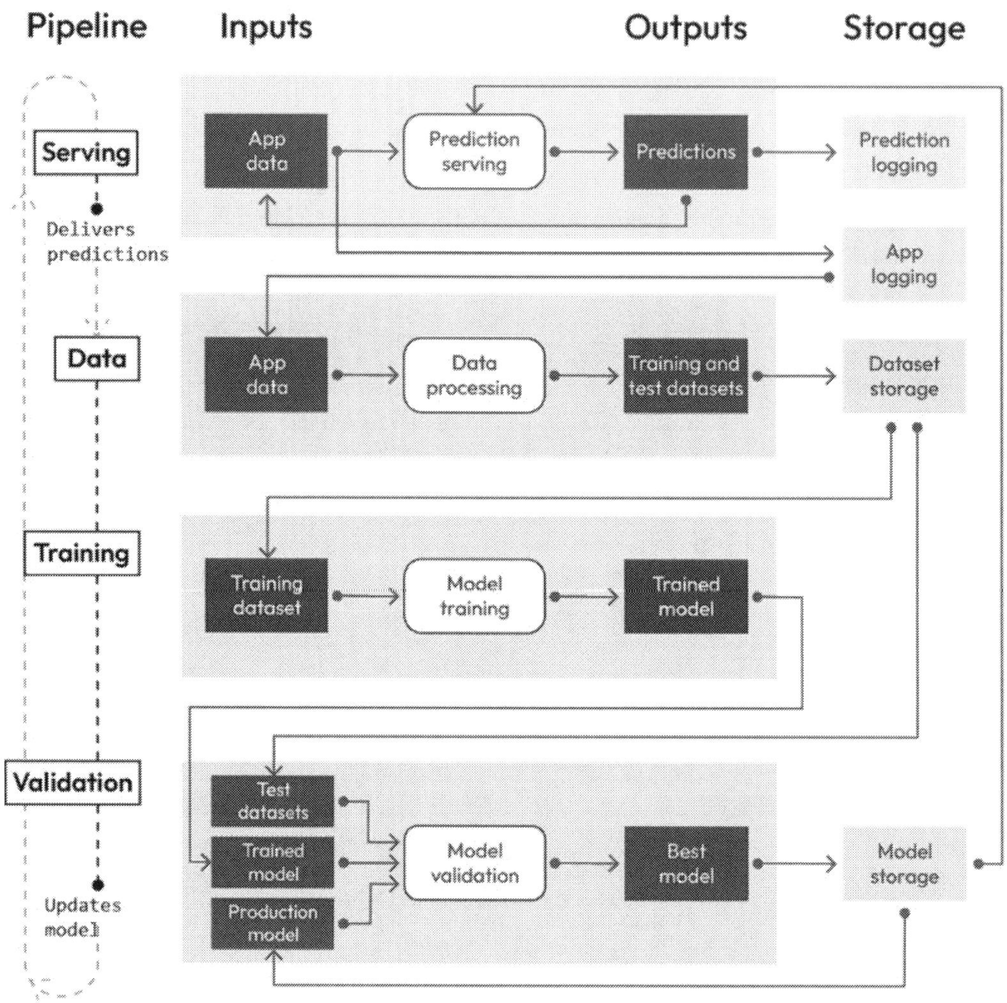

Figure 5.2 – ML pipelines automate different processes across model development (source: https://developers.google.com/machine-learning/managing-ml-projects/pipelines)

The idea behind an ML pipeline is simple: you organize the whole workflow as code (as a directed acyclic graph), and you can easily manage all artifacts that different parts of your pipeline produce. For example, you can cache various steps of the pipeline (when you're experimenting with the model's architecture, you don't need to preprocess data each time; you can use cached output from the preprocessing steps).

Modern ML pipeline frameworks such as Kubeflow, MLflow, Amazon Sagemaker, and many others give a developer a high-level API to manage their workflows and produce artifacts, execute these workflows, manage underlying hardware, visualize, and manage experimental runs. And automation of ML engineering and data science work is the key. This automation happens in two stages. First, you automate the model's training (as displayed in *Figure 5.3*). That means you develop a pipeline that automates all steps that include data extraction, validation, preparation, and later model training and evaluation. You can run the same pipeline in both the dev and prod environments. Such environments can even have slightly different data (for example, you can keep only sampled and/or anonymized data in dev).

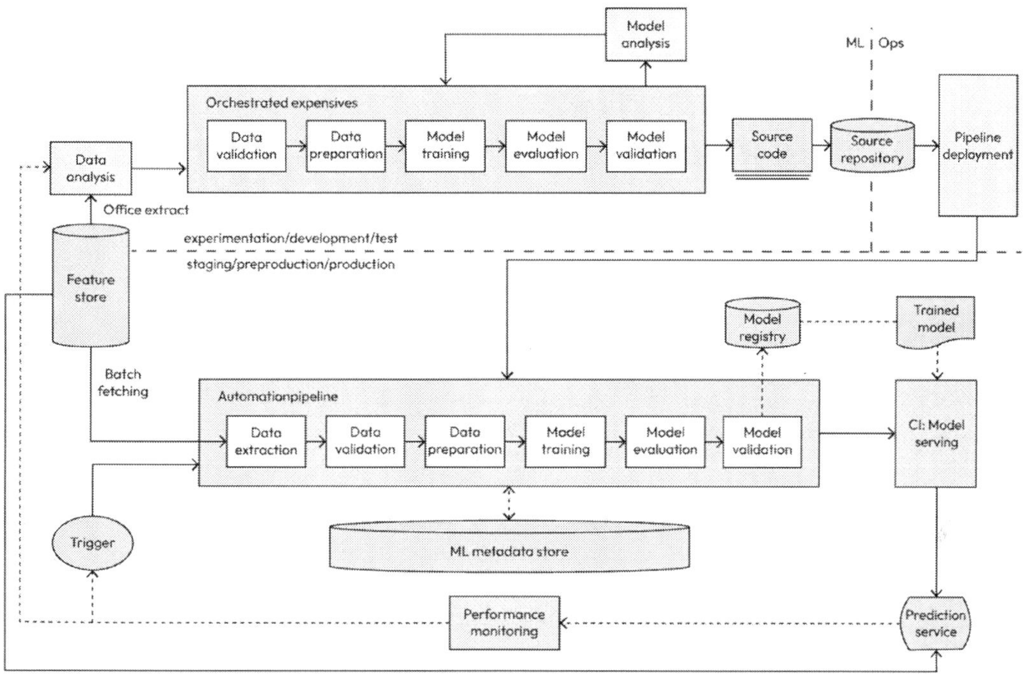

Figure 5.3 – Automating continuous training with ML pipeline (source: https://cloud.google.com/architecture/mlops-continuous-delivery-and-automation-pipelines-in-machine-learning)

Your ultimate goal is *continuous training*, so that you can retrain your model in production automatically.

> **Note**
>
> Continuous training is an MLOps practice that refers to the automated process of training an ML model in production to address concept drift and data drift (`https://developers.google.com/machine-learning/managing-ml-projects/pipelines`).
>
> Data drift occurs when the statistical properties of the data used to train the model have significantly changed relative to the production data used for inference. It might happen for many reasons, from changes in data collection to changes in the outside world (for example, related to seasonality or global changes such as a pandemic). Read more at `https://www.evidentlyai.com/ml-in-production/data-drift`.
>
> Concept drift occurs when an underlying relationship between input data (features) and a target variable changes, not just the data distribution itself (for example, spammers adapt to spam detection systems and start using other techniques). Read more at `evidentlyai.com/ml-in-production/concept-drift`.

There are two important questions we need to ask ourselves related to continuous training. First, why would you want to do it? The answer is to address **data drift** and **concept drift**. We briefly discussed this in *Chapter 2* when we discussed the need for evaluation and the concept of generalization in ML. To remind you, an ML model is good only while the data it has been trained on is a representative sample of the actual data it sees during the prediction time. Once the data distribution changes, we want to retrain the model automatically (or, in some domains such as ads, we just tell ourselves something like "*the world is changing too fast, let's retrain the model daily since effectively we're doing a memoization at scale*").

Second, what consequences does continuous training have for the ML team's setup? Once you start retraining the model and automatically pushing it to production, you need to put a lot of attention on the automatic evaluation to be able to detect all kinds of errors through the full flow, starting from the data arriving until the model has been trained. What would be easily spotted by a data scientist during manual retraining can be overlooked by an automated pipeline, and a garbage model would be promoted to `prod`. There are a lot of specialized MLOps tools, components, and approaches to ML monitoring to detect such problems. Adopting continuous training requires certain choices on automated monitoring, blending "old" and "new" data, automating code delivery, and so on. If you are interested, you can take a look at articles such as `https://neptune.ai/blog/retraining-model-during-deployment-continuous-training-continuous-testing` and `https://dl.acm.org/doi/10.1145/3550356.3561568`.

But we can take it a step further. What if we not only automate the model training (the pipeline part), but also add a CI/CD job to the pipeline itself? In other words, all a data scientist or ML engineer needs to do now is write the experimentation code, and an ML pipeline would be automatically built, tested, deployed, and executed, and the results would be collected and visualized in an experiment tracking system, as shown in *Figure 5.4*. A CI/CD will test and package our pipeline's code, run the pipeline deployment, then execute the pipeline, validate the ML model it produces, and push it to production if it passes the automated checks.

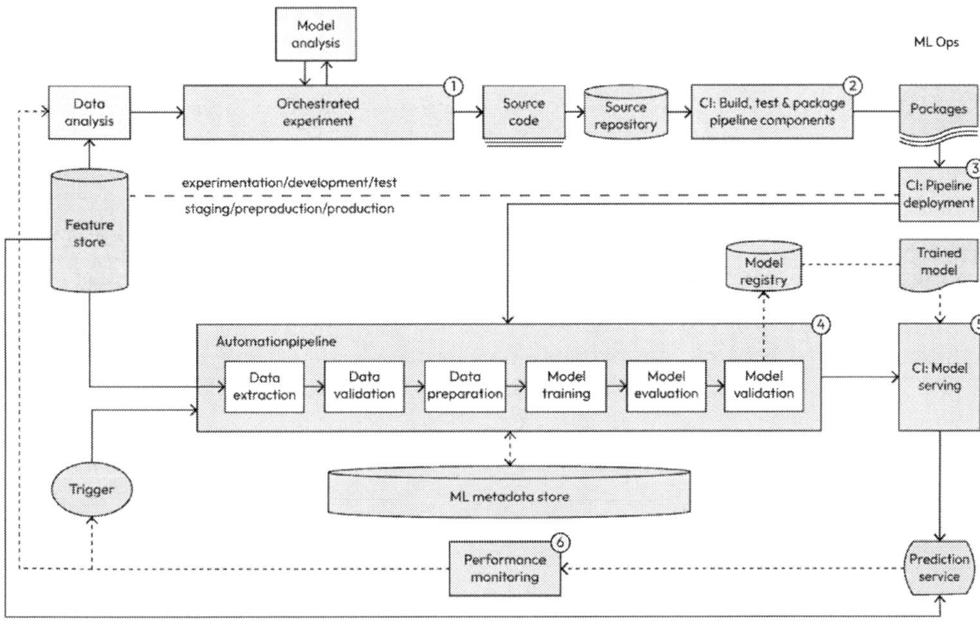

Figure 5.4 – ML pipeline CI/CD automation (source: https://cloud.google.com/architecture/mlops-continuous-delivery-and-automation-pipelines-in-machine-learning)

Last but not least, besides ML pipeline frameworks themselves, there exist dozens of specialized MLOps tools that automate various aspects of ML development. Looking over them might be a useful exercise since it helps to build an intuition of what might be useful for your team.

All the aforementioned is very good and useful, and these are best practices. But as with any best practices, it depends on your use case. Ask yourselves, what problem are you trying to solve? I've seen multiple times very capable ML/DS teams at large enterprises that were training small XGBoost models in their Jupyter notebooks, and they made a real impact on the business. At a certain point, somebody decided that they needed to adopt the best MLOps practices and build an MLOps platform. It's a very good decision, especially for people like myself, who were in the business of helping to build MLOps platforms. Seriously, start with the definition of the business problem you want to solve, for example, your models are too slow, you have measurable difficulties with reliability, or you want to run 10x more experiments than your current team has time for (and you have a backlog with these experiments). Otherwise, you might get the opposite results: your team would start wasting time learning Kubeflow or some other framework, modularizing their small Jupyter notebooks, and complaining about slow startup times of remote nodes when executing a pipeline. Start with the business problem first, as usual, and let the engineering team find a solution (MLOps practices will be one in many, but not in all cases).

What are success metrics?

A good question to ask yourselves when you're adopting MLOps practices is *Why am I doing so?* and *What are the success metrics?* Examples might include the following:

- To increase the efficiency of ML engineers and data scientists (measured as the number of models deployed, the number of products using ML, the number of experiments performed in a unit of time, etc.)
- To decrease the TCO (total cost of ownership) of your ML workloads (as you operate at scale, certain hardware and software optimizations in the training and inference pipeline might start eating your profit margin). In the GenAI domain, costs per one GenAI interaction might be high (and volatile), and reducing overall costs and/or the variance of costs per transaction might bring a high impact.
- To increase the reliability of your ML products (measured as the number of failures, number of incidents related to model degradation in production, latency, or error rate in production). We'll talk more about reliability metrics in *Chapter 8*.

Now that we've discussed DevOps and MLOps in detail, you might still ask why these topics are relevant for GenAI. The same concepts apply to the GenAI space, and we'll face the same problems when we start talking about operationalizing GenAI pipelines. And as you might have guessed, MLOps has evolved to LLMOps, or GenOps. So now, let's look into the specifics of increasing the developer's efficiency when building GenAI applications.

LLMOps

We have discussed how DevOps and then MLOps have made the ML engineer experience better. As you can guess, **LLMOps (large language model operations)** is a set of tools and practices that help to manage the lifecycle of LLMs and GenAI applications from development to production. There's still no universally accepted definition of *LLMOps* across the industry. It's clearly a subset of MLOps that focuses on the operationalization of LLMs and LLM-based applications. You might also have heard about **GenOps** and even **AgentOps**. In most cases, these terms are used interchangeably, but sometimes it's a hint at a focus: GenOps includes all

GenAI applications, not only LLM-based, and AgentOps focuses on complexity related to agents.

You might ask why DevOps or MLOps is not enough, and why we have to talk about LLMOps now. Let's discuss how the experience has changed for developers building GenAI applications.

How has GenAI changed the developer's experience?

We discussed the additional challenges faced by application teams (in *Chapters 1*, *2*, and *4*) who are developing GenAI applications earlier, and we will continue the discussion and will be addressing some other aspects later in this book. For now, let's summarize these challenges:

- **Increased complexity of the data**: GenAI applications depend on data; they need smaller but more complex datasets. Sometimes GenAI assistants and agents become a gateway to all enterprise data, from sales data in Salesforce to discussions on Microsoft Teams. Managing this at scale becomes a new challenge for data and security teams.
- **More complex evaluations**: Especially in the agentic world, evaluations constantly become more complex and sophisticated. You need to not only deal with non-deterministic outputs, but also with non-deterministic trajectories of your agent and multi-step workflows (each step being non-deterministic and its output influencing the outcome).
- **Importance of cost tracking and control**: LLMs can consume unpredictably many resources, and many agentic applications are reused across the organization. That means we move out of the decoupled microservices world where each team has its own budget and manages its own infrastructure. A larger portion of resources is reused, and that brings additional importance to tracking costs and usage.
- **Increased complexity of computing that you need to manage (if any)**: Not all, but some teams are hosting their own versions of LLMs, or are fine-tuning them and doing some other operations that require them to operate **high-performance computing** (**HPC**) clusters.
- **Security and ethics safeguards**: These are needed to prevent intentional or unintentional harmful usage of applications using GenAI.
- **Rapid evolution of the industry**: Software development has always been a fast-changing industry, but the speed of advancements in recent years has increased tremendously. For example, on SWE-bench, AI systems could solve just 4.4% of coding problems in 2023, but 71.7% in 2024 (that's a huge increase that completely changes how you think about the applicability of AI-based code assistants), according to the *2025 AI Index Report* (`https://hai.stanford.edu/ai-index/2025-ai-index-report`).

To address all of these challenges, we use various LLMOps tools that help us to manage evaluation, data governance, our compute capacity, and so on. Let's look deeper into LLMOps practice.

What is the value behind LLMOps?

Is LLMOps a hype? Why do we need yet another *Ops* (and not even one *Ops*)? On one side, during the gold rush in California in the 19th century, there was a saying, "*During a gold rush, sell shovels*." When a new large industry emerges, a lot of start-ups try to start building new tools for this industry, and an LLMOps story helps them to sell by convincing customers that they ultimately need new tooling to succeed in this race.

On the other hand, as we've already seen in previous chapters, and we will continue to look at other aspects throughout the book, GenAI changes the nature of enterprise applications and classical software development processes. New important and difficult challenges arise, and they need new tooling and a change in how we, as developers, build products.

I totally agree with the sentiment that GenAI product development needs new tooling, but *some* new tooling, not *all* new tooling. And I can only repeat my advice that I've been repeating multiple times across this book. Do not adopt LLMOps for the sake of adopting LLMOps. Stick to the first principles of computer science, look carefully at the problem you're going to solve, and then find the right tool. If you have a single application, maybe you don't need an LLMOps platform yet. Try to find a product-market fit, don't be afraid to fail, or do some hacks and sacrifice performance and efficiency. And only when you scale and face challenges related to scaling do you start solving these specific problems. In the *MLOps* section, we touched on success metrics that you might want to consider when introducing MLOps practices. They are the same for LLMOps. Hence, answer what problem you want to solve by adopting this or another *Ops* approach and tooling.

In the next section, we will discuss key LLMOps tools or components of a general LLMOps platform. But first, let's briefly touch on a "buy versus build" dilemma.

Choosing LLMOps tools

An important question that might be in front of you is a *buy versus build* decision. What LLMOps tool should you buy, and what should you build yourselves? This is an old dilemma in software engineering in general, and there are three main criteria to keep in mind:

- **Competitive advantage**: When you buy a piece of software, or in our case, you adopt an existing LLMOps tool, you get benefits such as faster deployment, lower initial costs, and access to best practices. But you won't get such flexibility as with an in-house tool; you might run into increased costs as you scale and into some integration issues. Ask yourself how critical this component is for your business, and whether it gives you a competitive advantage. One rule of thumb is to build in-house components that are crucial and distinguish you from your competitors, and buy everything else. For example, if you're a GenAI start-up, you most probably don't want to build your own telemetry platform, but you might end up developing your own evaluation tools. Or another example, if you're a start-up, you most likely use a pool of crowdsourcing annotators and integrate with such a platform, but if you're an enterprise automating some manual operations, only your in-house SMEs know how to do the labeling and evaluation, and you most probably will end up building a labeling tool for them yourself.

- **Business requirements**: Do your own benchmarking and work on your requirements. Adopting an LLMOps tool based on marketing materials or market opinion might not be the best idea. But keep in mind that figuring out your requirements is tricky. A lot of limitations and challenges can be discovered only when you start trying things in production (since you'll run into scenarios that you have never imagined before). Hence, do proofs-of-concept and thorough life testing before making a final decision.
- **Reliability**: Evaluate the reliability of a third-party service for your business. How difficult would it be for you to switch if the vendor gets out of the business or changes its strategy? If you're adopting an open source tool, check how large the community is, how often they publish new releases, and so on.

Thoughtworks published a good essay on this if you're interested in getting a more holistic view: `https://www.thoughtworks.com/insights/e-books/build-versus-buy-strategic-framework-for-evaluating-third-party-solutions`.

Before we complete this chapter, let's look at one specific example of how GenAI complicated the "classical" deployment approach, and why we need special LLMOps practices and tools to address it.

Case study: CI/CD job for RAG

Let's look at one specific example of complexity that LLMOps try to address. **Retrieval-augmented generation** (**RAG**) architecture is an important pattern in GenAI. You ground an LLM on your data during generation by retrieving context related to the input query from your database. That means, in production, there are two or more indices of your data (e.g., one with dense and another with sparse embeddings), a retrieval mechanism, and a generation mechanism.

Now, imagine you have changed the way you chunk your data, which affected the retrieval step, and now you want to deploy your changes to prod. The CI/CD job should perform five steps:

1. Initially, in production, there are our indices and the RAG pipeline itself:

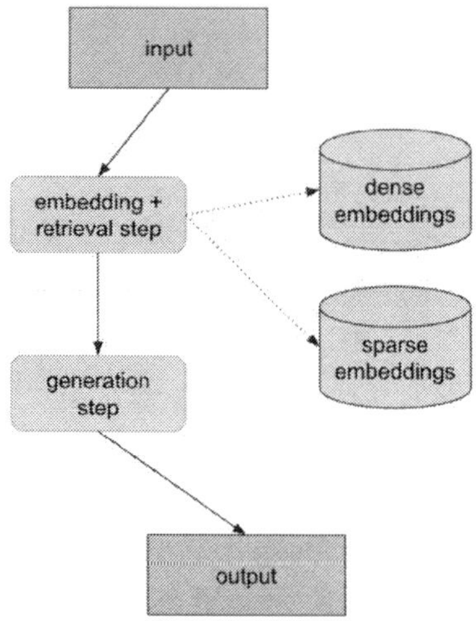

Figure 5.5 – RAG pipeline before deployment

2. Re-index the data in a new manner in production (or promote an existing updated index to production). Re-indexing takes hours, so you need to maintain two versions of indices (that means, you should deploy additional infrastructure to production).

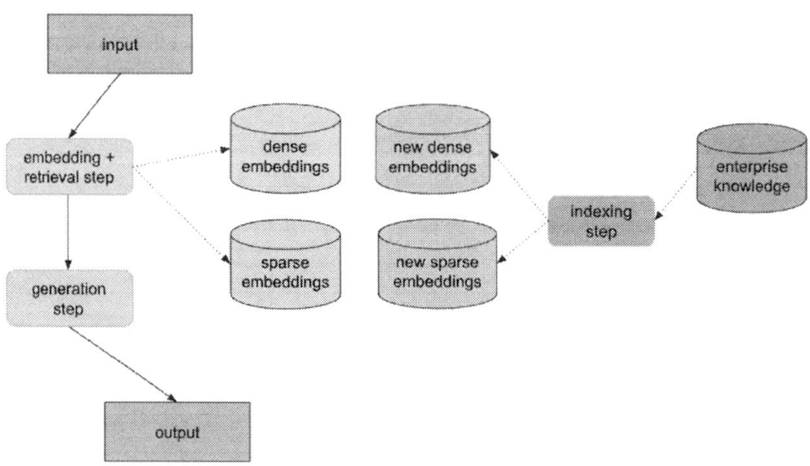

Figure 5.6 – During deployment, we run an indexing pipeline and create additional indices with dense and sparse embeddings. Indexing might take a few minutes or even hours

3. After the re-indexing job has been completed, you need to test the new index.
4. Then, you deploy a new version of your RAG code and point it to the new index (we'll be talking more about deployment strategies in *Chapter 6*).

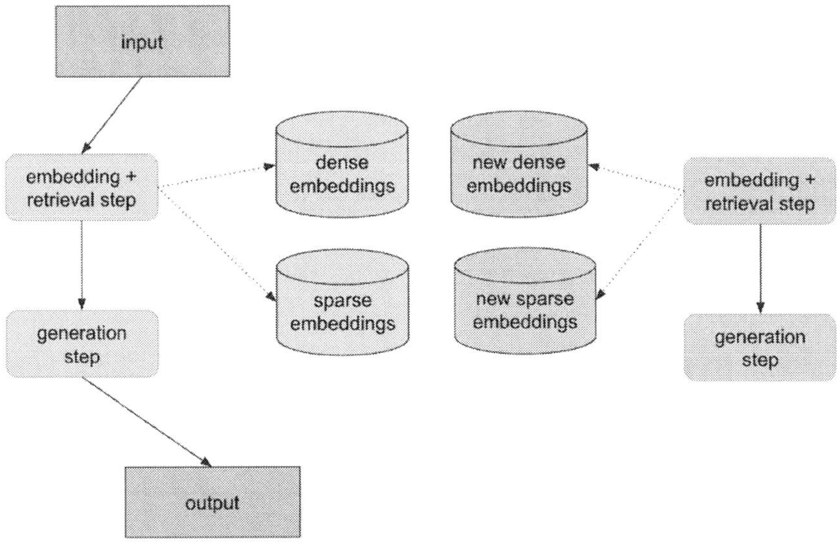

Figure 5.7 – After we have verified that the new test indices work properly, we deploy the new embeddings and generation pieces of our pipeline (and still keep previous ones since they serve the production traffic)

5. You wait for some time until you are sure that the new solution is working well, and you don't need to roll out your changes quickly. You start switching production traffic to the new RAG pipeline (and during the rollout, you keep both versions of indices and both versions of your code in production).
6. Only now can you delete the old index.

In other words, your code becomes even more tightly connected to the data it's using. This is uncommon for "classical" software applications. Yes, you might have one or two configuration tables in your database, but typically, data is detached from the application itself, and the application manages only the data structure during a release. In the ML world, data is more connected to the application itself. You use some post-processed binaries, such as scalers, hot-encoders, and the model's weights themselves, during the release. But still, your ML code produces the model and its binaries based on the data, and after that, during the release process, these artifacts are detached from the data. Search applications were the only category of applications where data was part of the release process, and they were highly connected with the code. Search teams knew how to manage this complexity, but it was a very niche business in software development. GenAI applications, in many cases, are very similar to search applications in this regard, so many developers need to learn and adapt this new way of managing the deployment of applications, coupled with the data they're using.

Summary

In this chapter, we learned that modern software development is heavily reliant on automation and collaboration, stemming from the practices of DevOps. We saw that DevOps is built on two pillars: a culture of shared responsibility (for the quality of software in the eyes of a user) and the automation of deployment and code delivery processes, which is commonly referred to as CI/CD. CI/CD practices, which involve frequent and automatic testing and deployment, are crucial for speed, scalability, and reducing errors in software releases.

We discussed how these core principles evolved into MLOps. MLOps focuses on streamlining the process of taking ML models to production, maintaining, and monitoring them, with a heavy emphasis on ensuring the reproducibility of ML models and automating the entire workflow through ML pipelines. This is essential for addressing issues such as data drift and concept drift through continuous training. However, we also discussed the importance of only adopting MLOps practices when they solve a specific business problem, rather than for the sake of adoption itself.

Finally, we explored how LLMOps (or GenOps/AgentOps) is evolving as a specialized subset of MLOps, necessitated by the unique complexities of building GenAI applications. These challenges include increased complexity of data and evaluation, the critical need for cost tracking, and the tight connection between code and data (as illustrated by the CI/CD job for RAG architecture). We concluded with the evergreen "buy versus build" dilemma for LLMOps tooling, advising that components offering a competitive advantage should be built in-house, and reiterating the core principle that all operational practices should be driven by a clear business need.

In the next chapter, we'll discuss some aspects (such as infrastructure as code, configuration and secrets management, scalability, etc.) of deploying your application to production.

> **Note**
>
> The three key outcomes to remember are as follows:
>
> - DevOps is a set of practices and tools to automate the delivery of software to production. Fundamentally, it's built on two pillars: a culture of shared responsibility and automation of operational work.
> - As we evolve from "classical" software to ML models, we meet new complexity and requirements. Hence, we introduce an additional DevOps subpractice called MLOps, which addresses corresponding challenges (such as experimentation, managing datasets, running multi-step workflows, etc.). MLOps helps increase the productivity of ML teams, decrease the cost of ownership of ML models, and improve stability and quality.
> - GenAI, in turn, introduces a new set of challenges (such as a more complex evaluation pipeline, different requirements for training a dataset, tight coupling of code with the data, and the importance of cost tracking), which brings us to the LLMOps subpractices that address these challenges.

Further reading

- ML pipelines: `https://developers.google.com/machine-learning/managing-ml-projects/pipelines`
- Komolafe, A. *Retraining Machine Learning Models*: `https://akhinoz.medium.com/retraining-machine-learning-models-2c41ccf23ba3`
- Sculley, D., Holt, G., Golovin, D., et al. *Hidden Technical Debt in Machine Learning Systems*, Advances in Neural Information Processing Systems 28 (NIPS 2015): `https://papers.nips.cc/paper_files/paper/2015/hash/86df7dcfd896fcaf2674f757a2463eba-Abstract.html`
- A curated list of awesome MLOps tools: `https://github.com/kelvins/awesome-mlops`

- *LLMOps: What It Is And How It Works*: https://cloud.google.com/discover/what-is-llmops
- *The Ultimate List Of Internal AI and ML Platforms*: https://www.evidentlyai.com/ml-platforms (if you want to read about real-world production challenges in MLOps and LLMOps)

Get This Book's PDF Version and Exclusive Extras

Scan the QR code (or go to packtpub.com/unlock). Search for this book by name, confirm the edition, and then follow the steps on the page.

UNLOCK NOW

Note: Keep your invoice handy. Purchases made directly from Packt don't require an invoice.

6

Deploying Your Application

We will begin by understanding the crucial concept of **statelessness** and its necessity in modern horizontal scaling with a load balancer. We will then introduce core deployment best practices, including adopting **infrastructure as code** (**IaC**) with tools such as Terraform and implementing secure **secret and configuration management**. The discussion will then shift to packaging and orchestration, where we detail how to wrap your application as a high-performance web API using frameworks such as FastAPI, how to leverage **Kubernetes** for container orchestration, and how to utilize specialized platforms such as LangSmith to deploy and manage durable agents. Finally, we will explore key scaling patterns such as caching, as well as the implications of the **consistency**, **availability**, and **partition tolerance** (**CAP**) theorem.

- Stateless and stateful applications
- Best practices for deploying your application
- Deployments
- Best practices for scaling your application

Stateless and stateful applications

Prototypes are often **stateful**, which means they retain and utilize information from previous interactions. This information is called an application's **state**. Let's take a look at a simple example. Let's assume we've developed a chatbot based on an LLM. The state of the chatbot is a history of previous conversations. Foundational models don't retain state, and they expose a stateless API. This means you need to memorize a history of messages yourself, and each time you invoke the API, you send not just the last message but the full history of your messages. Many prototypes are stateful, especially if you build them with a framework such as Gradio or Streamlit. Let's continue with the simple example of a chatbot application. If you develop a quick prototype of an assistant, you keep your chat instance and the history in memory, which means your application can serve only one user at a time. That can be a problem when it comes to deployment.

> **Note**
>
> A stateful application keeps and uses the state (the information from previous interactions) with the user. A stateless application processes any request without the need to memorize a state.

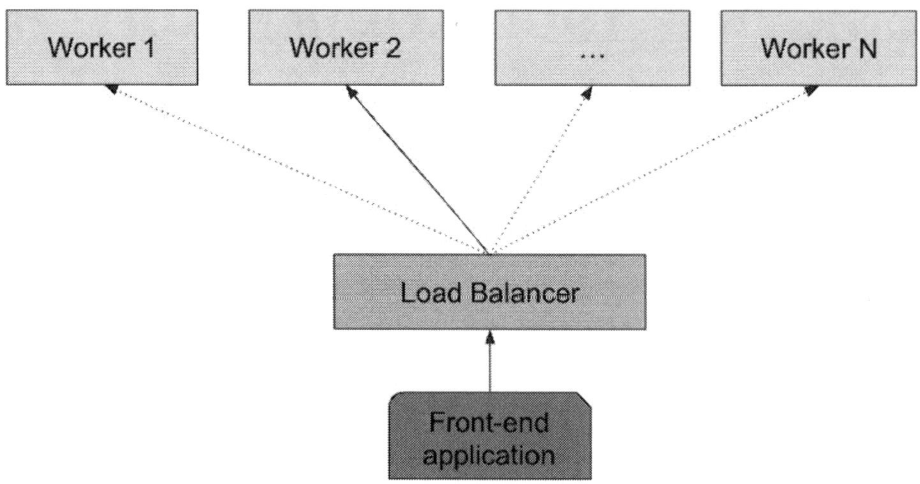

Figure 6.1 – Load-balancing traffic across multiple containers running your application

As shown in the figure, there are multiple workers behind the load balancer, each running copies of an application. A request from a user hits the load balancer first (to be fair, first the DNS address needs to be resolved, but these details are not relevant to this chapter), and the load balancer decides which worker to send the request to. There are two significant benefits of this kind of architecture:

- **Flexibility**: If one worker is suddenly busy with handling a particular user request, it isn't overloaded too much since the load balancer would recognize this and redirect traffic to other workers
- **Scalability**: If your load suddenly increases and you get more users, you can simply add another worker, which would run another copy of your application, and notify the load balancer when this worker is available, and it would start sending traffic to it too

The only issue? Your application should be stateless since you can't guarantee that the request from this particular user would be redirected to this specific worker. Actually, you can, but it would require a more nuanced configuration, which would increase the cost and latency of load balancing, so you don't want to do it. And what would you do if your worker (this specific instance) suddenly stopped handling requests because of some hardware failure? Should you just stop handling requests for all affected users instead of redirecting them to other workers?

Deployment best practices

We discussed in *Chapter 4* that as our application matures from a prototype to production-ready, we need to take care of aspects such as ease of maintenance and reliability. Choosing an appropriate deployment strategy is an important aspect of achieving such goals.

Infrastructure as code

Use tools such as Terraform that allow you to describe all your IaC. Keep track of all your dependencies with container management tools such as Docker and environment management tools for Python, such as Poetry. Otherwise, you will eventually run into the "it works on my machine" (or on your server) problem because you manually installed some libraries or enabled some APIs, but you can't even remember what exactly you did, and it would take you a lot of time to reproduce the same steps.

> Note
>
> **IaC** means that the setup and management of your infrastructure (setting up virtual networks, creating servers, setting permissions, enabling APIs, etc.) is done through code (configuration files) and not through manual processes. It enables you to easily reproduce the same environment each time, and to effectively manage (review, test, apply, and roll back) your changes.

Terraform (created by HashiCorp) is currently one of the key IaC software tools. It is very good at managing cloud resources, but you can also use it with a traditional on-premises data center with virtualized environments or to manage bare-metal servers. If you're new to Terraform, ask your operational team to create an initial setup for you, but it's worth spending some time learning the basics. The documentation at `https://developer.hashicorp.com/terraform/intro` is a great starting point, and it might enable you and your team to manage the infrastructure yourself. Let's take a quick look at how Terraform works. The following diagram shows the tasks that Terraform helps you to manage.

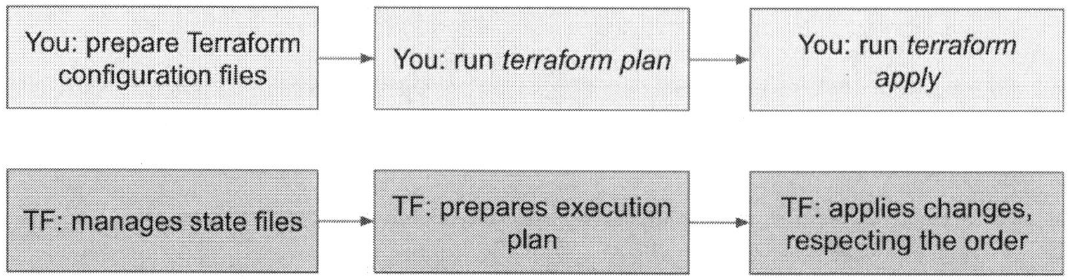

Figure 6.2 – How Terraform helps manage the deployment process

In the first stage, you describe your desired state in a declarative manner using **HashiCorp Configuration Language** (**HCL**). A declarative manner means that you just describe what you want in special `.tf` files. This approach naturally allows for version control and promotes modularity and reusability of your code since you can create modules and reuse them across your repository. On the other hand, Terraform maintains a special `.tfstate` JSON file that describes the current state of your infrastructure.

The next stage is the *planning* phase. When you run this special command `terraform plan` (`https://developer.hashicorp.com/terraform/cli/commands/plan`), Terraform creates an execution plan for you that you can validate. An important note is that the planning phase includes an implicit refresh where Terraform checks that what it knows about your infrastructure is actually true (if you made some changes manually, it would inform you about the discrepancies and whether they're critical).

> **Note**
>
> With Terraform, you first describe your infrastructure resources in configuration files, then you check the execution plan prepared by Terraform (Terraform informs you what resources would be destroyed, created, or changed). Once you confirm the changes, Terraform applies them by computing the correct order given the dependencies.

The last phase is the *apply* phase. You confirm the changes, and Terraform rolls them out to your environment. It allows you to easily test your changes in the `development` or `stage` environment before rolling them out to production. One important term is **Terraform provider**. You can think about it as a specific library or plugin that converts declarative Terraform code into the specific API calls required to manage resources on a particular platform. It implements the **create, update, delete, and read** (**CRUD**) operations on these resources so that Terraform can effectively manage them.

> **Note**
>
> A Terraform provider refers to a plugin that maps your Terraform configuration to a specific technology or service.

An interesting practical question is: should the Terraform code be part of your code repository, or should it stay in a separate repository? The answer is *it depends*. Different organizations use different practices. If you have a separate infrastructure team, it might be a good idea to have a separate infrastructure repository (or maybe an infrastructure repository per microservice). These repositories would have separate CI/CD jobs and permissions (for example, your team might create pull requests, but they should be approved by a member of the infrastructure team; also, rollout to production can be executed only under the manual supervision of an infrastructure team member).

Secret management

This might sound obvious, but do not put your API keys in your code or configuration files. You might laugh at this, but there are still many cases where API keys are leaked through code repositories.

Of course, proper secret management goes beyond that. An application these days might have many different secrets: API keys and tokens, database credentials (usernames and passwords), SSL/TLS certificates for securing web traffic, private service accounts or SSH keys, encryption keys, sensitive configuration values (for example, a "salt" used to hash user passwords), and so on.

> **Note**
>
> A secret refers to any sensitive information that grants access or privileges to a system. The defining characteristic of a secret is that its exposure could compromise the confidentiality, integrity, or availability of your application and its data. Secrets require special, accurate management.

If you believe that your application doesn't have any secrets, double-check. You might be running a GitHub action that is authorized by your cloud provider to run integration tests, and it uses an authorization key for that.

Choose a secret management tool (or check whether your organization has adopted one already). You can use managed services offered by cloud providers, or you can use a specialized tool such as HashiCorp Vault. For a very simple setup, you can stick to environment variables by setting them on a server where your application is running (still, make sure you separate this setup from the code!). Of course, GitHub, GitLab, and other code-managing systems offer their own secret manager that you can use. However, be aware that such secrets can be visible in logs or to anyone with access to the server, so it's a good starting point but unlikely to be a long-term solution.

These principles might be helpful for you:

- Identify all your secrets and keep them in one place. Make sure you secure your CI/CD jobs or your Jupyter notebooks even during the prototyping phase.
- Separate secrets by environment. Your development, staging, and production environments should have their own sets of secrets.
- Inject secrets at runtime. Your application should be configured to pull secrets from your chosen secret management tool when it starts up.
- Control access to define who and what can access which secrets.
- Regularly rotate your secrets (for example, replace API keys with new ones).
- When appropriate, add alerts on spikes in secret consumption. For example, if you use an API key to be authorized by an LLM provider, configure spending limits and alerts to be notified about a sudden spike in API key consumption.
- Separate API keys by application. Using the same example as the previous point, if you use an API key to be authorized by an LLM provider, then each application should have its own API key, and don't use the same API keys across multiple applications.
- Follow the least-privilege principle. Any entity (it can be a human, such as a developer, or a machine identity, such as a service account) should only be able to access a secret required for its legitimate purpose, only for the shortest time necessary, and this secret should grant the minimum amount of permissions required. In other words, do not use one secret for all possible purposes used by different identities.
- Make sure you add to the `.gitignore` file all files that contain secrets (for example, local files with tokens used by a cloud provider to authorize). Depending on your workflow, you might need to add such restrictions to `.dockerignore`, `.geminiignore`, and so on to avoid copying secrets into Docker images or the LLM's context.

Configuration management

Your application, especially as its complexity increases, will use many different settings, such as database connections, foundational model versions, prompts, and thresholds. Some settings are repeated multiple times across the whole code base. You need an easy way to manage these settings: change, version, test, and roll them out in different environments. That leads us to a need for configuration management, or a good way to handle all the settings that your applications need.

First, start by defining a constant only once. A common issue is defining the same thing multiple times across your code (remember, we discussed this in *Chapter 4*). For example, when you use a `gemini-3.0-pro` LLM, define its name once as a constant and maybe even create a singleton or use a factory method to create a client to use this model. When you switch to another model or adjust the way you initiate it, you don't want to search through the application's code base and make a dozen similar changes.

Second, how do you store your settings? You start simple, with files such as `config.py`, where you define your Python constants, or `.ini` files that define key-value pairs (you can read these files with the built-in Python `configparser` library or any advanced versions of it). It might be a good idea to organize config files hierarchically, so that production or stage values override development ones when needed. As your application advances, you can add more complex config validators with libraries such as Pydantic, or even use specialized frameworks such as Hydra to manage hierarchical configurations.

Some settings, however, do not define a state of your application, but they depend on the environment. For example, a database connection URL would be different in development, testing, and production environments. Hence, it's not a constant, but a configuration setting. You can define it as an environment variable so that an application will read the value from the environment during runtime. This allows you to separate your configuration from your code base in a secure way. Both Docker and cloud platforms allow you to set environment variables during deployment configuration setup. For local development, a possible way is to create a `.env` file (do not forget to add it to the `.gitignore` file!) and load it during runtime, for example, using a `dotenv` library (if you develop with Python):

```
import os
from dotenv import load_dotenv
load_dotenv()
DATABASE_CONNECTION_URL = os.environ.get("DATABASE_CONNECTION_URL")
```

Deploying an application

Imagine you have your GenAI agent ready. Let's discuss what options you have to actually deploy it to production and expose it as an API to end users or other services.

Wrapping code as a web API

In most cases, you need to expose a backend API that would make your application accessible through standard web protocols such as HTTP(S). A web API is called a **wrapper** since it is the communication layer. It defines a set of rules (endpoints, request/response formats) for how external clients can interact with your GenAI application. It takes an incoming HTTP request, extracts the necessary inputs, passes them to the application, gets the output, and then packages it back in an HTTP response to send back to the client.

> **Note**
>
> A web API wrapper is a communication layer that allows external applications of various sorts to easily interact with yours by sending an HTTP request and getting an HTTP response back.

There are a few things to take into account when creating a backend service that exposes such an API:

- Carefully consider the specifications of your API. Designing a good **Representational State Transfer** (**REST**) API is not easy, and so I highly recommend the excellent (and free!) e-book on API design by my ex-colleague Sergei Konstantinov (`https://github.com/twirl/The-API-Book`). Why do I recommend it? Because designing a good API is way more difficult than many of us think, and we engineers often don't focus enough on it (think about it, you've just trained a very complex ML model or developed a brilliant AI agent; what can be difficult about wrapping it as a web API?!). I often observe misused HTTP methods or statuses, inconsistent error handling and response formats, and other issues in APIs that wrap various ML and AI applications. At the end of the day, your application is only as good as the value it brings to users, which means the quality of the end-to-end solution matters the most (and a poor API design might hinder the best user experience).

  A good practice is to create your API specification (including authorization schemes and other details) in OpenAPI format and adopt a tool such as Swagger to validate it. Share this specification with teams who may end up using your API, and incorporate their feedback.

  > **Note**
  >
  > A REST API is an architectural style (or set of rules) that refers to a set of design principles that covers an abstract distributed client-server architecture (that is not bound to either HTTP or URL) and allows you to develop a good API for your programs to interact over the internet. It was initially developed in 2000 by R. Fielding, one of the authors of the HTTP and URI specifications.

- Pick a framework to adopt. A typical choice is Flask or FastAPI. Keep in mind that these frameworks are implementations on top of different (but related) interfaces that define how a Python application should interact with a web server. When you're deploying a Flask or FastAPI application to production, you'll essentially be running a web server and a gateway interface implementation on top of it (refer to *Figure 6.3* for more details).

FastAPI is considered to be more modern, and it has built-in support for asynchronous requests and request schema validation, but it's still a matter of personal preference when it comes to which framework to use.

> Note
>
> Both Flask and FastAPI are lightweight Python implementations of **Web Server Gateway Interface** (**WSGI**) and **Asynchronous Server Gateway Interface** (**ASGI**), which refer to interfaces for how web servers communicate with Python web applications. WSGI was initially defined in PEP-0333 (`https://peps.python.org/pep-0333`), and ASGI is mainly driven by the Django team, so refer to its official documentation page for additional info (`https://asgi.readthedocs.io/en/latest`).

Let's take a look at what actually happens when we deploy a Flask application that wraps our GenAI agent (or another application):

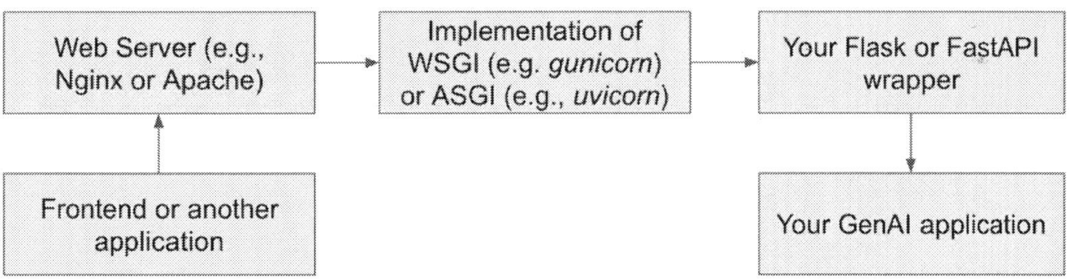

Figure 6.3 – What Flask deployment looks like

- Think about whether you need an asynchronous API and/or streaming. If you're going to utilize streaming, think about whether you need true bidirectional streaming with WebSocket.
- Follow all other best practices of scaling web applications: add input and output schema validations, proper exception handling and logging, and so on.
- Containerize your application with Docker and follow Docker best practices.
- If you use singletons, make sure your application code is thread-safe.

Before we move on, let's discuss how exactly we should package our application into a Docker container and wrap it with FastAPI. A very simplified version of the Docker file would look similar to this (keep in mind, as discussed in the previous section, that if you have many unnecessary files or dependencies in your application, it's a good idea to keep your image slim, for example, with the help of `.dockerignore`). We start from an existing Docker image, copy our code and requirements, install them, expose a port, and start our application:

```
# Pick a specific version of the base image
FROM ...
# Set the working directory inside the container
WORKDIR /app

# Copy the requirements file into the container (of course, you can use poetry or
any other dependency management framework)
COPY requirements.txt .

# Install Python dependencies (you can also install missing Unix dependencies with
apt-get)
RUN pip install --no-cache-dir -r requirements.txt

# Copy your application code into the container
COPY ...

# Expose the port your application will listen on (if it's a web service)
EXPOSE 8000

# Command to run your application when the container starts
["python", "my_genai_application.py"]
```

In reality, your Docker file would look more complex since you would most likely like to set up environment variables, pass credentials, install more complex dependencies, and so on. What would be inside your FastAPI application? The easiest way to wrap your GenAI agent with FastAPI is to add a simple `app.py` wrapper to your application that might look similar to this (it's a simplified version):

```
from fastapi import FastAPI, HTTPException
from fastapi.responses import StreamingResponse
from pydantic import BaseModel
import uvicorn import asyncio
```

```
# Import your application logic
from some_module import process_request
from schemas import AgentResponse
app = FastAPI(
    title="My first generative AI agent",
    description="..",
    version="...", )

@app.post("/your_path", response_model=AgentResponse)
async def invoke_agent(request: QueryRequest):
    try:
        response_text = process_request(request.query)
        return AgentResponse(
            response=response_text, session_id=request.session_id)
    except Exception as exc:
        raise HTTPException(
            status_code=500, detail=f"Error invoking agent: {str(exc)}")
```

This is why we call it a wrapper. We just wrapped an existing application with a very lightweight service that processes incoming HTTP requests (and, in turn, this wrapper uses the FastAPI framework for managing HTTP requests), invokes our application with corresponding input parameters, and transforms the output back to the HTTP response.

There's an alternative way of packaging your GenAI application, but before we look into it, let's briefly discuss how to deploy a Docker container that you've created on Kubernetes.

Deploying your container on Kubernetes

Many of you will be familiar with Kubernetes, which is an open source container orchestration system. It was initially released by Google in 2014, and it has gained wide adoption and strong community support since then. It's now truly portable, and you can run it in almost any cloud, on-premises, or hybrid environment, which prevents vendor lock-in. Kubernetes has gained strong developer support because of the level of flexibility and automation it provides to manage your applications (which, in turn, allows you to easily achieve a high level of reliability and resource utilization) and its high availability (because of its self-recovery features that decrease the downtime).

If you're an engineer who deals with production applications, you have most probably worked with Kubernetes or you will during your career. I'm not saying that you should become an experienced DevOps engineer, but I believe understanding the basics and mastering some simple commands and ways to work with Kubernetes would make your life much easier.

But let's take a step back. Why would you need Kubernetes at all? These days, a common practice is the **containerization** of applications (that's what we discussed in the previous section when we packaged our FastAPI application with Docker). A container is an isolated entity that allows running the application consistently and reliably across different environments, regardless of the operating system or hardware.

> **Note**
>
> Containerization technology allows you to package software code and all of the needed dependencies into a single, self-contained unit called a container.

But when we have a container, we need to manage it to make our application production-ready. This includes, but is not limited to, the following tasks:

- Deploying containers to hardware or virtual machines in the cloud environment
- Load balancing and horizontally scaling the number of running containers up and down, depending on the current load on your application
- Managing updates and rollbacks, identifying failed containers and restarting them, or replacing them with new ones

There are many good courses on Kubernetes available online (both free and paid). If you're a GenAI developer, you most probably do not need to go into the details on how to set up and manage the Kubernetes cluster itself. It is useful to understand that a Kubernetes cluster consists of two main types of Pods. Some system Pods run the control plane components, while others run worker Pods. The control plane manages the cluster and its state, and users interact with it through the API server. In this chapter, we are not going to go into the details of the other services that the control plane runs and what tasks it performs. Just know that you can use a command-line interface called **kubectl** to interact with Kubernetes; a good starting point is looking at the cheat sheet at `https://kubernetes.io/docs/reference/kubectl/quick-reference/`. I have come across some developers who didn't know the basics of kubectl, and it made it very difficult for them to manage their applications. With kubectl, you can easily apply changes to your cluster and schedule new workloads, inspect existing ones, take a look at container logs, SSH within the container for debugging, and do many other things with one line. Learning the fundamentals of the Kubernetes control plane is crucial; once learned, you will be able to use any visual tools to simplify cluster management. There are plenty of options, but to name a few, take a look at visual managers such as K9s or Lens, or VSCode extensions and plugins for other IDEs, such as IntelliJ from JetBrains.

We describe our application deployment in the Kubernetes manifest. This is just a YAML or JSON file that defines the state of our deployment in a declarative way. Kubernetes will take care of the deployment of the application (it's similar to what we learned about Terraform configuration, isn't it?). Each Kubernetes cluster consists of node pools, or groups of nodes of the same hardware configuration. A node is a virtual machine, and you can have multiple node pools with different hardware configurations in your cluster (for example, you can have a high-memory node pool and a GPU-enabled node pool). Another important concept is a **Pod**. A Pod is a single deployable unit; that is, when you're running an application, you define a Pod. It can be one or multiple containers running together. You define Pods for your application in the Kubernetes configuration file, including so-called node selectors and affinity rules, which define which node pools your Pod can be (or are prohibited from being) deployed to. In other words, you define hardware requirements in your manifest, and Kubernetes takes care of scheduling a required number of Pods to nodes in such a way that it optimizes the overall hardware utilization.

Each Pod has its own internal IP address that is automatically assigned. For other applications to communicate with your application, you define it as a Kubernetes **Service**. If you're using any cloud service, then you would choose a LoadBalancer type of service (other ways to define a Kubernetes Service exist, but that's the easiest way to connect your internal cluster and cloud provider's networking infrastructure). It exposes the Service externally using the cloud provider's load balancer and provides a stable network endpoint (with a consistent IP address and a DNS name).

To summarize, if you're using Kubernetes for deployment, you need to be able to read and understand Kubernetes manifests and have a brief understanding of what you can achieve with this platform and how to manage and debug your applications with **kubectl**. Ask your DevOps team to help you with the initial setup, but again, you need to know what questions to ask them (or how to prompt them, if you wish). You need to understand the requirements (such as CPU, memory, and disk limits of your application) to put them in front of your DevOps team. You also deploy your application as a Service by composing a Kubernetes manifest. In that way, Kubernetes would care about load balancing, scaling your application, recovering unhealthy Pods, bringing secrets to your applications, rotating service account keys, and other operational tasks.

Kubernetes allows you to describe the underlying infrastructure for your application as YAML manifests. To move beyond basic restarts of a service, Kubernetes offers several rollout patterns:

- The default is a rolling update strategy that gradually replaces old Pods with new ones, ensuring some instances are always running

- An alternative is a blue/green strategy that deploys a full version of your application (called *green*) alongside the running production one (called *blue*). Once verified, traffic is switched instantly
- Another alternative is a canary deployment that releases the new version of an application to a tiny subset of users first to monitor for issues before a full (gradual) rollout

To ensure zero downtime in production, consider following these basic principles:

- Include readiness probes in your application (you configure a deployment manifest by instructing Kubernetes not to send traffic to a Pod until it's fully initialized by making a certain probe `HTTP API` available).
- Define the `RollingUpdate` strategy in your manifest by setting `maxUnavailable` Pods to `0` and `maxSurge` to `1` (or more) so that new Pods are ready before old ones are killed.
- Ensure your app handles the `SIGTERM` signal to finish active requests before shutting down (this pattern is called graceful termination).
- Use autoscaling appropriately. Kubernetes offers three ways to scale your application:
  - **HorizontalPodAutoscaler**: Automatically increases or decreases the number of Pods based on metrics such as CPU or memory usage. The scaling behavior can be configured in the manifest, for example, by setting minimum and maximum Pod limits.
  - **VerticalPodAutoscaler**: Automatically adjusts the resources of individual Pods, such as the amount of memory or CPU consumed.
  - **Cluster Autoscaler**: Automatically provisions (or detaches) actual virtual machines (Kubernetes nodes) when the cluster runs out of resources or when existing nodes are underutilized.

To simplify Kubernetes manifests, you can use Helm Charts (or any alternative tools). These are reusable templates that bundle all your YAML manifests into a single package. In production, this avoids the friction of manual configuration and "copy-paste" errors across different environments (development, staging, and production), allowing for versioned releases and easy rollbacks.

As you can see, deploying on Kubernetes gives you a lot of flexibility, but it requires quite some configuration (you need to wrap your agent with Flask or FastAPI, build a Docker image, configure a Kubernetes cluster, and deploy your application there). Now, let's look at an alternative way of deploying your GenAI application. There exist managed services that take care of all this burden. With one click or CLI command, you get a ready application, and all this work of packaging your code and deploying it will be done under the hood.

Deploying with a managed service such as LangSmith

As we have seen, we can follow the standard process of developing a custom API and containerization of our GenAI application. But there are multiple problems that we need to solve:

- Developing a custom REST API for every agent
- Taking care of the horizontal scaling of our application, given that some runs might be stateful
- Allowing asynchronous job execution for long-running tasks (where a client schedules a task and doesn't maintain an open connection with the backend until the task is completed)
- Gracefully handling interruptions (both expected, such as human-in-the-loop, and unexpected, such as a random failure of an agent) and rerunning subparts of the flow only
- Implementing long-term and short-term memory stores to handle agent state and memory
- Supporting real-time streaming, cancellation of tasks, and other features that are a must-have for a GenAI application

Cloud providers (including Azure, AWS, and Google Cloud) and smaller vertical start-ups offer **software-as-a-service** (**SaaS**) options to deploy GenAI applications without the need to follow a fully custom route. One such example is LangSmith Deployment, which is a SaaS offering developed by LangChain (as a company, not as a framework).

> **Note**
>
> LangSmith Deployment is a SaaS offering from LangChain (as a company) that helps developers develop and deploy LangGraph applications by making them reliable and scalable. It has a strong focus on developing agentic applications and provides tools and components to develop and manage the user experience around GenAI agents. You can read a blog post on the reasoning behind LangSmith Deployment at `https://blog.langchain.com/why-langgraph-platform/`.

We are not going to go into the details of LangSmith Deployment itself, but I'd like to explain how such platforms typically work so that you get an idea, and you can use any such platform of your choice (if you decide to go down the managed service route). You only need to develop your GenAI application; then, these deployment platforms will automatically package your code and deploy it. How does the packaging work? There are multiple options:

- The platform copies your local file or multiple files (folders) to the server, and these files are added to the Docker image that is automatically built. You only need to specify a path to your files and high-level functions that implement certain functionality (they should follow an interface defined by the platform).
- You can specify additional dependencies in your configuration. For example, you can tell it which libraries should be additionally installed.

That's it! You just need to develop your agent and expose a certain interface, and you don't need to care about anything else. The LangGraph platform (and, again, it's just mentioned as an example) would automatically package, deploy, and manage it, and it would expose an out-of-the-box API to execute with your agent, since we can be opinionated about how an API for submitting a task to an agent should look. It also simplifies the use of your agents by downstream services, since each new agent exposes the same API. If you need a custom output API format, you can always define your own custom route in the configuration of your application deployed to the LangGraph platform.

Before moving on to discuss reliability and observability in the next chapter, let's look at a few simple but important techniques that can help you to scale your application and prepare it for a high load.

Best practices for scaling your application

In this section, we will discuss a few architectural patterns that will help you to prepare your application for a high load and make it more robust.

Caching

In classical system design, a **cache** is a storage layer that sits between a backend application and a permanent storage layer (a database). Caching helps with the following:

- It decreases the overall latency because it's faster than retrieving data from a database
- It decreases the load on a database, and that in turn improves the scalability of your system (or decreases the cost of ownership since you can handle a higher number of requests with the same hardware)

Cache has two distinct characteristics. First, it's fast, and that's why it decreases the latency. Second, it's temporary. There is no guarantee that every request will be fulfilled by a cache (or it will *hit* the cache). Why is that? Why can't we always serve any request from the cache (or, at least, any *read* request)? An answer is that cache is designed for speed, not for persistence and durability. In other words, a cache is volatile, or it might crash, and you might lose all your data (in that case, you re-create a cache from a database). In terms of **hit ratio**, which is the percentage of queries that were served from a cache (without the need to go to a database), the higher the hit ratio, the better. However, a too high hit ratio might mean that you cache too much data, your cache size is large, and the cost of ownership is also high.

There are several strategies for determining when to add records to a cache. One of the most commonly used approaches is **lazy loading**, where a record is added to the cache only after a cache miss occurs. In this case, the system retrieves the data from the source and stores it in the cache for future requests. Cached records are usually assigned a **time to live** (**TTL**). If a record is not accessed for a specified period, it expires and is removed from the cache to help control its size.

> **Note**
>
> Caching is a classical system design pattern that adds a high-speed but volatile storage layer to reduce the load on a database (which is designed for persistence and durability). A cache contains only a subset of the data that exists in a database, and data loss is acceptable (a cache can always be rebuilt). Caching parameters such as time to expire help to balance the cache size (or cost of ownership) with the cache hit ratio.

From the preceding description, you might think that a cache is always a key-value storage. While this is a very common cache architecture, there is also different caching. A very simple example is a **least recently used** (**LRU**) cache, which you might know from the Python `functools` module. Caching is a classical design pattern in software engineering that helps to reduce the latency and infrastructure costs.

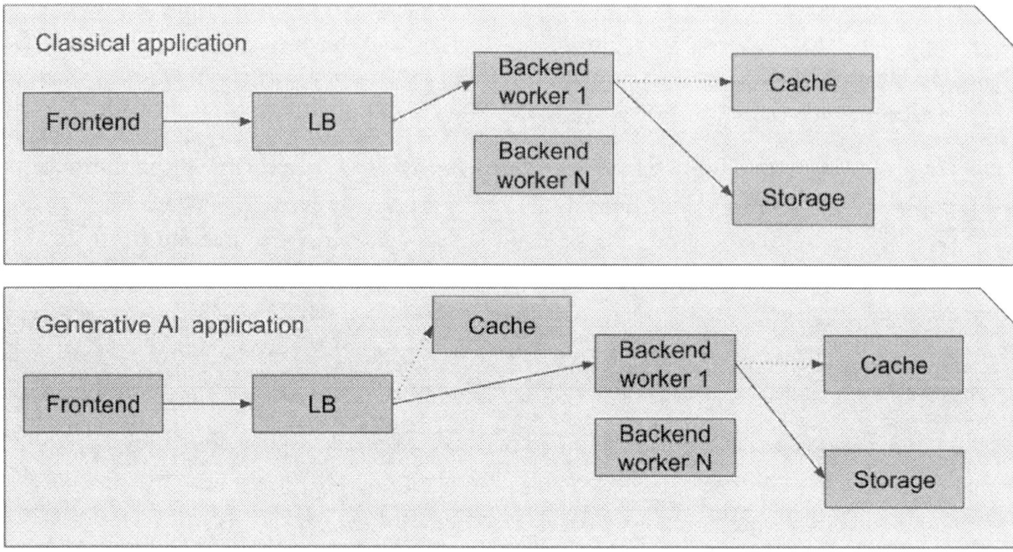

Figure 6.4 – Using cache in your GenAI application

How can caching be used to design GenAI applications? First, GenAI applications might use a cache in a "classical" manner. For example, if you need to display images or large PDF files as evidence of your answers, loading them from the storage each time might be slow and expensive, so you can introduce a cache just to store supporting documents that are often used. Besides that, one example might be **semantic caching**. We could cache responses to the most frequent user queries without the need to run a complex pipeline involving an LLM, or we can cache the most frequent context retrieved from our complex retrieval systems to speed up the question-answering pipeline. But instead of looking for an exact match between a new user input and a cached one, we can use an embeddings-based similarity search in our cache.

Consider a customer support chatbot for a smartphone. If you cache an answer to the input "*What are the new features of the latest iPhone?*" and you then give it the input "*Tell me about the upgrades in the newest iPhone model,*" a traditional cache would see these as two different queries, and a cache miss would occur. A semantic cache (using ANN and KNN, which we discussed in Chapter 3), however, would recognize their similar intent and, if the answer to the first query is cached, could serve it for the second query as well, avoiding a costly call to the LLM.

Another example (and note that it's not a key-value cache!) is caching complex data structures and execution plans. If you're developing a code assistant that should be aware of your specific code base, you need to build a complex structure called an **abstract syntax tree** (**AST**) that is a tree representation of the code's syntactic structure, capturing the relationships between functions, variables, and statements. You typically cache such a structure and rebuild it from time to time.

A third example is caching complex generation plans. Imagine you're developing an application that generates a Google Slides deck based on a document provided. Most probably, it would be a complex multi-step pipeline that includes stages such as outline generation and generating text and images for each slide. If a user wants to refine a specific slide and provides additional instructions, you don't want to re-generate the whole plan, but you'll use the cached one.

As we scale our applications, sooner or later, we'll need to use a distributed storage layer; hence, let's discuss the potential limitations of caching that we need to deal with.

CAP theorem

If you're using caching, you have, by default, built a distributed data-processing system, even if the cache and persistent database are each represented by a single worker. We need to be aware of a fundamental limitation that any distributed data store faces. This limitation is described by the so-called CAP theorem, which states that with any distributed data store, we can get only two of the following three guarantees:

- **Consistency**: Each operation receives the most recent version of the data. With a caching system, we might first write an update to a persistent database, and until we have updated the cache, our application will receive an outdated version of the data served from the cache.
- **Availability**: Serving requests without an error. In our case, this means if there's a failure in communication between cache and persistent storage, we still continue operating without errors.
- **Partition tolerance**: The system works even if the communication between nodes drops.

We almost always want partition tolerance in distributed data systems, which means we have to choose between availability and consistency. Without going too deep into the consequences of this choice, I want you to be aware of this fundamental limitation and take it into account when designing distributed systems. If you choose high availability, your workers might be out of sync for a moment; hence, some parts of your applications might receive stale data. Otherwise, if you always want consistency, you should be prepared for short downtimes since you can't guarantee 100% availability. If you reach a certain amount of traffic, you can scale your storage layer only by using a distributed design. If you're interested in learning more about the application of the CAP theorem to system design, take a look at the PACELC design principle.

> **Note**
>
> The **PACELC design principle** is an implementation of the CAP theorem. It states that if there's a network partition (*P*) in a distributed system, you face a trade-off between availability (*A*) and consistency (*C*); else (*E*) (if there's no partition), you face a trade-off between latency (*L*) and consistency (*C*).

Now, we'll look into another caching example, but this time related to context caching, which works on the server side during an LLM inference.

Context caching

One important aspect of the caching pattern is **context caching**. Depending on the LLM provider, two types of cache may be used: a **prefill cache** and a **preprocess cache**. A prefill cache decreases the time to first token. If we simplify things, a transformer computes large matrices (called key-value matrices) based on the input as part of the inference process. Since an LLM generates output autoregressively, we can cache these KV (key-value) matrices and pass them to the transformer directly during inference. Most modern LLM providers and inference servers enable this by default nowadays.

A preprocess cache uses a similar idea. Complex multi-modal inputs (such as images, audio, and large texts) are tokenized, postprocessed, and cached across different inference requests. This saves inference time if we re-use such large multi-model inputs next time.

- **Implicit context caching**: No saving guaranteed; an LLM provider decides whether to use caching or not on a best-effort basis, without any additional instructions from a user
- **Explicit context caching**: When a user instructs an LLM to use a specific cache when serving a request, and puts data into the cache first, latency and cost decreases are guaranteed, but maintaining a cache incurs extra costs

The explicit prefill context caching and long context window that modern models offer allow us to use **cache-augmented generation** (**CAG**) techniques. We discussed in *Chapter 3* that if your knowledge fits in the LLM's context window, you can skip the retrieval phase. The next logical step would be to put all your knowledge in the cache, which means you append additional dynamic instructions (including the question itself) to the system message. Such an approach would significantly reduce response times.

Now that we have discussed caching and scaling our storage layer, let's look at other aspects of designing our applications for scale.

Failing gracefully

Do not neglect failures when designing your application. We tend to forget that failures will always happen, and we design only for the best scenario. There are two aspects of a graceful failure.

First, error messages should be informative for the user. For example, the error message "*Something went wrong*" can clearly be improved. "*Your input exceeds the context window*" is a better one, but it still lacks some information. "*Your input exceeds the maximum allowed size (XXX tokens), trace-id AAA-BBB*" is even better since it clearly explains to the user what system limitations they have hit, and it provides additional debug information for an engineer to look into the issue (if still needed). Do not crash on exceptions, but log the issue with the `error` mode and return a corresponding error status to the user. That means that you shouldn't have `assert` statements in the production code (but rather raise a corresponding exception instead).

We should not only fail gracefully but also be prepared to keep our application alive when a spike of traffic occurs. Let's see how we can do that.

Request throttling

Your system should continue to function even when it's overloaded with incoming requests. Request throttling helps to keep your system at least partially functional when you get a spike in traffic. The ways of handling too many requests are limited:

- **Scale up your application horizontally (by adding more workers)**: Horizontal scaling would incur additional costs; hence, you need to set up the limits for this scaling. Some examples of things you need to take care of are performing capacity planning (if you use specific hardware such as rare GPUs), checking your quotas in the cloud project, checking historic throughput of your application (whether there are periods with high or low incoming traffic), implementing scale-up and scale-down triggers on your container management platform (think about whether you scale based on the number of requests, CPU load, or any other operational metric), and working on reducing start-up times of new containers (we briefly touched on this previously, but a good starting point is the Docker documentation: `https://docs.docker.com/build-cloud/optimization/`).
- **Reject excessive requests**: Ideally, this rejection should support a fair resource allocation and equitable distribution of resources among all users; hence, you block or limit only users who send too many requests. Again, your decision might depend, since you might choose a different prioritization approach depending on the business requirements. For example, requests from some departments or functions might be more important for the business, and you should add such priorities to your

application. For example, if you have a slide generation assistant and it's overloaded before the annual report call, you would probably like to prioritize requests from the department that prepares slides for the annual conference (although they're clearly overloading the system), and temporarily limit all other users. Of course, needless to say, to implement rate limits, you need to have a system that can compute and enforce such limits. In fact, rate limiting is one way of implementing request throttling, but dynamic prioritization is a more flexible and dynamic approach to handling traffic spikes (and the easiest and fastest approach to begin with it just to reject any excessive request).

- **Delay excessive requests by queuing them**: If a traffic spike is a temporary one, you can queue your request without rejecting it. Do not forget to inform the user of what's happening. If you care about a share of requests being handled within a defined SLI (faster than *X* seconds), you might use a **last-in, first-out** (**LIFO**) order, that is, you handle the latest incoming requests first, instead of **first-in, first-out** (**FIFO**), which is often considered to be fairer. You can read more about this in a great Medium post, *FIFO considered harmful* (`https://medium.com/swlh/fifo-considered-harmful-793b76f98374`).
- **Degrade functionally and keep only the most critical features**: Consider a simple example: if your image generation model is overloaded, you might switch to generating images of a lower quality (or decrease the maximum output size for your text generation model). In other words, think about what features are the most important for the user and try to keep them working by limiting everything else.

Cascading failures

A cascading failure is a failure that grows over time as a result of positive feedback (*Site Reliability Engineering* by Beyer et al., 2016). Complex software systems often have a lot of internal interdependencies. When one part of a system fails, it might lead to a domino effect.

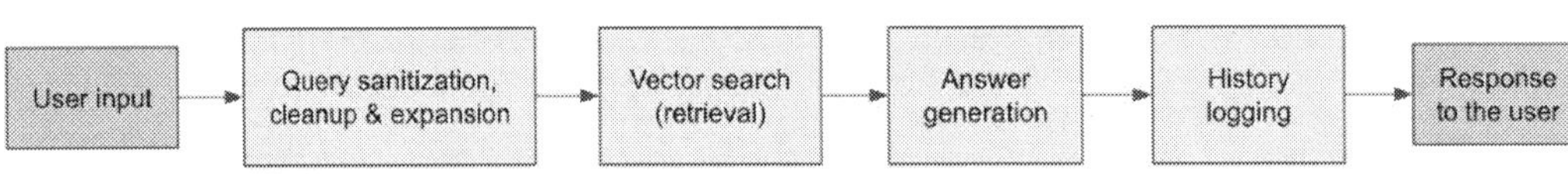

Figure 6.5 – An example of a service that handles customer support inquiries

Let's imagine that a history logging service has a bug that causes it to fail on average on every 20th request. The worker starts crashing, which immediately leads to two problems. First, Kubernetes is instructed to horizontally scale this service on a best-effort basis, so it starts increasing the number of workers and consumes all the CPUs available on the server. On the other hand, logging service crashes lead to immediate retries on the backend side since it's configured to do so without any exponential backoff. That, in turn, increases the load on the system and causes even more crashes. During peak hours, traffic to the customer support bot increases, and it leads to a need to scale up the query sanitization service, but there's no free capacity left on the server. The query expansion server becomes overloaded with the requests, its processing times increase, and it starts crashing too because of out-of-memory errors. The backend was configured in such a way that it sends unprocessed queries to the retrieval server if it doesn't get an answer from the query expansion server. But it turns out that raw queries overload the retrieval service too, because we now get 10 times more output items, and each search takes longer because the search query doesn't have any enriched metadata that was used for pre-filtering. Wrongly retrieved snippets are passed to the answer generation service, and it starts experiencing delays (because of a significantly larger context window), and also, the answer quality drops because of a noisy context. The share of hallucinations and irrelevant answers that are passed to the user increases.

In other words, a minor failure caused a major outage (our bot is slow, it often times out and doesn't respond at all, and if it responds, the answer quality is significantly worse than usual). This happened because of a positive feedback loop in our system. The system was designed in such a way that an attempt to recover from a failure led to an increased number of errors and worsened the overall situation.

Multiple patterns can help you to prevent cascading failure issues. Let's look at them briefly:

- The **circuit breaker** pattern adds an intermediate layer between upstream and downstream services. The circuit breaker can be in an open, closed, or half-open state. The default is the closed state, when it passes all requests to the downstream services and monitors the number of failures over a certain interval of time. If this amount increases above the threshold, it opens and breaks the connection. It terminates all the requests, but this gives time to the downstream service to recover and prevents it from being overwhelmed by the amount of traffic. After a certain timeout, the circuit breaker goes into a half-open state and checks whether the service has recovered by passing a small fraction of traffic to it. For example, imagine a customer support bot that retrieves knowledge from a database to ground an LLM. If the database suddenly starts failing, a circuit breaker will stop any additional load on the database, and it will respond to the user with something such as, "*service is currently unavailable, try later or call our support line at XXX-XX-XX.*" After a timeout (for example, 60 seconds), it will allow one or two (not all the queued requests) to pass through, and if it sees that the database has recovered, it will gradually open the breaker again and restore the service.
- The **bulkhead pattern** recommends isolating application components to contain failures and prevent them from spreading. It isolates system resources (such as connection pools, thread pools, or memory) for different services. For example, Kubernetes has many built-in ways to implement this pattern by limiting the amount

of resources that each service can consume and by physically placing different services on different virtual machines with configuration options, such as resource requests and limits, Pod affinity and anti-affinity, taints, and namespace isolation.

- The **timeout** pattern recommends that a service should never wait for a response indefinitely, but raise an error after a timeout. At the same time, using retries with a randomized exponential backoff allows the system to recover from temporary issues and failures. But it's crucial to retry a limited number of times, add a small random delay (called jitter), and exponentially increase the pause before sequential retries to prevent cascading failures. For example, if a chatbot sends a request to a foundational LLM, it should always define a timeout and retry policy if the request is not returned on time, instead of waiting for a response forever.
- The **fan-out** pattern involves a single source distributing work to multiple parallel workers by decomposing the task into smaller subtasks. As a simple example, if you're developing a news summarization service, consider not adding all relevant news to produce a summary into an LLM's context and send a single large prompt to an LLM, but summarize each news item in parallel and then just merge these summaries into the final report.

Many other system design patterns can help you to build scalable and reliable systems; we've just scratched the surface. Hopefully, that gives you a good overview and an idea of the potential directions to explore these topics further.

Summary

In this chapter, we tackled the critical transition from a local, often stateful prototype to a production-ready, horizontally scalable application. We learned that a scalable deployment of a web service requires multiple containers running behind a load balancer. Hence, our applications must be stateless to ensure flexibility and scalability. To achieve reliable and reproducible environments, we emphasized adopting key deployment best practices. Specifically, we dove into IaC using tools such as Terraform, which allows us to manage infrastructure declaratively. Crucially, we also covered secure secret management, detailing principles such as separating secrets by environment and following the least-privilege rule, as well as effective configuration management to handle dynamic application settings.

We then explored the necessary steps for packaging and orchestration. We learned how to wrap our GenAI application as a high-performance web API using modern frameworks such as FastAPI. We also discussed the importance of proper REST API design and specification. Following that, we introduced Kubernetes as the de facto container orchestration system, giving an overview of core concepts such as containers, Pods, and services, as well as the utility of the kubectl command-line tool. Finally, we looked at alternative, specialized SaaS deployment solutions, exemplified by the LangGraph platform, which abstracts away much of the infrastructure complexity.

To prepare our applications for high load, we discussed key architectural patterns. We learned about caching, both the classical approach to decrease latency and database load and the more advanced concept of semantic caching for GenAI to avoid costly LLM calls by recognizing similar user intent. Lastly, we introduced the fundamental constraints of distributed systems via the CAP theorem, understanding the unavoidable trade-off between consistency and availability when maintaining partition tolerance. These patterns and practices are essential for building robust, high-performance, and reliable systems.

In the next chapter, we'll look into various aspects related to the security of AI applications and so-called AI fairness (if this term is new to you, no worries; we'll dig into this in detail!).

Note

The three key outcomes to remember are as follows:

- Your applications should be stateless to enable horizontal scaling. Keep state in a separate storage layer.
- Make everything repeatable and reproducible, including ML pipelines or provisioning infrastructure. Keep your application settings in a single configuration file. Never store secrets in your code, use a secret manager for that.
- Design for scalability and graceful degradation. Provide an informative error message to the user, and use techniques such as horizontal scaling, request throttling, degradation of functionality, etc.

Further reading

- Beyer, B., Jones, C., Petoff, J., Murphy, N.R. *Site Reliability Engineering*, O'Reilly, `https://sre.google/sre-book/table-of-contents/`
- Beyer, B., Murphy, N.R., Rensin, D.K. *The Site Reliability Workbook: Practical Ways to Implement SRE*, O'Reilly, `https://sre.google/workbook/table-of-contents/`
- Adkins, H., Beyer, B., Blankinship, P., et al. *Building Secure and Reliable Systems: Best Practices for Designing, Implementing, and Maintaining Systems*, O'Reilly, `https://google.github.io/building-secure-and-reliable-systems/raw/toc.html`
- Google Cloud, *The Art of SLOs*, `https://sre.google/resources/practices-and-processes/art-of-slos/`

Subscribe for a free eBook

New frameworks, evolving architectures, research drops, production breakdowns—*AI_Distilled* filters the noise into a weekly briefing for engineers and researchers working hands-on with LLMs and generative AI systems. Subscribe now and receive a free eBook, along with weekly insights that help you stay focused and informed.

Subscribe at `https://packt.link/8Oz6Y` or scan the QR code below.

7

Ethics and Security

I believe that for any tech and product leader in the AI space, understanding **Responsible AI** is not just a regulatory requirement, but a core component of building sustainable and impactful products. The influence of AI systems on society has grown exponentially in size and impact, making the issues of potential unfairness, harm, and unintended consequences more critical than ever. In this chapter, we will dive into how we, as the designers of these powerful systems, must approach this great responsibility.

We will first establish a foundational understanding of Responsible AI, its rationale, and the practical methods engineers can employ to address these challenges in their daily work. Then, we will explore the four crucial dimensions that define a responsible AI system: **fairness**, **explainability**, **safety and security**, and **privacy**. We will also explore bias in machine learning models, how it can be measured using fairness indicators, and techniques for mitigating it. We will also discuss how GenAI systems introduce additional concerns, such as toxicity and preference bias.

Next, we will clarify the differences between **explainability**, **interpretability**, and **transparency**, and review methods such as feature attribution and mechanistic interpretability for both classical machine learning models and large language models.

We will then examine robustness and safety, including prediction monitoring, model alignment, and risks specific to GenAI, such as jailbreaking attacks and the role of red teams in identifying vulnerabilities.

Finally, we will discuss privacy and data governance, covering approaches such as differential privacy and federated learning, and how GenAI systems introduce new privacy risks during both training and inference.

In this chapter, we'll be covering the following topics:

- The basics of Responsible AI
- Fairness
- Explainability
- Safety and security
- Privacy

The basics of Responsible AI

What is Responsible AI? The Responsible AI topic started to gain popularity across the world (tech companies, large enterprises, and policymakers) a few years ago. The following definition from a paper published in 2016 by Google Brain, OpenAI, and Stanford describes it very well:

"AI technologies are likely to be overwhelmingly beneficial for humanity, but we also believe that it is worth giving serious thought to potential challenges and risks. We strongly support work on privacy, security, fairness, economics, and policy, ... another class of problem which we believe is also relevant to the societal impacts of AI: the problem of accidents in machine learning systems" (`https://arxiv.org/abs/1606.06565`).

Let's understand the reasons behind concerns related to Responsible AI, since it would help us to discuss the same considerations related to GenAI.

To begin with, AI was initially used for use cases such as retail recommendations or ad click-through rates that influenced our lives, but maybe not as much as engineers working on ads would like to think. However, the impact of AI across society continued to increase, and AI started to be used for more critical tasks. Hence, policymakers realized that we should invest effort into making AI systems more fair and inclusive for all. For example, according to a report from the Pew Research Center, only 3% of US adults used a dating site or app in 2008, compared to more than 30% in 2019 (`https://www.pewresearch.org/internet/2020/02/06/the-virtues-and-downsides-of-online-dating/`). Of course, when the industry has grown more than 10 times in 10 years (and across some slices, has become even more influential; for example, more than half of adults under 30 are using dating apps), potential unfairness or harm coming from AI would affect society in a larger way.

> **Note**
>
> As Google, one of the pioneers in Responsible AI, defines it, "Responsible AI considers the societal impact of the development and scale of these technologies, including potential harms and benefits" (`https://developers.google.com/machine-learning/guides/intro-responsible-ai`).

The AI Incident Database states that *"like similar databases in aviation and computer security," its goal is to "learn from experience so we can prevent or mitigate bad outcomes," and collect "history of harms or near harms realized in the real world by the deployment of artificial intelligence systems"* (`https://incidentdatabase.ai/`). According to the Stanford AI Index Report 2025, the number of reported AI incidents has increased 10x in the last decade and reached 233 incidents per year in 2023 (+56% increase year on year).

In other words, as AI and classical machine learning have advanced, researchers, scientists, and engineers have increasingly realized that, as the saying goes, "with great power comes great responsibility." The second aspect (partially related to the first one) is the issue of potential biases. As we already discussed in *Chapters 1* and *2*, ML models are only as good as the labelled dataset they were trained on. If there is an inherent bias in the training dataset, ML models will incorporate it. For example, in the next section, I provide an example of how medical vision models trained on a dataset that had mostly people with lighter skin tones performed poorly on people with darker skin tones.

> **Note**
>
> In ML, bias refers to systematic errors that lead to skewed or unfair outcomes.

From what we have learned so far in this book, we can easily assume what options engineers have to address Responsible AI issues in practice.

First, be clear in your objectives. Google uses the so-called **AI Principles** as a framework to determine objectives for AI applications and to determine which applications it *"will not pursue in the development of AI systems"* (`https://developers.google.com/machine-learning/guides/intro-responsible-ai`). You can find these AI principles online together with multiple examples of how Google uses them in action (`https://ai.google/responsibility/principles`).

Second, invest effort in better datasets and benchmarks to address your goals related to responsible AI. Last but not least, build tools to detect biases and other issues at scale. Let's see these issues in more detail in the upcoming sections, where we look at Responsible AI across four dimensions: fairness, explainability, safety, and privacy.

Fairness

Let's begin ML models">idx_b0097466 with fairness. ML models learn from labelled datasets, and these datasets are collected from the real world. A model can learn, and even amplify, an existing bias. For example, historically, some racial groups were "less likely to receive laboratory tests," and because of that, medical models "developed to predict clinic outcomes ... were potentially amplifying inequities in clinical care" (`https://pubmed.ncbi.nlm.nih.gov/39475953/`). Moreover, it is challenging to build a system that is fair across all possible situations and cultures. The challenge begins with defining what *fair* actually means. Mathematically, it can be done by selecting a fairness metric and picking one or many slices of your dataset to be analyzed.

> **Note**
>
> A **fairness indicator** is a mathematical definition of fairness that makes it measurable. There are different fairness metrics, and they might contradict each other, but once we've picked one, we can measure fairness and improve on it. You can find some definitions and Python implementations of fairness indicators revealed by Google in 2019 here: `https://research.google/blog/fairness-indicators-scalable-infrastructure-for-fair-ml-systems`.

Improving fairness

Improving the fairness of your ML systems is always a work across multiple dimensions, such as the following:

- Product discovery and data analysis, which includes detecting unexpected segments of the population that have started using your application.
- Investments in training and evaluation datasets and building new benchmarks. For example, in 2018, it *"became apparent that ... computer vision systems struggled to detect people with darker skin tones, and performed particularly poorly for women with darker skin tones,"* and researchers released a new **Monk Skin Tone** (MST) scale and a new MST-E dataset with labelled annotations (`https://research.google/blog/consensus-and-subjectivity-of-skin-tone-annotation-for-ml-fairness/`).

- Improving evaluation and monitoring systems to catch slices of the population on which models underperform as early as possible, since the big challenge in this domain is actually to detect that the problem exists and to quantify it.
- ML remediation techniques, which are specialized methods used to improve fairness in ML systems. These techniques can be applied during pre-training (through data preprocessing), training (by modifying the learning algorithm or adjusting model weights during training), or post-processing (by modifying model outputs after the main training phase). The goal is to improve performance across selected fairness indicators without significantly degrading performance on the original objective (`https://arxiv.org/abs/1610.02413`).

If you are interested in ML fairness, you can read a case study, *Attacking discrimination with smarter machine learning*, published by Google on tuning the fairness of a binary classification ML model that decides whether a loan should be granted to a person.

Fairness in GenAI

Now that we have introduced this aspect of Responsible AI, let us briefly discuss what new biases and fairness-related challenges GenAI has introduced.

GenAI is good at generating text, images, or other content. Many such systems do suffer from severe **toxicity** (partially, since they're often trained on social media data), and the problem begins with how to define toxicity and align across human raters providing feedback to the model during the alignment phase.

> **Note**
>
> Toxicity in the context of GenAI means harmful content, including hate speech, insults, profanities, and threats (`https://arxiv.org/abs/2109.07445`).

Stereotypical toxicity is related to the bias that an LLM might inherit from the training data. Large amounts of training data scraped mostly from the internet might inherit bias towards various identity groups that might be traditionally subject to bias and discrimination (such as gender, age, and religion). Another important bias to address is **preference bias** in socio-political and other topics. A big ethical challenge is whether we want an LLM to always be neutral and factual, and then how to achieve this in practice (`https://arxiv.org/abs/2308.05374`).

> **Note**
>
> A preference bias refers to a tendency to favor certain options, ideas, people, or information over others. For example, an LLM might favor certain political opinions or parties, or it could just favor movies that were the most popular at the time data was collected.

Last but not least, it's important to consider the **performance bias**. Ideally, we want GenAI systems to perform well across all socio-cultural groups (across multiple languages, cultures, ages, etc.), but as many studies have demonstrated, it might not always be the case.

The challenge is to detect and address such content, and this is typically done at three stages:

- Cleaning and filtering content that is used in training
- An additional alignment phase during post-training that reduces toxicity and harmfulness
- Applying safety and toxicity detection filters during inference

Detecting and addressing such biases is an ongoing research effort, but the practical considerations for us, engineers developing AI systems based on LLMs, are that GenAI amplifies fairness issues, and we should significantly increase our evaluation effort. At least, fairness concerns should influence our choice of a foundational model.

Explainability

AI systems are probabilistic by design, and that implies a certain level of uncertainty in their decisions. It might be difficult for a user to interpret this implicit level of uncertainty, and because of that, we need to guide users and help them understand how these systems work, especially if users are new to such systems and they have not developed their own intuition yet. This is known as **explainability**, which is the ability to provide humans with understandable reasons for decisions made by AI systems. Hence, explainability and trust are inherently interconnected. This sounds familiar, doesn't it? We ran into these challenges when we were widely adopting ML systems, but it took us 5–10 years to get there, and now we're observing the same issues with GenAI. The big difference, though, is the accelerated speed of users' adoption.

> **Note**
>
> It is important to distinguish explainability from the following terms:
>
> - **Interpretability**: Understanding of techniques used to explain how specific AI systems make decisions
> - **Transparency**: Sharing enough information about the behavior of AI systems with users

In this section, we'll first look at how explainability can be improved and then focus specifically on LLMs.

Improving explainability

We can adjust ML models to make them more understandable, and we can also help users to calibrate their trust in specific predictions. As usual, as we can see, it's a mix of working on user experience and improving algorithms. Sometimes we can improve things a lot by adjusting the interface. For example, we can show a user a confidence score of the model or provide some kind of explanation on how the decision has been produced. We can do this in three ways:

- Through *in-the-moment explanations*, by providing clarity on every decision. For example, a knowledge assistant can cite sources for its answers and give guidance to a user to decide whether the answer can be trusted or not.
- Through *product explanations*, by improving onboarding, FAQs, user interfaces, and so on. For example, when a user first starts using an enterprise knowledge assistant, they might be offered an interactive tutorial that introduces the concept of hallucinations, how to verify answers, and what kind of questions the assistant is supposed to help with.
- Through experience *beyond the product*, by raising awareness about certain topics through marketing and educational campaigns. For example, when launching a corporate knowledge assistant, the product team might introduce a few all-hands educating colleagues on Gen AI, hallucinations, and how to work with such products in a proper way.

Of course, realistically, as product leaders, we have a direct influence only on the first two ways.

On the other hand, there is ongoing work on explainability in "classical" ML that addresses both working on better explainable model architectures and developing post hoc explainers that help us understand existing models. Some ML model architectures are naturally explainable by looking at the trained model. For example, think about a linear regression or a decision tree model; you can explore the weights to explain its predictions. There are certain research efforts to develop more powerful explainable architectures, such as TabNet.

> Note
>
> **Explainable Artificial Intelligence (XAI)** refers to a set of methods and techniques that make the predictions made by AI systems understandable to humans.

The challenge, though, is that the most powerful models (such as deep neural networks and LLMs in particular) are difficult to inspect and understand why they make certain predictions. This makes it difficult for engineers to improve the models (how can you improve something you don't fully understand?) and for decision makers to trust their predictions (how can you trust something you can't explain, and you can't validate the associated risks?). That's why the focus of today for XAI is post hoc explainers, or an attempt to explain the model's behavior by using the trained model to extract the relationship between the feature values and predictions. To give you an idea of how this can be done, let's take two examples (but there are many more different algorithms that you can study if you're interested in the topic; please refer to the papers listed in the *Further reading* section as a starting point).

One method is the **feature-attribution method**. For every prediction, we assign to each feature a score that characterizes the importance of this feature for this prediction. There are different ways to produce such scores – for example, using gradient-based methods, evaluating each feature's contribution to the prediction value with the Shapley score. Then, we visualize these scores and analyze them. For example, for image recognition tasks, we can plot each pixel's importance, and for text classification tasks, we can understand the contribution of each word or token to the prediction. Such analysis not only helps to debug the model and get some insights but also establishes additional trust in its predictions. Feature importance can also be used for monitoring purposes (you can use a sudden change in the distribution of feature importance as an alert).

A quick note, without going into too much detail: be aware that it's very easy to misinterpret feature attribution. It is not an explanation of reality; it's just an explanation of how the (actual) function from inputs to labels was approximated when the model was trained. For example, if you remove one feature (or add another), you might get very similar predictions but with very different attributions. The reality has not changed, but your approximation has. Of course, a correlation does not imply causation. You might get a high attribution score without actual causal dependency between the output and the given feature.

Second, we can explore **example-based explanations**. The idea behind this method is to find the most similar examples from the training dataset that generate the same prediction as the one for the new input. It works well for image, text, and tabular data. It can help to debug the model's behavior (for example, you might identify flaws in your training dataset or a need for additional data collection) or to explain the model's predictions to stakeholders.

Explainability of LLMs

LLMs have billions of weights and a complex architecture, and their capabilities came as a surprise to many researchers a few years ago. But we now understand the importance of the explainability of AI systems. Can we understand how an LLM operates, instead of treating it as a "*black box*" system? This is a hot research topic, and there are certain advances in this area.

One direction of research is **mechanistic interpretability**. In October 2023, Anthropic released a study, *Towards Monosemanticity: Decomposing Language Models With Dictionary Learning*, in which they demonstrated that a single neuron is not a good unit of analysis to understand the behavior of an LLM since it's fired on many different inputs. Instead, they suggested algorithms to find a set of sparse and interpretable features in a one-layer transformer model. You can explore online examples of features they found. Other researchers continued their work, and in 2024, researchers from Google DeepMind demonstrated how to apply sparse autoencoders to discover interpretable sparse sets of features in an LLM that has up to 7B parameters.

> Note
>
> **Mechanistic interpretability** is a direction of interpretability research that aims to identify individual components of an LLM to figure out how they interact to perform specific tasks or represent specific knowledge.

Initially, these studies were performed on small language models because of engineering challenges to scale the computations. But in May 2024, Anthropic applied similar methods to their Claude 3 Sonnet model, an actual medium-sized production LLM that was one of the leaders at that time. In only 8 months, the scaling challenges of applying sparse auto-encoders to large transformer-based models were solved, and these impressive results tell a lot about the speed of development in this area.

Of course, there are many other alternatives and research directions. For example, some researchers reuse the feature attribution method we discussed in the previous section. In *Figure 7.1*, you can see an example of how Shapley values were used to interpret the importance of each token in the LLM input.

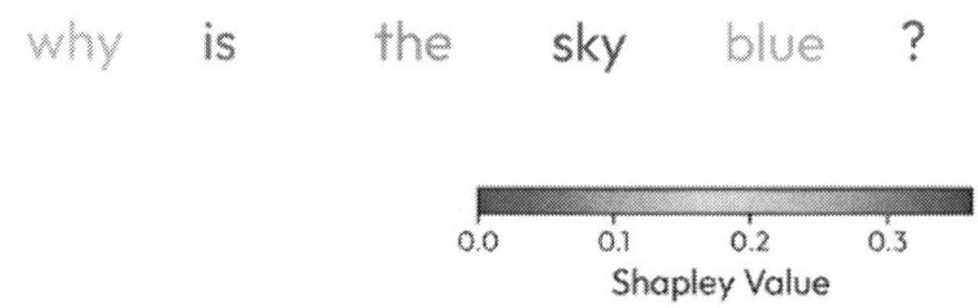

Figure 7.1 – Visualization of Shapley values for each input token (source: https://arxiv.org/abs/2407.10114)

We have discussed the importance of explainability of AI systems to build users' trust and help researchers to debug and better understand the model's behavior, what the key challenges are in LLMs' explainability, and how researchers attack this problem. Now let's discuss the next important aspect of Responsible AI: safety and security.

Safety and security

There are many aspects of AI security, and one of them is **AI safety**. Our goal is to design systems that don't cause any harm. In order to do so, we need to identify potential threats, including unintended consequences, and then find ways to combat these threats. Potential vulnerabilities become increasingly concerning as we deploy AI systems across critical domains. We will see a very similar reasoning when we talk about GenAI security later in this section; that's why it's important to spend some time discussing what the industry has stood for in the pre-GenAI era.

> **Note**
>
> An **incident** is an unintended and harmful behavior that may emerge from machine learning systems due to poor design (`https://arxiv.org/abs/1606.06565`).

Safety in the classical ML era

Researchers at UC Berkeley, Google, and OpenAI published a joint paper in 2021, *Unsolved Problems in ML Safety*, where they proposed four classes of security challenges and related ways of addressing them:

- **Creating robust models that can withstand adversarial attacks and sudden changes in environments (so-called "black swan" effects):** ML models are trained on existing datasets, which makes it hard to adequately incorporate long-tail (improbable) events and even test for them.

> **Note**
>
> A popular author and a former Wall Street trader, Nassim Taleb, popularized in his books a *black swan* event – a very rare (and, because of that, an unpredictable) event that has a major impact on a system. The COVID-19 pandemic or the dissolution of the Soviet Union are examples of such events. One example related to computer and AI systems is the 2010 Flash Crash event, which was a trillion-dollar US market crash that lasted 32 minutes and was supposedly caused by HFT systems (`https://en.wikipedia.org/wiki/2010_flash_crash`).

- **Predictions monitoring that allows for the detection of malicious use and discovery of unexpected model behavior**: By perturbing inputs, adversaries might influence the ML system's decisions. One example is attacking computer vision models. With a relatively easy manipulation of pixels of an image, you can fool an image recognition model so that it changes the classification label of this specific example. It becomes easier if you attack an open-weighted model (i.e., you know the model's architecture and its weights). You can find simple tutorials online that demonstrate simple vectors of attacks in a matter of minutes (for example, `https://christophm.github.io/interpretable-ml-book/adversarial.html`). *Backdoor* is another example; somebody can train a model that behaves as expected in most scenarios, and hide a backdoor that is very difficult to detect.

> **Note**
>
> The *adversarial robustness* of AI systems refers to the prevention of adversaries from manipulating and exploiting vulnerabilities in AI systems.

- **ML model alignment or developing models that represent human values**: First, it's hard to define some human values. *"Encoding human goals and intent is challenging. Lawmakers know this well, as laws specified by stacks of pages still often require that people interpret the spirit of the law. Many human values, such as happiness, good judgment, meaningful experiences, human autonomy, and so on, are hard to define and measure"* (`https://arxiv.org/abs/2109.13916`). Secondly, it's difficult to align such values with objective functions that are used to train and evaluate complex AI systems.
- **Ensuring the safety of the environment in which they operate**: Cybersecurity risks are deeply connected to AI security since malicious actors could exploit cybersecurity

vulnerabilities and gain control over AI systems. Another aspect of this is decision-making. If we get powerful systems that are safe, per se, but we make bad decisions, it makes the overall environment unsafe.

An important note is that we, as technical leaders, should not rely on regulation only when we're thinking about security and safety. The industry is developing rapidly, and regulation is typically behind it. "*Robust safety regulation is almost always developed only after a catastrophe—a common saying in aviation is that "aviation regulations are written in blood." While waiting for catastrophes to spur regulators can reduce the likelihood of repeating the same failure, this approach cannot prevent catastrophic events from occurring in the first place*" (`https://arxiv.org/abs/2109.13916`).

If you're interested in the topic, please take a look at the provided papers and also at more comprehensive reports that you can find at the end of this chapter.

GenAI safety

The widespread adoption of GenAI has brought about concerns about associated security and safety risks. I want you to remember that AI systems present new types of such risks.

Let's start with a simple example: a jailbreaking attack. LLMs can solve a broad set of tasks, and it becomes not only a strength but a vulnerability. When we release a corporate chatbot based on an LLM, we don't want it to give health advice or harmful advice. But if a user manipulates an input prompt, in theory, they could convince an LLM to do harmful or unintended things. One famous incident is when a car dealer released a ChatGPT-based chatbot on its site, and a driver convinced this bot to sell them a new Chevrolet Tahoe for only one dollar when the list price was more than $75,000 (`https://www.aiaaic.org/aiaaic-repository/ai-algorithmic-and-automation-incidents/driver-persuades-chatbot-to-sell-car-for-usd-1`).

> **Note**
>
> Jailbreaking in GenAI is bypassing built-in security measures and generating non-desired outputs by manipulating the prompt sent to an LLM.

How can jailbreaking be mitigated? Of course, it's an ongoing battle between an attacker and a defender, but general mechanisms include measures such as developing real-time safety filters (testing both inputs and outputs in real time), introducing advanced systems to block malicious activity (for example, users with a high rate of blocked requests), improving the robustness of the system in general, comparing prompts with known jailbreaking candidates, and so on. You can take a look at a recent study on jailbreaking from Palo Alto at `https://unit42.paloaltonetworks.com/jailbreaking-generative-ai-web-products`.

Jailbreaking is just one example of a unique risk born with the wave of GenAI. In 2024, a group of researchers from Stanford University and other US universities and start-ups revealed a study on AI risk categorization (AIR 2024) and suggested a taxonomy with more than 314 risk categories across four main categories: system and operational risks, content safety risks, societal risks, and legal and rights-related risks. You're welcome to look at the risks listed yourselves, but now let us focus on another question. Why are safety and security risks related to GenAI high and worth a separate discussion? Anthropic answers this very well in its program post about AI safety: *"it may be tricky to build safe, reliable, and steerable systems when those systems are starting to become as intelligent and as aware of their surroundings as their designers... Second, rapid AI progress would be very disruptive, changing employment, macroeconomics, and power structures both within and between nations"* (`anthropic.com/news/core-views-on-ai-safety`).

> **Note**
>
> A red team is a dedicated team that performs proactive and adversarial testing of AI systems. Such a team tries to simulate real-world attacks and find vulnerabilities that could cause potential misuse or bias of such systems.

The goals of current research in the GenAI safety field are oriented towards better methods to develop safe AI systems (which include extensive evaluation methods and datasets) and, at the same time, towards better detection techniques to assess how safe (or unsafe) such systems are. One of the ideas is to formulate a set of principles that Anthropic calls **constitutional AI**.

> **Note**
>
> Constitutional AI is an approach to train LLMs with alignment with human values, ethical principles, and desired behaviors without solely relying on extensive direct human feedback. The only human oversight provided to the training process is a list of principles and values (`https://arxiv.org/abs/2212.08073`).

My goal is not to make you wary, but to make you aware and to make you appreciate the risks associated with this new technology and take them into account when designing AI solutions. From my experience, for many years, application development security has been treated by some engineers as "something that will be taken care of by the security team," but this has changed. As engineering leaders, we should be aware and work proactively with security teams when designing and developing products. Some of these risks (such as risks related to content safety or privacy) are very relevant in the short term and we should include them in our risk analysis when developing products today; other risks are more relevant in the coming years (or maybe even on the scale of the next decade), but it shouldn't prevent us from discussing them and working on preventing them.

When discussing the security of generative AI applications, we cannot ignore the rise of agentic workflows. Our AI applications are not encapsulated anymore; they consume external and internal APIs and services, and this brings a lot of questions and concerns related to authentication, permissions, and the security of such systems as a whole. A good starting point is an article from the Red Hat blog on security concerns related to the use of MCP servers: `https://www.redhat.com/en/blog/model-context-protocol-mcp-understanding-security-risks-and-controls`.

Privacy

Machine learning relies on data, and this data is often collected from users. Much of this data is personal and sensitive, especially in domains such as HRtech, healthtech, fintech, and so on. Security experts from KPMG and many other companies have raised concerns that a lack of privacy protections increases risks that private data will be exposed to unauthorized misuse, which would cause harm to individuals (`https://kpmg.com/xx/en/our-insights/ai-and-technology/privacy-in-the-new-world-of-ai.html`).

Tech companies have been taking privacy risks very seriously, but sometimes I observe a certain lack of awareness across engineering and product leads, which causes a certain lack of focus on privacy, especially in small teams and start-ups.

Privacy is one of the core focuses of many regulations, such as the **General Data Protection Regulation** (**GDPR**) in the EU, initially published in 2016, the **California Consumer Privacy Act** (**CCPA**) in California, and the **Personal Information Protection Law** (**PIPL**) in China. Let's ask ourselves, why is privacy so important? For a few reasons. First, we want to avoid any unauthorized access to private data. Secondly, we want to prevent any misuse of private data, such as a secondary use of collected data without the explicit consent of users or understanding how their data is used. Last but not least, we want users to keep trusting AI systems and interact with them without any concerns for their data being misused.

Improving privacy

What can we do as engineers? As usual, we have two ways of doing this at our disposal: better processes and more sophisticated algorithms. First, we need to establish strict data governance in how we collect and handle any private data. A good start is to ask ourselves whether we really need to collect this specific attribute each time we get an idea to enhance logging. Yes, we know that ML models benefit from more data, but we should take privacy into account and find the right balance.

> **Note**
>
> Data governance is a system of processes, tools, and standards across an organization that enables the effective and secure use of data throughout its entire lifecycle (from collection to disposal). It covers aspects such as access management and access control, data discoverability, data management, and so on (`https://www.databricks.com/discover/data-governance`).

Besides improving our processes and tools to establish data governance, we can use more sophisticated algorithms to protect privacy. Let's look at three examples to get an idea.

The first is about **deanonymization** and improving data collection and analytics. When collecting data, use aggregation, sampling, or redaction techniques. For instance, Chrome collects users' data by using histograms. It groups data points into bins and collects distribution values from a random sample of users instead of collecting individual events (`https://chromium.googlesource.com/chromium/src/+show/master/tools/metrics/histograms/README.md`).

The second example that we'll look at is **differential privacy**. It involves a complicated mathematical algorithm, which we're not going to discuss in detail. If you're interested, look at the original paper *Learning Statistics with Privacy, aided by the Flip of a Coin* (you can find the link in the *Further reading* section at the end of the chapter), or take a look at a more popularized explanation, such as the one on a Cloudflare blog (`https://blog.cloudflare.com/have-your-data-and-hide-it-too-an-introduction-to-differential-privacy`).

> **Note**
>
> Differential privacy is an algorithm of data collection that protects the privacy of individual users but still allows for performing data analysis by aggregating information on a group level without sharing any individual data points.

The idea is relatively simple. Imagine I'm a professor and I want to find out how many students in my group use Gemini to do their homework. The important part is that I know exactly what kind of information I need. I need only to see the percentage of the group that used GenAI. Another implicit assumption is that my class is big enough (so let's imagine for a moment I have thousands of students visiting my online classes). What should I do? First, I should ask every student to flip a coin. In other words, each student would be randomly assigned to one of two groups, and the important fact is that I can't determine which student is in which group. Now it becomes tricky. I would ask students to raise their hand if they got a tail *or* if they got a head, and if they used Gemini to prepare their homework. What happens now? Looking at every individual student, I can't guess whether they used Gemini or not. Since the hand raised might indicate multiple things: a student got a tail, or they cheated (and got a head). Let's take a look at example:

Student	Used Gemini or no	Coin flip outcome	Action
Student A	used Gemini	tail	raise a hand
Student B	used Gemini	head	do not raise a hand
Student C	did themselves	tail	raise a hand
Student D	did themselves	head	do not raise a hand

Table 7.1 - Student responses based on coin flip and Gemini use

So my estimation will be 2/4 = 50% of the students used Gemini for their homework, but I can't guess who exactly these students were just by looking at their actions. Of course, this example is simplified, and in real life we might not get exact numbers, but if our sample is large enough, we'll get a pretty good estimation of a variable we're interested in.

But looking at the overall share of raised hands, I can derive (assuming my group is large enough) a share of students using GenAI for their homework with a high degree of confidence. This is a very simple explanation, and it helps you to get the idea, but the actual algorithm behind it is a little bit more complex, and you're welcome to read the links provided if interested.

The third example is **federated machine learning** (**FML**). These are algorithms that allow for training an ML model in a distributed manner without consolidating data from clients (users). This is a complex set of techniques, but large tech companies such as Apple and Google have successfully utilized it to evaluate and train deep learning models on devices for use cases such as news personalization, speech recognition, or predicting next words by GBoard.

To give you a straightforward idea, let's look at the principles behind the FedAvg algorithm (although other alternatives exist, and there are many more details; please refer to the *Further reading* section if you're interested). It's actually similar to a distributed training scenario. Imagine that each device (or client) keeps its own data, and a server keeps track of a model's weights. A server initializes the model, sends it to the client, and they train for one (or a few steps) on their own data. Then it sends the weights' updates to the server. The server performs an aggregation step, combining all weights into a single model, and sends the updated global weights to devices to continue the training.

Of course, there are many difficulties in ensuring a stable training process in practice. We're not going to dive into the details of FML since you could write a whole book (or a few) about FML. If you're interested in the topic, please refer to specialized papers or take a look at frameworks such as TensorFlow Federated, Flower, PySift, and so on.

There are two more things that an ML engineer should keep in mind when thinking about privacy. First, preserving privacy is not only about data governance and using advanced algorithms. It's also about how you design the user experience to keep users safe. Here's a simple example: imagine you're building an app to find a breakfast place, and you're gathering community reviews for that. Even if a user agrees to share their full name, you might unintentionally reveal their habits (and the time and location where they usually have their breakfast) to the whole world.

Another aspect is that if you use sensitive data (such as private messages) to train deep learning models, these models could memorize the data in unexpected ways, and an attacker could reveal this data from them.

Additional privacy concerns in GenAI

After discussing general privacy issues related to AI systems, let's ask ourselves, how do GenAI systems change these risks?

First, LLMs are trained on large amounts of data, which creates risks of exposing sensitive data collected during training in an unpredictable way. For example, in 2023, a group of researchers demonstrated the effect of extractable memorization. A new attack vector allowed the effective extraction of large blocks of training data from open sourced and closed LLMs. As always, the biggest concern was not that it was possible (the issue has been mostly mitigated), but that this was an unexpected vector of attack discovered after the model had been released. There is continuous research that demonstrates this kind of attack is efficient against transformer-based models (both output generation and embeddings).

Another aspect is issues related to **LLM inference**. Chatbots and agents collect a large amount of information about our private lives, and they can infer some sensitive details from memory. Users might unintentionally share private information in their prompts or by giving agents access to additional data or tools (such as files or access to databases).

Another still debated aspect is **copyright**. I'm not going to dive into the details, but datasets for model training are also collected through web scraping, which raises certain privacy concerns. Then, modern models can generate high-quality, impersonated content (such as texts, music, images) that might violate the privacy of the author of the original content. There are a lot of ethical and privacy challenges that society needs to discuss and recalibrate.

Last but not least, the power of GenAI can amplify all the privacy risks we have discussed earlier. Such systems could help malicious actors to perform better in phishing, generating harmful or fake content, impersonation, and so on.

According to article 22 of the GDPR, "the data subject shall have the right not to be subject to a decision based solely on automated processing, including profiling." Depending on the use case, some GenAI agents can be qualified this way, and that creates additional privacy and legal concerns. In general, the ability of such systems to process large amounts of data fast, cheaply, and efficiently raises large additional privacy concerns. We should be responsible for what we're creating. I will finish this chapter by repeating, *"with great power comes great responsibility."*

Summary

In this chapter, we learned that Responsible AI is not merely a regulatory requirement but a core element of building sustainable and impactful products, especially given the exponential growth and societal influence of AI systems. We established a foundational understanding of this responsibility by diving into the four crucial dimensions that define an ethical AI system: fairness, explainability, safety and security, and privacy. We saw that our role, as technical leaders, is grounded in being clear on our objectives, investing in better datasets and benchmarks, and building tools to detect issues at scale.

In exploring the four dimensions, we learned about the practical application of these concepts and how GenAI fundamentally changes the picture. For fairness, we examined how traditional ML models can amplify bias and saw that LLMs introduce new challenges such as severe toxicity, stereotypical bias, and the complex issue of preference bias. We then addressed explainability by differentiating it from interpretability and transparency, exploring methods such as feature-attribution, and discussing the rapid progress in mechanistic interpretability for complex LLMs. Our review of safety and security covered the need for robustness, monitoring, and model alignment, with the rise of unique GenAI risks such as jailbreaking and the necessity of red teams for adversarial testing.

Finally, we learned that privacy requires strict data governance and sophisticated algorithmic techniques such as differential privacy and FML. GenAI significantly amplifies these concerns through risks such as extractable memorization and the potential for misuse in phishing or impersonation. We concluded that the industry is developing at a pace that outstrips regulation, and therefore, we must be proactively aware of these security and ethical challenges, taking them into account when designing any new AI solution.

To repeat again, as we create these powerful systems, we must remember that *"with great power comes great responsibility."*

In the next chapter, we will look into a definition of reliability, the basics of developing highly reliable systems, and what role observability plays in software development.

> **Note**
>
> The three key outcomes to remember are as follows:
>
> - Responsible AI is a core component for building sustainable and impactful products, especially given the exponential societal influence of AI systems.
> - GenAI amplifies existing risks and introduces additional ethical concerns, privacy risks, and security vulnerabilities.
> - Industry progress outpaces regulation, and proactive effort is required. Technical and product leaders must incorporate Responsible AI considerations into their priorities when designing new AI solutions.

Further reading

- Amodei, D, Olah, C, Steinhardt, J., et al. (2016) *Concrete Problems in AI Safety*: `https://arxiv.org/abs/1606.06565`
- *Artificial Intelligence Incident Database*: `https://incidentdatabase.ai/`
- *Google AI - AI Principles*: `https://ai.google/responsibility/principles`
- Chang, T., Nuppnau, M., He, Y., Kocher, K.E., et al. (2024) *Racial Differences in Laboratory Testing as a Potential Mechanism for Bias In AI: A Matched Cohort Analysis in Emergency Department Visits*: `https://pubmed.ncbi.nlm.nih.gov/39475953/`
- *Fairness Indicators: Scalable Infrastructure for Fair ML Systems*: `https://research.google/blog/fairness-indicators-scalable-infrastructure-for-fair-ml-systems`
- *Consensus and subjectivity of skin tone annotation for ML fairness*: `https://research.google/blog/consensus-and-subjectivity-of-skin-tone-annotation-for-ml-fairness`
- Hardt, M., Price, E., Srebro, N. (2016) *Equality of Opportunity in Supervised Learning*: `https://arxiv.org/abs/1610.02413`

- *Attack discrimination with smarter machine learning*: https://research.google.com/bigpicture/attacking-discrimination-in-ml
- Welbl, J., Glaese, A., Uesato, J., et al. (2021) *Challenges in Detoxifying Language Models*: https://arxiv.org/abs/2109.07445
- Liu, Y, Yao Y, Ton J-F, et al. (2023) *Trustworthy LLMs: A Survey and Guideline for Evaluating Large Language Models' Alignment*: https://arxiv.org/abs/2308.05374
- Arik, S.O., Pfister, T. (2019) *TabNet: Attentive Interpretable Tabular Learning*: https://arxiv.org/abs/1908.07442
- Li, Y., Zhang, Y., Kawaguchi, K., Khakzar, A., Bischl, B., Rezaei, M. (2023) *A Dual-Perspective Approach to Evaluating Feature Attribution Methods,* https://arxiv.org/abs/2308.08949
- *Towards Monosemanticity: Decomposing Language Models With Dictionary Learning*: https://transformer-circuits.pub/2023/monosemantic-features/index.html
- Rajamanoharan, S., Conmy, A., Smith, L., Lieberum, T., Varma, V., Kramár, J., Shah, R., Nanda, N. (2024) *Improving Dictionary Learning with Gated Sparse Autoencoders*: https://arxiv.org/abs/2404.16014
- *Scaling Monosemanticity: Extracting Interpretable Features from Claude 3 Sonnet*: https://transformer-circuits.pub/2024/scaling-monosemanticity/index.htm
- Goldshmidt, R., Horovicz, M. (2024) *TokenSHAP: Interpreting Large Language Models with Monte Carlo Shapley Value Estimation*: https://arxiv.org/abs/2407.10114
- Hendrycks, D., Carlini, N., Schulman, J., Steinhardt, J. (2021) *Unsolved Problems in ML Safety*: https://arxiv.org/abs/2109.13916
- *Adversarial Examples – Interpretable Machine Learning*: https://christophm.github.io/interpretable-ml-book/adversarial.html
- Brundage, M., Avin, S., Clark, J., et al. (2024) *The Malicious Use of Artificial Intelligence: Forecasting, Prevention, and Mitigation*: https://arxiv.org/abs/1802.07228
- Bai, Y., Kadavath, S., Kundu, S., et al. (2022) *Constitutional AI: Harmlessness from AI Feedback*: https://arxiv.org/abs/2212.08073
- *Learning Statistics with Privacy, aided by the Flip of a Coin*: https://research.google/blog/learning-statistics-with-privacy-aided-by-the-flip-of-a-coin
- Paulik, M., Seigel, M., Mason H., et al. (2021) *Federated Evaluation and Tuning for On-Device Personalization: System Design & Applications*: https://arxiv.org/abs/2102.08503

- *Federated Learning with Formal Differential Privacy Guarantees*: `https://research.google/blog/federated-learning-with-formal-differential-privacy-guarantees`
- Carlini, N., Liu, C, Erlingsson, Ú., Kos J, Song, D. (2019) *The Secret Sharer: Evaluating and Testing Unintended Memorization in Neural Networks*: `https://arxiv.org/abs/1802.08232`
- Shokri, R., Stronati, M., Song, C., et al. (2017) *Membership Inference Attacks against Machine Learning Models*: `https://arxiv.org/abs/1610.05820`
- Nasr, M., Carlini N., Hayase, J., et al. (2023) *Scalable Extraction of Training Data from (Production) Language Models*: `https://arxiv.org/abs/2311.17035`
- Derner, E., Batistič, K. (2023) *Beyond the Safeguards: Exploring the Security Risks of ChatGPT*: `https://arxiv.org/abs/2305.08005`

Get This Book's PDF Version and Exclusive Extras

8

Observability and Reliability

After discussing the challenges related to our app going to production in *Chapters 2, 4, 5,* and *6*, we turn our focus to the key element of long-term operational success: **reliability**. As engineers, we know that a service that does not fulfill user needs is useless. This chapter is dedicated to the core principles and practices that enable us to build, deploy, monitor, and maintain highly reliable systems at scale. We will look at **site reliability engineering** (**SRE**), an approach pioneered by Google, and break down how the SRE mindset and engineering practices fundamentally change how we run our operations.

We will dive deep into the philosophy of reliability, learning why 100% uptime is the wrong target and how to measure and manage acceptable failure. We will define the concepts of **service-level indicators** (**SLIs**) and **service-level objectives** (**SLOs**), and most importantly, understand how the error budget transforms reliability from an abstract goal into a practical tool for prioritizing work. Finally, we will explore the complementary discipline of observability, which provides the capability to not just know that something is wrong (monitoring), but to understand why it is wrong (debugging) by examining our system's telemetry data.

In this chapter, we'll be covering the following topics:

- What is site reliability engineering?
- Achieving high reliability
- Observability
- GenAI observability
- Instrumenting your application

What is site reliability engineering?

SRE is the way in which Google runs its production systems. Why did it become famous? For many years, Google has been running online products at a huge scale, worldwide, and serving billions of users. It's not only Google Search but also YouTube, Google Play Store, Google Maps, Google Drive, Gmail, and others. Many people, including engineers, appreciate the scale and the reliability of these products, and Google popularized its approach to SRE by publishing a great book called *Site Reliability Engineering* in 2016. This book is an easy and enjoyable read, and it explains how the SRE team "*enabled the company to successfully build, deploy, monitor, and maintain some of the largest software systems in the world.*" Another good read is *The Site Reliability Workbook*, the details of which you can find in the *Further reading* section. Google has made these books available for free online reading at `https://sre.google/books/`.

> Note
>
> According to the definition from the IEEE Computer Library, **reliability** is "*the ability of a system or component to function under stated conditions for a specified period of time*" (`https://csrc.nist.gov/glossary/term/reliability`).

So, how does Google define SRE? It's Google's way to run production systems, or to organize IT operations, or Ops. In other words, it's Google's way to address the challenges related to going to production that we described in *Chapters 4* and *5*.

> Note
>
> **SRE** "*is a job function, a mindset, and a set of engineering practices to run reliable production systems*" (`https://research.google/pubs/sre-principles`).

How is SRE different from DevOps? Let's just say that SRE is one of many ways to implement DevOps. That's why I'm not saying you should ultimately implement the SRE function at your organization. But understanding the core principles behind SRE is useful, and it can help us to understand the trade-offs around reliability.

Achieving reliability

Let's try to dive deeper into the SRE philosophy on reliability. From an SRE perspective, reliability is the ability of a system or a service to perform its intended functions. According to that definition, reliability is the most important aspect of any service because if the service is not fulfilling users' needs, it's useless. But now it gets tricky. First, we need to find a way to measure reliability. And second, one of the core SRE mantras is that you shouldn't aim for 100% reliability of your service. Even aiming for 99.999% (the so-called *5 nines reliability*) might be the wrong goal, since increasing your reliability becomes exponentially harder as you add an additional nine.

> **Note**
>
> 100% is the wrong reliability target for basically everything (pacemakers and anti-lock brakes being notable exceptions). The marginal difference between 99.999% and 100% gets lost in the noise of other unavailability, and the user receives no benefit from the enormous effort required to add that last 0.001% of availability.

But for engineers to discuss reliability, we need to agree on how to measure it first. SRE practice suggests defining SLIs, or a performance metric that we believe is important.

SLIs, SLOs, and SLAs

We start by defining SLIs for our service. An SLI is an aspect of our service that has a direct impact on a user, and we define it in such a way that we can measure or count it numerically. For example, we want a service to be fast. But that's subjective, isn't it? Instead of saying "the service should be fast", we can define our SLI as the "latency of API calls defined at the load-balancer level" (i.e., not taking into account network delays between the user and our backend systems). Why did we define it on the load balancer? Because that's what we control (network delay might depend on the user's location, device type, and network performance, and if there's an external fluctuation, it's beyond your control). Of course, you can use your own definition of latency, and you might want to investigate end-user latency from the product perspective, and you might find out that some of your mobile users experience significant latency, which would inspire you to change the user journey or make some other changes. But that's different from how you define your SLI. Be careful and do not introduce too many SLIs. Irrelevant SLIs are bad since you invest your effort in things the business doesn't really need, and it becomes difficult to manage the entire system and stay focused.

The definition of an SLI is closely related to the definition of an SLO, so let's look at them together to understand the distinction. Once you have defined an SLI, you can take the next step and define an SLO. It's a target value or range for an SLI. An SLO defines the accepted level of failures, or unreliability. SLIs and SLOs focus on specific characteristics of the service that directly impact the user experience. You need to pick the right SLIs, and then, for each SLI, you define SLOs so that if you meet them, you'll keep your average user happy. But if you don't, your users would be unhappy (on average). SLOs that are too low are bad since you end up not meeting users' expectations. In other words, you can't have too ambitious SLOs (like "I want to serve 99.99% of all requests within 150ms"), and, at the same time, you can't have them too weak ("I want to serve 10% of all requests within 150ms" also doesn't look like a good target). Defining them in such a way is more like an art than a science. Without going into too much detail, let's look at some examples:

- **SLI**: Server-side latency of an API call.
  SLO: Server-side latency of 99% of API requests is below 150 ms.
- **SLI**: A proportion of API requests without an error.
  SLO: 99% of API requests are successful and don't throw an error. (Please note that we have given a clear definition of success. Results might still be poor or not liked by a user, but what's important from a reliability standpoint is that we return these results to the user.)

> Note
>
> An **SLI** is a quantifiable measure of some aspect of the level of service that is provided by a service. An **SLO** defines a target value for this metric.

Do not aim for too many SLIs. First, identify your core user journey and then define two to five SLIs per user journey.

People often use the term **service-level agreement (SLA)** when talking about SLOs and SLIs.

Remember, when determining how to measure reliability, we start with SLIs and identify what is important for our service and how we are going to measure it. Then, we continue with defining SLOs, or targets. An SLA is a legally binding part of your contract. SLAs can't be more strict than SLOs; your external SLA targets should be lower than your internal SLOs. And while engineering and operations teams should meet SLAs, in everyday life, they're using SLOs and SLIs, and SLAs are for legal teams and business teams (both on your and your customer's sides).

> Note
>
> **SLA** is the promise you make to your customer, and there are repercussions if you don't deliver on this promise. SLO is the internal goal that helps you to keep this promise and make the customer happy.

Another SRE mantra is that failures are not optional, and a failure doesn't mean that the team has done a poor job. Failures happen. That's inevitable! Again, failures happen: you would have bugs in production applications, and your users would be impacted. It is a fact that's beyond your control. The only thing you can control is the impact of these failures that are to come: how often your service fails, how fast you recover from this failure, how many users would be affected, and so on. To decrease the negative impact, SRE suggests using multiple methods that change how you organize your processes, what tools you use, and what your team's culture is like. Let's start with the processes, and one of the most important is balancing product and technical work using the error budget.

Error budget

A key concept in SRE practices is the error budget. Technically speaking, it's just *1 - your SLO*. For example, if your SLO is 99% availability of an API, then your error budget is 1%. But you need a second component, a rolling measurement window. You translate your SLO into a measurable allowance for failures, so you say, "I'm allowed to fail 1% over the next 28 days." The typical size of the rolling window is 28, 30, or 90 days. Sometimes, teams use a smaller or a larger window size (7, 14, or 180 days), but in my experience, a short window creates too much noise and a large window has too much inertia.

Now, let's look at some examples in the following table before we jump into a discussion about how to use the error budget. We can see that with a rolling window of 28 days, our error budget for 99.999% reliability is only 24.2 seconds! What does this mean in practice? If there's a failure or some downtime, the team should detect it almost immediately and automatically (and very quickly) roll out the change or roll back the erroneous release. That's an additional illustration of why a high level of reliability requires a ton of effort invested in infrastructure, tooling, and training the team.

SLO	Rolling window 28 days	Rolling window 90 days
99%	6.72 hours	21.6 hours
99.9%	40.3 min	2.16 hours
99.99%	4.03 min	12.96 min
99.999%	24.2 sec	1.30 min

Table 8.1 – Total downtime durations allowed depending on the SLO and a rolling window

Now, let's discuss how to use the error budget. First, we need instrumentation to automatically compute and monitor it. Second, we need to make decisions about how to balance work on reliability improvement and product development. Our development resources are always limited, and there's always a need to prioritize between building new features and reliability work, such as reducing technical debt, bug fixes, or infrastructure improvements. In other words, an error budget becomes a way to prioritize work. It accommodates such things as new releases (that increase the probability of things going wrong) and risky experiments, failures in dependencies such as network, hardware, and downstream APIs, as well as planned downtimes, and so on.

Thinking in terms of error budget, or how much your services are allowed to fail, helps you to prioritize work between new features and reliability improvement. How do we prioritize the team's work with an error budget? We compute a consumed budget, or how much we have violated the budget in the last *N* days (where *N* is the size of the rolling window). Let's look at the examples in the following table:

Consumed budget << planned budget	GREEN	That's an ideal state. The team continues to innovate, release new features, run experiments, and perform planned maintenance. Velocity is prioritized.
Consumed budget ~ planned budget	YELLOW	The team should reduce velocity or become more cautious with new feature releases. It should start prioritizing reliability by shifting focus to addressing reliability issues, perhaps by dedicating a portion of sprint capacity to reliability tasks (tech debt, bug fixes, performance improvements) and it should conduct initial investigations into the causes of budget consumption.
Consumed budget >> planned budget	RED	Announce a code read and a feature freeze. All new feature deployments are immediately frozen. The team should focus entirely on restoring reliability; only critical bug fixes and security patches are allowed to be deployed. Perform intensive debugging and root cause analysis, and develop targeted fixes to improve SLIs. Investigate major incidents that consumed a significant part of the error budget.

Table 8.2 – Applying error budget to manage teams' priorities between product features and reducing technical debt

Thinking in terms of an error budget amplifies the understanding that 100% reliability is not possible (yes, you might be lucky once or twice!) and, at the same time, achieving reasonably high reliability requires additional resources and effort. Just defining an SLO won't help, and it would remain wishful thinking if you don't adjust your processes.

We have discussed how we can make reliability measurable with SLIs and SLOs and use the error budget to make management decisions. Now, let's discuss other principles and processes that might help to improve the overall reliability of our application.

Other SRE principles

SLOs and an error budget mindset help transform reliability from an abstract concept into a measurable, manageable target. As application requirements continuously evolve, so does the ideal architecture; there's no such thing as a perfect system. Instead, teams must constantly balance reducing technical debt with delivering new features. Fortunately, a set of proven practices (***SRE principles***) can help minimize maintenance effort and free up more time for product development. I highly recommend that you read the SRE books cited previously if you are interested in the topic. They will introduce you to other SRE principles, such as the following:

- **Eliminating toil**: This is possible through identifying toil and constantly working on automation. Toil, or operational work, is any repetitive manual work that is reactive. One interesting aspect of something being considered as toil is that if the amount of manual work grows linearly as a service scales, that's a sign of a problem and a lack of automation. The SRE team is an operational team, but Google tries to keep SRE teams busy with toil less than 50% of their time.
- **Monitoring**: You can't improve what you don't measure, and you don't know about. We will discuss some best practices around monitoring later in this section.
- **Automation**: This applies to everything from deployments and configuration management to incident response and remediation. Automation increases consistency and speed and reduces human error.
- **Constant improvement in release engineering**: This focuses on consistency, repeatability, and safety in releases, and includes such practices as automated builds and tests, CI/CD, and frequent, small, and automated deployments, canary deployments, and gradual rollouts, reducing the blast radius of potential issues, fast rollback capabilities, and being able to quickly revert to a stable state if a problem is detected.
- **Designing and building systems that are as simple as possible**: Complex systems are harder to understand, operate, and make reliable. Simplicity reduces the cognitive load on engineers, minimizes potential points of failure, and makes debugging and troubleshooting easier. This often means pushing back against unnecessary features or architectural complexity. One of my favorite design principles is to postpone design

decisions and simplify things as much as possible, since we might later face slightly different requirements and know better what kind of system we're building.

In practice, these principles are harder to apply than they sound. Sometimes, teams don't pay attention at all to the level of technical debt and the system's quality (and there comes a moment when everything falls apart), and sometimes they overengineer too much, sacrificing product development without a clear need. When advising start-ups, I sometimes see that they are surprised. They aim for complex architectures designed for scale and flexibility from the very beginning, and they seem offended when I recommend using a simple solution. But the truth is that their product will change a few times before they reach the amount of traffic where they need to think about scalability, and spending time now on unnecessary things is a waste of resources right now and in the future (since it increases the cost of maintenance).

Finalizing our discussion of SRE, it's very important to mention the culture of blameless postmortems. When incidents occur, the focus should be on learning from failures to improve the system and processes, not on assigning blame to individuals.

Firstly, a postmortem should be truly blameless since a famous saying is that *people can make mistakes, and if a mistake is made, it's a failure of a process*. We should think about how to eliminate the possibility of such a mistake, not how to punish an engineer. Talking is easier than doing, but once you've adopted a blameless culture, you'll see how the team starts discussing issues with deep honesty and think about how to fix the root cause.

> **Note**
>
> A *postmortem*, or an *incident retrospective*, is a practice of learning from incidents, outages, or any significant operational event that impacted a system or service. The team goes through the incident and tries to understand why something happened and how to prevent similar issues in the future.

Secondly, an important part of conducting a postmortem is a deep analysis of the root cause. You typically start by carefully documenting what happened, and it requires a certain amount of effort to recollect all the information. Then, you look at the data you collected and start an analysis of what really happened, what went wrong, and where you got lucky. Such a deep analysis allows you to uncover the actual root causes and suggest how they can be addressed. The whole idea is that you should be truly learning from a postmortem, and, again, it's a big cultural shift:

> *"Introducing postmortems into an organization is as much a cultural change as it is a technical one. ... Don't emerge from an incident hoping that your systems will eventually remedy themselves. You can start small by introducing a very basic*

> *postmortem procedure, and then reflect and tune your process to best suit your organization—as with many things, no one size fits all" (the SRE Workbook).*

The Site Reliability Workbook has a good example of a postmortem in *Chapter 10*, and you can also find some good examples of public postmortems on the internet; for example, there's a good collection on GitHub: `https://github.com/danluu/post-mortems`.

We have briefly discussed the technical and cultural changes that SRE adoption brings with it in an organization, and let me repeat that these are only suggestions; the implementation in your organization and your team might vary. Feel free to adopt practices that work and adjust what is not working for you. Let's move on and discuss observability, since it helps us to make reliability measurable. We can't manage what we cannot measure.

Managing production application

Observability, monitoring, and alerting are terms that often go together, and some people use them interchangeably. In fact, monitoring helps us to understand that something is wrong, alerting helps us to be notified when something is wrong, and observability helps us to understand why something is wrong. While monitoring focuses on collecting and visualizing pre-defined metrics, observability focuses on a deep understanding and debugging of the internals of your system and answering complex questions.

> **Note**
>
> Observability is the ability to understand the internal state and behavior of a complex system by examining the data it outputs.

The confusion is also related to the fact that monitoring, alerting, and observability are based on the same telemetry data, and there is an interconnected set of tools despite the fact that they answer different questions. You need all three components to develop a reliable system. Let's start with telemetry data and instrumentation, and then we'll look into monitoring, alerting, and observability.

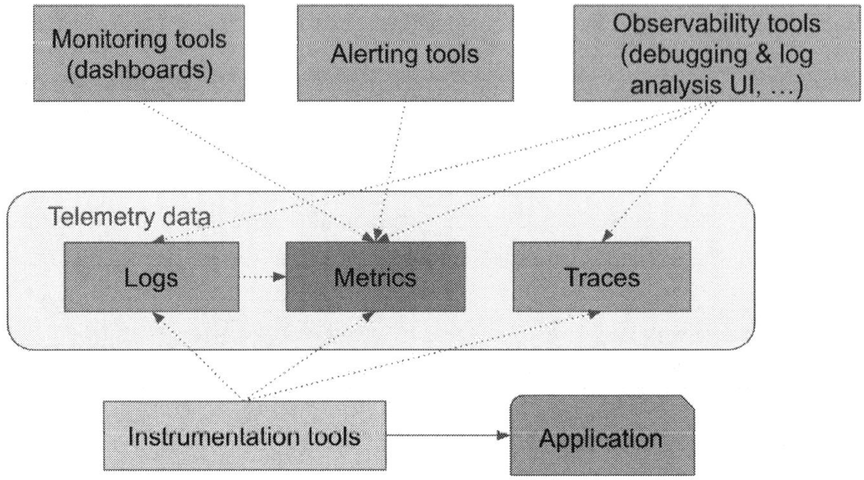

Figure 8.1 – How monitoring, alerting, and observability tools help to manage a production application

Telemetry data

Logs, metrics, and traces are three key pillars of telemetry data that we need to manage applications in production.

Logs

Logs are time-stamped records of events, messages, or errors produced by software systems. Logs are typically structured. What is the most important thing to say about logging? Just collect logs, including error messages with stack traces, warnings, and information about your application! Remember that good logging provides rich context and is essential for root cause analysis and debugging. Logs capture the narrative of what the system was doing, making them vital for postmortems and security forensics. Effective logging includes details that help pinpoint the exact cause of an issue. If you're interested in more details, you can take a look at logging best practices published by New Relic (`https://newrelic.com/blog/log/best-log-management-practices`).

You need to not only generate logs. You need to collect them from all hosts where your application is running and insert them into the centralized log system for processing. There are many ways to organize such a log collection, but the easiest way (and the most popular) is to make an application running in a Docker container write logs to standard output streams of the operating system (`stdout` or `stderr`). Container orchestrators (such as Kubernetes) and special logging agents (such as `OpenTelemetry`, `Fluentd`, and `Logstash`) process these logs.

You typically need to configure these yourself since your infrastructure has implemented them once and for all services deployed across your organization, but it's always useful to understand how the system works.

> **Note**
>
> Log entries are collected from your applications and sent to the central log system (which processes at scale, stores, and visualizes them). In many cases, log collection is organized in the following way: a container writes logs to a `stdout` or `stderr` stream, and special logging agents process these logs and send them to the log system.
>
> A *logging agent* is a lightweight software component installed on each host or alongside application containers, and it is for tailing log files, capturing `stdout/stderr` streams, and forwarding them to a centralized logging system.

When configuring logging, you always face a tradeoff. On the one hand, you don't want to collect too many logs (since it might become quite costly quickly). For example, Google Cloud Logging charges you $0.50 per GB of collected logs (and the first 50 GB are free). It seems like you can ignore the price, but I have seen systems that produced terabytes of logs in a short period of time, and costs suddenly became quite significant. Anyway, don't forget to adjust the retention period of your logs (typically, retention for more than 30 days costs additionally with most cloud systems, and in most cases, you don't need old logs). So, again, we're facing a design question regarding how long we want to retain logs, but this doesn't have a direct answer, and an answer is "it depends."

> **Tip**
>
> - Do not emit log entries with a print statement; use logging instead
> - Use an appropriate log level to emit logs: `logging.warning`, `logging.error`, or `logging.info`
> - Adjust the configuration of a log entry to the one expected by your logging system
> - Think carefully about what kind of logs should be collected
> - Handle exceptions and emit full tracebacks

On the other hand, you don't need most of the logs until an incident has occurred. When an incident happens, you will explore, correlate, and analyze logs in order to find out what happened.

Metrics

Metrics are another important source of telemetry data. Metrics are numerical measurements collected over time that reflect the state or performance of a system. For example, they could be CPU or GPU utilization, GPU temperature, latency of API response, network throughput, or cache hit ratio. Metrics provide a quick, quantitative overview of system health and performance trends. There are three key types of metrics:

- **Counter**: A counter is a cumulative metric that represents an always-increasing quantity, as you can tell from its name. A counter is always collected and sent to the metric system based on a scheduled interval. For example, it could count the number of requests or errors.
- **Gauge**: A gauge represents an arbitrary numeric value, including a counter that can go up and down. Unlike a counter, a gauge provides a snapshot of a value at any given point, and it's collected according to the scheduling interval (every 5 seconds or every minute). GPU temperature, CPU or memory utilization, number of active connections, and queue size are examples of gauge metrics.
- **Histogram**: A histogram represents a distribution of a numeric value across many observations (across a counter or a gauge). A good example is latency. You're interested in the distribution of a latency: for example, average latency, or latency at p90 or p95. When we define a histogram metric, we need to define buckets for which we collect values (sometimes, modern observability systems adjust these buckets dynamically).

> **Note**
>
> Latency is commonly measured at a given percentile, for example, p50, p90, p95, or p99. In statistics, a *percentile* indicates the value below which a given percentage of observations in a sample fall. Hence, latency at p90 (or @p90) refers to the 90th percentile. In other words, if we quote latency @p90 over the last week equals 110 ms, that means that 90% of the requests last week were served faster than 110 ms.

Metrics are typically collected at regular intervals and are well suited for trend analysis, dashboards, and alerts. You can also compute metrics in real time based on log events. Modern observability systems such as OpenTelemetry, Prometheus, and Datadog have a lot of preconfigured metrics (also natively integrated with cloud services and engines such as

Kubernetes). You get quite a lot of metrics out of the box, but if you need some customization, it's important to understand how they are collected.

> **Note**
>
> Many common metrics, such as counters, gauges, and histograms, are predefined by your observability tools, but if you need a custom metric, you need to configure its type, what value it collects, and the interval at which it collects values.

Traces

Traces are the last pillar of telemetry data. A trace represents an end-to-end journey of a request as it propagates through a distributed system. Traces provide a detailed view of how different services interact and the latency at each step, and you use them to troubleshoot performance bottlenecks, understand service dependencies, and pinpoint the root cause of issues across multiple services. Traces are typically used for debugging.

The process of adding code to your application to capture and emit this trace data is called instrumentation. The most popular library for distributed tracing is OpenTelemetry. It is a pretty broad option for automatic instrumentation, but in many cases, you still need to add small snippets of code to create better spans and manage the context. Without going into too much detail, let's briefly discuss how distributed tracing works.

Within your application, you create spans. A span is a single unit of work within a distributed system, and essentially, it unites a few log entries with common log fields such as `span_id` and `trace_id`. Your telemetry framework automatically sets these fields when emitting log entries, and it also emits metadata for a span, such as its name, start and end timestamps, status of the operation, and other key-value pairs called tags (which can be SQL queries, the content of the HTTP request, size, user ID, or something else). You can instruct your application how to organize various steps into spans (or many frameworks and libraries have extensive support for automatic instrumentation). Spans can also have a child-parent relationship (one span can originate within another span), and by organizing your execution steps into logical spans, you simplify later analyses.

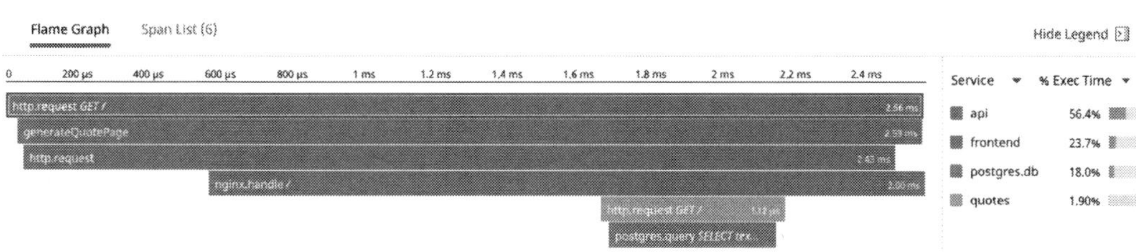

Figure 8.2 – Datadog trace example (source: https://github.com/DataDog/trace-examples)

If you invoke another service (for example, with an HTTP request), the telemetry framework adds special HTTP headers to your request, and these headers are propagated further by the telemetry library on the downstream service (and this allows us to collect the entire trace). It creates a new span that inherits from the original one, and the tracing service that you're using later collects all these spans into one single trace.

As with monitoring, you typically run a standalone telemetry collector. It's a separate service (it can be run in another container or just nearby your application) that collects emitted traces, processes them, and sends them to the telemetry server to be processed, stored, and visualized.

Monitoring

Effective monitoring is crucial for understanding your system's health, identifying issues, and ensuring a good user experience. Think about what kind of question you want to answer, and be prepared by building dashboards and tools to dive deeper into your application's performance. First, you want to know whether your application is performing well or not. Second, once something is wrong, you want to understand what exactly is happening. Think of your monitoring dashboards as your control center. You don't want too many dashboards; if you have too many, you may get distracted. Also, you don't want your dashboards to be too complex since you need to operate quickly when things go wrong.

Effective production monitoring typically covers three domains: application performance, infrastructure health, and log-based dashboards. **Application performance monitoring (APM)** covers the user's experience, and you track the flow of requests through your application, from the moment a user interacts with it to the responses from your database and external services, with metrics such as latency (at p50, p90, or p95, for example), request throughput, error rates, and so on.

Infrastructure monitoring collects data on CPU utilization and memory usage, disk I/O, network performance of your workers, and so on. It helps you to understand whether something is wrong (for example, a sudden spike in CPU consumption might be a sign of a changed user behavior or problems with processing certain types of user requests).

The third type of monitoring is log-based. Be aware that any monitoring system (such as Prometheus, Grafana, and Google Cloud Observability) has its own version of logging query language. You don't need to become a master of it (and you can always use an LLM to write a logging query for you!), but you need to know it exists, and it allows you to develop complex queries to filter, group, and transform large amounts of logs in order to develop your own dashboards and alerts. One very popular example is a dashboard with the most common errors that occur in your application (by normalizing and grouping error messages, you can quickly spot patterns, such as a sudden spike in a specific error type, which often signals that something is going wrong.).

Alerting

When you deploy your first application to production, you need to think about the support model. Is your application supposed to work only within the working hours of your team, or should it be available for users 24/7? If you have an established Ops team in your organization, they will ask you all these questions and guide you through preparation to production. But if not, or if you're building a start-up, these are the questions you should ask.

A key aspect of alerting is automating monitoring. With good alerting, you don't need to manually check for issues on your monitoring dashboards. An automated alerting system can check for issues in application and infrastructure health and notify the team. All you need is to configure your alerts and alerting mechanism.

Building a good alerting system takes time, and it's typically a combination of trial and error. Good alerts should be actionable, timely, and relevant. Any incident that consumes your error budget has two components: time to detect and time to recover. With a good alerting system, you can decrease the time to detect from dozens of minutes or even hours to a few dozen seconds or minutes.

On the other hand, you don't want to get too many alerts. Too many false alarms take time from your team and decrease their awareness of alerts. If I, as an engineer, have closed 49 out of 50 alerts, next time I might not be as focused and miss a critical incident. Iterate on your alerts, adjust alerting schedules if needed, and work on alerts that cause too many false positives.

Think about alerting mechanisms and your on-call schedule. Do you need on-call? If yes, is it 24/7, or do you provide support only within working hours? Don't rush to answer "yes, we need 24/7 on-call" since it has certain implications on your engineers' availability and how much time they will be able to spend on product development.

> **Note**
>
> *On-call* refers to a period during which an employee is required to be available to respond to urgent issues outside of their regular working hours. This ensures that critical systems remain operational and that emergencies are addressed promptly, 24/7. Typically, the response time to an incident should be 15 minutes (or less), and team members should rotate through their on-call shifts. Do not forget to discuss with the engineering and HR teams all additional issues related to on-call, such as compensation and legal guidelines in your country of residence.

Depending on your on-call requirements, think about notification mechanisms for alerts. Should it be only email or Slack, or do you want to page an on-call engineer on their mobile phone? If they are not responding, how should an incident escalate? Who should be able to page an on-call engineer—only the alerting system, or other colleagues (including colleagues from customer support) too? If you're interested in further details, you can take a look at public guides on alerting published by Atlassian (`https://www.atlassian.com/incident-management/on-call/it-alerting`) and Pagerduty (`https://response.pagerduty.com/oncall/alerting_principles`).

Once you have implemented monitoring and alerting, you need to think about how your team will operate when an incident happens. This brings us to the last pillar: observability.

Observability

The third pillar is observability. To recap, observability allows you to debug or to deeply understand the internal state of your system by exploring telemetry data (logs, metrics, and traces) and to pinpoint the root cause of a detected problem. Observability is based on telemetry data; therefore, the key element of instrumenting observability in your application is collecting the right telemetry data and choosing the observability toolset.

Let's look at an example. Imagine you've developed a GenAI agent for customer support. What metric would you use for the main dashboard? It depends on the details of your use case, but I suggest the following ones would be a good start:

- CPU utilization of your workers and the number of workers
- Number of support requests handled per minute or hour
- A p50 and p90 resolution time (in seconds)
- Tokens per request
- Escalation to human rate
- Number of failed calls to external tools
- Number of errors (based on logs), including the number of "Max retries exceeded" or "Max recursion depth exceeded" errors (based on pattern matching of your log entries)

What alerts would you implement? You probably know the answer: it depends on the details of your use case, and you should iterate with a real application to tune alerts and thresholds, but sudden spikes in costs, latency, or error rates are good starting points:

- Alert if `latency_@p95` is more than once over the 5-minute interval
- Alert if `tokens_per_request` is more than two times over the 5-minute interval

- Alert if `error_rate` is more than three times over the 1-minute interval
- Alert if `human_escalation_rate` is more than four times over the 15-minute interval

You can add more alerts based on safety filters, errors in internal tools, and other things, but keep in mind that we don't want too many alerts; we want alerts that help us to detect incidents. Sometimes, teams distinguish alerts that are good to double-check during working hours and alerts that are escalated to an on-call engineer at any time.

Now, let's go to observability. Imagine an alert has been triggered. An engineer now needs to figure out what is wrong. First, they acknowledge an alert. Second, they start investigating service dashboards and correlating logs from different parts of the application. If there's a spike in CPU consumption, is there anything else happening (maybe error rate or the average amount of tokens per request has also increased)? They check for unusual errors and log records to try to figure out what's happening. A good idea is to also check for the recent releases and whether they could have affected the application. It's important to say that there are two tasks: fix the problem and understand what has happened. Sometimes, you can prioritize the first one without solving the other one. For example, rolling back a release or restarting a container might fix the problem, but after the service is restored, you still need to figure out the cause of the incident (you can do this in working hours, though). My team once had a problem with a Java application that experienced sudden CPU spikes (and corresponding error spikes) in production, and redeployment always helped. But in order to know the cause, we spent more than a week and simulated the problem in different ways before we found it.

Last but not least, an engineer tries to isolate the problem using distributed tracing. They look at traces of an agent for erroneous requests, explore the details of each step, and try to figure out the problem and how to fix it.

It's important to say that when an incident occurs, you are under pressure. That's why it's a good idea to prepare a playbook for an on-call engineer that describes common problems and ways to fix them, has a collection of useful links and commands, and contains other information. Trust me; during an incident, you will forget certain things, so it's better to have them in writing and to be prepared.

> **Note**
>
> Invest time and prepare *playbooks* for your applications. A playbook is a collection of step-by-step instructions that describe clear actions to be taken in case of an application failure. Playbooks have links to release and monitoring dashboards, describe high-level application architecture, what to check, and typical actions (for example, how to roll back a release or redeploy a worker).

Now, let's take a look at how GenAI applications are different and why they often require special observability tools.

GenAI observability

Instrumenting observability for GenAI applications is a challenge. Why is that the case? What is so special about these applications? There are two key characteristics of GenAI systems that make traditional observability approaches insufficient.

First, as we have already discussed many times in this book, GenAI applications exhibit probabilistic behavior instead of deterministic behavior. This is a huge paradigm shift from an observability perspective. Traditionally, we focused on applications operating on deterministic logic that takes a certain state and produces an output according to the algorithm. From that perspective, observability was about the verification of this logic. We looked at metrics such as CPU consumption, error rates, and latency, and we tried to find out when and why the actual application logic deviated from the expected one. As we discussed in *Chapter 2*, in the new GenAI world, the notion of a failure is different, and it's much more complicated to determine whether the system is in the correct state or not. We face failures such as LLM hallucinations, irrelevant responses (that are grammatically correct and the system functions normally), and biased or toxic responses. It becomes more challenging to determine when a failure happens, and then to find out what is the reason for this failure.

What does this mean from a practical perspective? We need to enrich our telemetry data to handle a semantic context, which significantly increases the number and size of collected logs. For example, for a RAG application, we would traditionally only monitor response times and errors from a database (retrieval) and generation (an LLM) components. But a RAG might function perfectly fine and provide a completely irrelevant response, which is a failure. To understand what's happening, we would like the full trace to include the actual content that was retrieved, ranking scores, the actual prompt that was passed to an LLM, inference parameters, and other important attributes. We want to collect a lot of data as part of our telemetry, and we need to inspect this data in a fast and convenient way, too, which imposes new requirements for traditional observability tools from the UX perspective. Our main goal is now to ensure not only reliability from an operational perspective (guaranteeing uptime from the point of view that an application is running correctly and effectively) but also from the semantic perspective (ensuring behavioral consistency and quality within an acceptable range).

Secondly, if we look at GenAI agents, they are composite systems that include an LLM, a memory, an orchestrator, and an integration layer with various tools. There are many integration points, and each of them can be a source of failure. An agent can fail in more dynamic and catastrophic ways than a traditional application. For example, it can get stuck in a repetitive loop, endlessly re-attempting the same failed action; it can fundamentally misunderstand the assigned task, leading it down a completely irrelevant path of execution; it can pass incorrect or malformed information between steps, causing a cascade of errors; it can fail to properly coordinate the use of multiple tools, leading to an incoherent or incomplete outcome; or in one of the agent's steps, an LLM might receive a poorly composed context that influences the whole further path of the agent.

As we can see, to effectively observe an agent or a complex GenAI application, it is no longer sufficient to look at the final output only. We also need to trace the entire execution path, visualizing the agent's internal reasoning, the sequence of tool calls it made, the data it passed between them, and the errors it encountered along the way. This requires a level of deep, granular logging and tracing that far exceeds the capabilities of traditional application performance monitoring. This also applies to the observability tools: we need new capabilities to monitor and evaluate the application, and to analyze and visualize the telemetry data. That's one of the reasons why there are so many new tools for observability of GenAI applications, such as LangSmith and Langfuse.

Instrumenting your application

When you start instrumenting observability in your application, you need to think about a few things:

- Select appropriate observability tools (take into account price, performance, support for your frameworks, and usability).
- Define what telemetry data you need to collect for effective monitoring and debugging.
- Check that you collect logs in the correct format.
- Ask yourself what kind of decisions you want to make based on monitoring. Implement the general monitoring dashboards and more detailed ones with additional metrics.
- Decide on your support model, how your on-call shifts are organized, where you track an on-call schedule, and what alerting mechanism you need (email, Slack, SMS, phone calls, etc.). Pick a tool for alerting that meets your requirements.
- Design an initial set of alerts and thresholds, and document them (to track changes later). Implement your alerts.
- Create an initial playbook and add it to the alerting message template.
- Pick observability tools and make sure your logs, traces, and metrics are accessible through this tool.

- Test the system. Simulate an incident and make sure you can go through the whole path to resolve it.
- Be calm and keep building great products!

One of my favorite SRE sayings is "Hope is not a strategy." Incidents always happen, but if you invest in observability, you significantly increase your reliability and your chance of recovering quickly from them.

Summary

We started this chapter by establishing that reliability is the most crucial aspect of any service. A service that fails to meet user needs is simply useless. We learned about SRE, Google's operational approach that helps run reliable production systems. A core takeaway was understanding why aiming for 100% reliability is a misguided and exponentially costly goal. Instead, we focused on defining and measuring acceptable unreliability through SLIs and SLOs. Most importantly, we defined the error budget (*1 - SLO*) and saw how this simple metric, when paired with a rolling window, becomes a powerful, practical tool for prioritizing work and balancing feature velocity against reliability improvements.

We also discussed other key SRE principles, including the cultural shift toward blameless postmortems to ensure learning from failure, and the need for continuous automation to eliminate repetitive manual toil. We then explored the crucial difference between monitoring, which tells us that something is wrong, and observability, which allows us to understand why it is wrong for deep debugging. This led us to the three foundational pillars of telemetry data: logs (time-stamped events), metrics (quantifiable measurements such as counters, gauges, and histograms), and traces (end-to-end request journeys in distributed systems). Finally, we examined the importance of having actionable, timely, and relevant alerts and documented playbooks to minimize the time to detect and recover from inevitable incidents.

We explored the new frontier of GenAI observability, recognizing that the probabilistic nature of LLMs presents unique challenges such as hallucinations and irrelevant-but-successful responses. We learned that to ensure behavioral and semantic consistency, we must enrich our telemetry data to capture contextual information, such as the full prompt and entire execution traces of composite AI agents. By collecting and analyzing this deep, granular data, we can move beyond traditional operational reliability to ensure the overall quality and trustworthiness of our GenAI applications.

In the next chapter, we're going to discuss the maintenance of GenAI applications and how a GenAI platform can offer repeatable pieces that improve reliability and decrease development time and the cost of maintaining such applications across an organization.

Note

There are three key outcomes to remember:

- 100% reliability is not achievable by definition, and aiming for higher reliability requires an exponentially higher effort and investment.
- Reliability should be measured and treated as an engineering goal. But defining SLOs and SLIs doesn't help if you don't use them to balance technical debt and reliability improvement effort versus product development.
- To reduce the duration of an incident, you need to minimize both time-to-detect and time-to-recover. Good observability includes monitoring that helps you to detect incidents more quickly, and debugging tools that help you to understand what's wrong with your application and restore it quickly.

Further reading

- Murphy, N.R., Beyer, B., Jones, C., et al. *Site Reliability Engineering: How Google Runs Production Systems*, O'Reilly Media, Inc.
- Beyer, B., Murphy, N.R., Rensin, D.K., et al. *The Site Reliability Workbook: Practical Ways to Implement SRE*. O'Reilly Media, Inc.
- *Site Reliability Engineering (SRE)*, Google Cloud. `https://cloud.google.com/sre`
- Mireles, Y., *See everything in your tech stack with these logging best practices*, New Relic. `https://newrelic.com/blog/log/best-log-management-practices`
- Atlassian. *Guide to IT alerting: practices and tools.* `https://www.atlassian.com/incident-management/on-call/it-alerting`
- PagerDuty. *Alerting Principles.* `https://response.pagerduty.com/oncall/alerting_principles`

Subscribe for a free eBook

New frameworks, evolving architectures, research drops, production breakdowns—*AI_Distilled* filters the noise into a weekly briefing for engineers and researchers working hands-on with LLMs and generative AI systems. Subscribe now and receive a free eBook, along with weekly insights that help you stay focused and informed.

Subscribe at `https://packt.link/8Oz6Y` or scan the QR code below.

9

Maintaining Your Application

You have successfully deployed your application, and you've onboarded first users. What happens next? The life cycle of a successful application rarely ends at deployment. For an enterprise, this success often triggers a massive acceleration of GenAI adoption, which, in turn, will shift your focus from a single application to building a foundational platform that enables multiple use cases across the organization. Even if you are working at a small start-up, you will quickly discover the need for a robust set of underlying tools to manage the complexity and rapid change inherent in the LLM landscape. We will now turn our attention to this critical stage: life after deployment.

In this chapter, we will discuss the role that platform teams play in this evolving landscape, comparing their function with that of a traditional product engineering team. We will then dive deep into the essential architectural building blocks required to support a scalable, reliable, and secure GenAI platform. These are the key LLMOps tools that you'll need, whether you're supporting an entire organization or just a single, complex agent. Finally, we will bring a product lens to this discussion by exploring the unique challenges and considerations when setting a product strategy and roadmap for GenAI products.

In this chapter, we'll be covering the following topics:

- Life after deployment
- How are platform teams different?
- What differentiates GenAI in this context?
- Product strategy and roadmap

Life after deployment

After your first GenAI application has been successfully deployed to production and you have onboarded first users, it's time to celebrate! Then you ask yourself, "What is next?" In an enterprise setup, two things might happen (together or separately). Firstly, your first successful prototype leads to further adoption of GenAI across the company. Secondly, your team soon realizes that you're developing a platform to enable multiple GenAI internal use cases.

An alternative is that your application tracks a large user base, and you'll see a lot of feature requests and bugs. This means you need to constantly develop and improve it, classic product engineering work. It's more likely to become a use case when you get a large internal or external user base. For example, you've developed an employee assistant or an external-facing chatbot. You're now in the business of deciding what your priorities are, how to ensure the reliability of your application, what new features to add, and so on.

There is also a third scenario: your application becomes a successful one in the sense that it's used every day, it solves its task reliably, and you and your team won't touch it for years. It's not rare in an enterprise. I've worked on a few migration projects from on-premises to cloud for large Fortune 500 companies. These projects involved thousands of legacy applications migrated in a lift-and-shift style, and you won't believe how often we have discovered applications running for years (and even for dozens of years!), doing an important job and having zero maintenance (everybody who knew how this application worked had already left the company). It's unlikely to be the case for a GenAI application, and we'll discuss why later in this chapter. But that's how success might look in an enterprise!

From my perspective, the third scenario is a pretty rare one for GenAI applications since the industry is rapidly evolving and certain foundational models have a relatively short lifetime of 1–2 years maximum (then they are decommissioned and replaced by newer ones). But remember, as we discussed earlier in this book, switching a foundational model is a time-consuming maintenance task since it requires running the full cycle of evaluations, adjusting the prompts, and so on.

Now, let's discuss some details of establishing a platform team.

How are platform teams different?

A platform team works on creating foundational tools and infrastructure for developers that improve their productivity, decrease time-to-market and cost of ownership of applications, and improve aspects such as reliability and security. As Red Hat defines, "*the overarching goal of platform engineering is to identify the pain points impacting development teams and mitigate them by providing common, reusable tools and capabilities via an internal developer platform (IDP)*" (`https://www.redhat.com/en/topics/devops/platform-engineering`).

> **Note**
>
> A *platform team* builds foundational tools and infrastructure for developers to improve the velocity and quality of software delivered.

A product engineering team is focused on designing and developing great software applications for a given group of end users. They're focused on improving this application and are responsible for its whole end-to-end life cycle, from idea and design to deployment and maintenance. In contrast, platform teams are focused on development and deployment phases as they develop foundational systems for software operations. Product engineering or application development teams are users for a platform team, and the value a platform team brings to the organization is related to their ability to influence these teams' ability to deliver better products faster (`https://www.hashicorp.com/en/resources/platform-teams-best-practices`).

One important question to keep in mind is that developing a platform is difficult since it goes beyond building a set of great tools. You need additional focus on aspects such as these:

- Integration of these tools so that they can work together seamlessly.
- Abstraction of tools' internals and providing a consistent user experience by exposing simple and user-friendly interfaces.
- Standardization and ensuring consistency to enforce best practices. This sometimes comes at the cost of opinionating (i.e., you select certain ways how things are done and enforce them across the whole organization).
- Focus on self-service so that developers can easily run complex tasks such as training an ML model or launching ML workflows without the need to involve the platform team for assistance.
- Maintenance, or keeping all platform components reliable, well integrated, and up to date. This is often underestimated but is critical for long-term success.

Now, let's look at what's special about GenAI platform teams.

What differentiates GenAI platform teams from regular platform teams?

First, when we talk about GenAI platform teams, the notion of a user expands. Users for a platform team are not only developers or data scientists, but every employee within the organization can also benefit from such a platform.

Second, we can learn lessons from the early days of designing ML platforms at large enterprises. Looking at the typical goals for an ML platform team, we can easily adapt them to the GenAI landscape. Let's compare the typical goals of an ML platform team to possible ones that a GenAI platform team can put in front of itself.

ML platform team	GenAI platform team
Adoption of ML to improve customer experience across different product areas across the organization	Adoption of GenAI tools to boost employee productivity and user experience across the organization
Establish common practices for developers to train and deploy ML models	Establish common practices for developers to build applications with LLMs
Make data accessible to data scientists and ML engineers	Make LLMs grounded on enterprise data respecting end user permissions, and also make enterprise tools available for any GenAI developer across the organization
Make ML models and pipelines discoverable and reusable across the organization	Make tools and specialized LLM-based agents discoverable across the organization
Make self-service capabilities for developers to build ML applications	Provide a no-code or low-code way for employees (even with little or zero knowledge of AI) to enhance their daily routines with LLMs
Improve the reliability of ML-based applications	Improve the security (for example, prompt injection defense) and quality (for example, hallucination mitigation) of GenAI applications
Educate developers on ML technology best practices and on how to effectively use the platform	Educate developers and non-technical employees on best practices working with LLMs in the enterprise context (both on their advantages, capabilities, and limitations)

ML platform team	GenAI platform team
Reduce TCO by implementing policies and providing cost transparency through showbacks and chargebacks	Reduce TCO by implementing tracking usage, introducing best practices (such as context caching or model selection), and providing cost transparency through showbacks and chargebacks
Educate developers on how to solve problems not algorithmically but with ML	Introduce new ways of working and automation across the IT organization (by introducing tools such as Copilot)
Unify ways of working and choose from a broad landscape of ML frameworks	Unify ways of working and choose not only from a broad landscape of GenAI frameworks, but also from many foundational models and special tools, such as vector databases

Table 9.1 – Evolution of goals across ML and GenAI platform team

Looking at *Table 9.1*, it might appear to be a straightforward adaptation of an ML platform team's scope to a GenAI platform team's scope, but there are a few aspects that are truly unique to a GenAI world:

- Unifying internal tools (i.e., APIs that are wrapped as an LLM tool) and agents, and making them truly discoverable across the organization.

  > **Note**
  >
  > As we discussed in *Chapter 3*, LLMs benefit a lot from access to tools (external capabilities or functions that allow them to perform tasks). An LLM can decide when to call a tool, generate a payload, and use the tool's output to continue solving the task. Moreover, LLMs benefit a lot from the decomposition of a complex task into smaller tasks, which means we end up with a lot of specialized, modular LLM-based agents. This means we now need to make not only data, but also tools and agents discoverable and reusable across the entire organization.

- Broad support for a non-technical group of users.
- Addressing the complexity related to grounding GenAI applications on enterprise data.

- Dealing with a situation with a lot of uncertainty, constant changes in the landscape, and a rapid evolution of the industry.
- New specific security threats and ethical concerns are being added to the overall picture.
- A GenAI platform might be less monolithic than a classic ML/MLOps one. At this stage, it looks more like a curated set of APIs (such as foundational models or guardrail services), vector databases, best-practice guidelines, and framework choices rather than a single integrated system.

It is truly challenging, but that's what makes our lives interesting!

GenAI platform building blocks

I expect a user to know what a RAG is and to be familiar with its architecture in general. If not, you can refer to *Chapter 3* for more details.

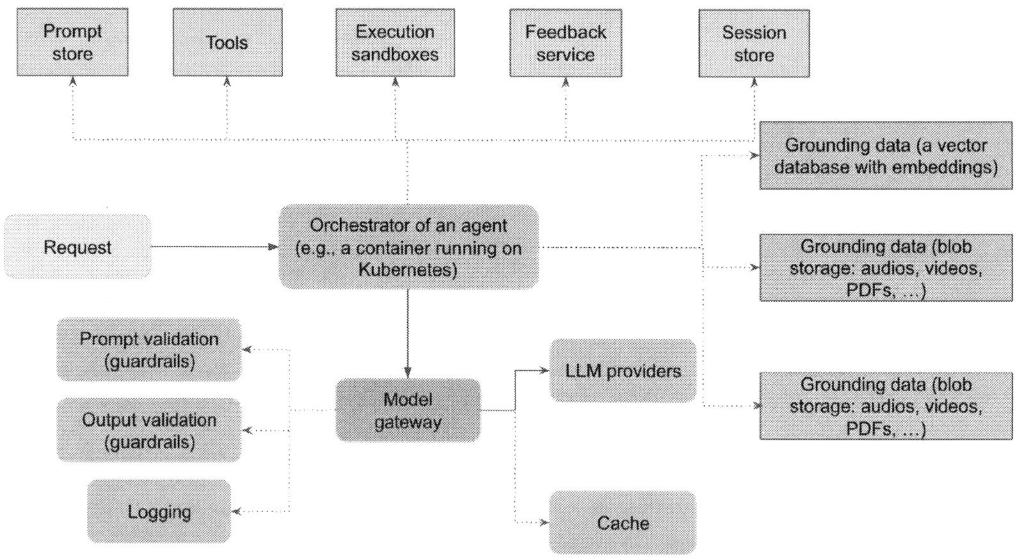

Figure 9.1 – GenAI platform building blocks (an example)

Figure 9.1 shows an example of what a GenAI platform could look like and how these building blocks relate to each other. Let's walk through these components and understand what roles they play in an enterprise platform.

Model gateway

A model gateway is an intermediary layer between applications and various LLMs they interact with. It is responsible for logging, content moderation, ensuring data sovereignty, allocating resources, and prioritizing requests. It could be a proxy to third-party model providers such as Anthropic, Google, or OpenAI, or it could expose self-hosted open source LLMs to achieve higher GPU utilization by combining all requests across organizations.

> **Note**
>
> A model gateway is responsible for "managing access to GenAI models, tracking usage, implementing security measures, and more" (`https://www.ml6.eu/blogpost/why-you-need-a-genai-gateway`).

The typical tasks of a model gateway are as follows:

- Abstraction of models and providers (if needed)
- Performance monitoring, cost management, and optimization (an API gateway can choose the best LLM to serve the request based on its nature, priority, or the current availability of third-party APIs)
- Load balancing, rate limiting, and handling failover of requests
- Request caching
- Trace logging (for compliance and other reasons), request validation, and policy enforcement (for example, an API gateway can check that users follow the internal terms of service)

Most SDKs of foundational models (from Anthropic, Google, OpenAI, etc.) or frameworks such as LangChain support an endpoint proxy as an additional parameter, which makes it easy to incorporate a model gateway pattern into the code base.

Prompt store

A prompt store, or a prompt registry, helps to manage prompt templates. It might look like overkill: why do you need a separate service for that? As we discussed in *Chapter 3*, typically, you define prompts directly in your code (or maybe, as you evolve and try to follow best practices, you start defining them as constants or put them separately in config files). A prompt store helps you to better handle and navigate your prompts.

> **Note**
>
> "A *prompt store* helps to decouple prompts from code, enable collaboration among technical and non-technical stakeholders, and streamline the prompt development lifecycle" (`https://docs.promptlayer.com/why-promptlayer/prompt-management`).

A prompt store serves as a central repository for all your prompts. It helps to decouple them from the code by separating prompts from the application logic (which makes it easier to maintain the code, allows changes to the prompts without changing the code itself), and allows versioning and experimenting with prompts (a prompt store might become the first no-code GenAI tool inside the organization). It fosters collaboration, allows you to more broadly reuse your prompts (also accessing them via API), and fosters modular design (since you can easily split large prompts into reusable snippets).

Tool registry

Agents are on the rise, and we see more and more agentic workloads in production. 2025 was called the year of agentic AI (`https://www.sequoiacap.com/article/ai-50-2025`). Two fundamental patterns behind agentic AI are tool calling and decomposition of tasks. We want to enhance LLMs with tools, and we want to build specialized agents that collaborate on complex tasks through multi-agentic workflows.

> **Note**
>
> A *tool* is an external function or an API that enhances LLMs and allows them to interact with the world and go beyond their knowledge incorporated during training (`https://python.langchain.com/docs/concepts/tool_calling/`).

That means that building tools becomes critical for the success of GenAI at the enterprise. And we want these tools to be *discoverable*; developers, researchers, and business users at the enterprise should easily search and discover new tools, and incorporate existing ones into their workflow.

> **Note**
>
> A tool registry is a centralized catalog that organizes information and provides access to tools available across organizations. Specialized agents are also tools, hence a tool registry is sometimes called an agent registry (`https://research.csiro.au/ss/science/projects/agent-design-pattern-catalogue/tool-agent-registry/`).

Another important aspect of a tool registry is to ensure the versioning of the tools. When you launch your first or second AI agent in the organization, things look good and easy. But imagine that you have dozens of tools (maintained by different teams) and dozens of agents (created not only by different teams but also by business users in a low-code style). Some underlying APIs would inevitably change (and sometimes it would be impossible to ensure backwards compatibility), and rolling out these changes to the entire organization might quickly lead to chaos. You need to understand which agents are using which specific tool, roll out the new versions of the tool, but keep the old one for a while, and notify all dependent teams to adjust their agents.

Since tools are used in many workflows across the entire organization, you want these tools to perform reliably, and you need to ensure a compliant usage of them (and at least you'd like to understand who and how is using a tool). Hence, a tool registry sometimes becomes responsible for hosting tools and managing them, similar to a model gateway. Everything we discussed about model gateways can be applied to tool registries, albeit in the context of a tool, not a foundation model. Our aim is to decouple production agents from specific tool providers by introducing an abstraction layer that enables load balancing and requests prioritization across tools and supports features such as caching, logging, and authentication.

Execution sandboxes

LLMs are good at writing code, and code-generated copilots such as Cursor are on the rise to help software engineers become more efficient. Moreover, in many cases, we can structure a problem as a code-writing one, and it improves an LLM's success rate in solving it. For example, DeepMind has demonstrated how this pattern can be used to solve optimization problems, and it even helped an LLM to make its first mathematical discovery.

> **Note**
>
> An *execution sandbox* is an isolated and secure environment that allows an LLM to execute a tool (for example, to run generated code) (`https://developer.nvidia.com/blog/sandboxing-agentic-ai-workflows-with-webassembly`).

Hence, GenAI workflows often need to execute the code generated by an LLM (to test for errors, to get a rendered visualization, etc.). The challenge is that LLM's output is non-deterministic, and we cannot guarantee that the generated code will not harm other systems or violate end-user permissions. What if a bad actor tasks an LLM to delete all the enterprise data instead of writing code for the website? GenAI teams need a secure and isolated environment where they can safely execute tools to mitigate security, privacy, and stability risks. By isolating, or sandboxing, such execution, you can keep the broader system safe and analyze the behavior and potential harm of your executable (`https://www.paloaltonetworks.co.uk/cyberpedia/sandboxing`).

And, of course, we can generalize this for other tools, too. For example, we want to run SQL queries (you can challenge me whether SQL can be treated as code, too) generated by an LLM, allow an LLM to securely use a browser to explore the internet, or take actions on a website, handle and analyze files, and interact with a filesystem.

Session store

When you move into an agentic world, your applications (or your agents) would need an external memory. First, an agent needs an external short-term memory to persist its state. It helps to maintain a conversation history and preserve user context, allows adding **human-in-the-loop** (**HITL**) elements to your workflow, and recovers if your agents fail in the middle of a long execution.

Secondly, more complex agents benefit from long-term memory. An external memory mechanism mitigates a limitation related to LLMs' "*inability to retain and retrieve relevant information from long-term interactions, which in turn limits their effectiveness in applications requiring sustained personalization*" (`https://arxiv.org/abs/2503.08026`).

Memory mechanisms can be unified across many agents and be exposed by a single GenAI platform.

Feedback service

AI and GenAI need labeled datasets. One of the great sources of data is user feedback. But collected feedback is useful only if you understand how to use it. I've seen multiple times how feedback has been incorporated into a GenAI product, and after a few months, the engineers realized that this feedback is not actionable. For example, one of the most obvious ways to introduce feedback on a GenAI answer in a question and answering system is to introduce likes. But think further. If you have millions of users, then likes and dislikes might be a good source because they can alert you to a degradation of a service (if you suddenly get a spike in a proportion of dislikes), you can find some content areas where the ratio of dislikes is high, or you can use a like/dislike ratio to A/B test different versions of your system. If you have a few dozen users a day (and that's the case for many enterprise assistants, especially in the early days of the rollout), all these won't work. Instead, ask yourselves what kind of feedback you want. It might be the case that you want to collect a golden answer, so ask a user to provide it to you! There are multiple ways to collect feedback besides likes, for example, valuation on specific scales, open questions, providing feedback on every source used for generation, and adding missing documents that were overseen by the retrieval. Start with the design of the data you'd like to collect and how you will use this data (what questions you want to answer), and then build a corresponding user experience.

The complexity of implementing a service for feedback collection is often underestimated, but it's a great source of labeled data. Think carefully about what kind of data you need to collect, and invest in designing good interfaces and an overall user journey to motivate users to spend time sending you the right signals and keep them engaged.

Developing a good feedback service is a complex task. You need a persistent data store, a backend service, and a good UI element. To encourage users to give feedback, it's a good idea to give them a follow-up on how their data would be used (e.g., send a *thank-you* email, explain that the answer provided would be added to the evaluation dataset, and then send another email when a new release comes out that uses an extended evaluation dataset). That's why providing building blocks and components that allow the easy introduction of different feedback mechanisms in an application might be owned by a platform team. And it's also pretty closely related to the next building block: HITL.

Human-in-the-loop

We've mentioned multiple times that data is a key component of any GenAI application. Such applications typically address complex use cases, and human annotators are involved in providing accurate labels for such data, and in manually validating models' outcomes during development or training (as we discussed in *Chapter 2*, human annotators are essential for the offline evaluation process).

Besides labeling the data, you can add HITL components directly to your GenAI agent to handle edge cases when the model's confidence is low, or to verify any outcome before the end user sees it. Another scenario where humans might be involved is to verify any tool call for sensitive tools (`https://python.langchain.com/docs/how_to/tools_human`).

One important point is that HITL differs from **human-over-the-loop** or **human-on-the-loop** (**HOTL**). HOTL is a process by which a human oversees an AI system through monitoring activities. Sometimes these concepts are used interchangeably since annotation processes look very similar. It makes sense to unify them under one platform block, but nevertheless, it's important to keep in mind that we have different goals and slightly different implementations in each case.

Serving infrastructure

Depending on the size and complexity of your organization, you might want to serve some open-weight models yourself (in the cloud, on-premises, or even on-edge). Organizing an optimal inference of LLMs is challenging. You need to choose a serving framework (such as vLLM or TensortRT), optimize inference settings for a given model, manage underlying hardware, and unify APIs to enable tool calling and other advanced capabilities. You don't want each of your team members to replicate this effort. By unifying this effort under a platform team and exposing an open-weighted model behind a unified *model gateway* (which we discussed earlier), you'll get efficiencies of scale and concentration of expertise in one place.

Training infrastructure

Training LLMs costs millions of dollars, and despite the progress in hardware, costs are increasing with the size and complexity of the models. Sam Altman claimed it cost around $100M to train the GPT-4 model (`https://www.wired.com/story/openai-ceo-sam-altman-the-age-of-giant-ai-models-is-already-over`). You might have heard that the DeepSeek team trained an extremely cheap LLM, and they did indeed (given the quality of the model they presented), but it's still a huge amount of money. Let's dive into it.

They spent 3M GPU-hours for a full-cycle training. According to their own estimation, it's $2 per GPU hour, so it's $6M (and most companies don't have such efficient clusters to reach $2 per GPU hour, it would be closer to $3–$4 per GPU hour). But they also conducted many experiments and ablation studies, and trained other models for more than a year until they reached the reported level of performance. Hence, I would estimate that they spent at least $20-$30 million to train DeepSeek v3.

So, most probably, you won't need your own training infrastructure since you don't want to be in the business of training LLMs (and if you are, I'm not sure you need to read this book). But your organization might still benefit from fine-tuning instruments. You might fine-tune open-weight models for your use cases, or use cloud tools to fine-tune proprietary foundational models with **parameter-efficient fine-tuning** (**PEFT**).

> **Note**
>
> **PEFT** is a collection of methods that allow LLMs to be fine-tuned efficiently, using only a small subset of weights and obtaining performance comparable to full fine-tuning. PEFT makes it possible to fine-tune LLMs on a smaller dataset and decreases the need for computational resources.

Now that we have discussed how the platform team's story is changing, let's talk about another important aspect that awaits us as the adoption of GenAI across organizations increases. After the first success and the first successful implementation, we need to answer the question "What are we going to build next?", and that's where the importance of a product vision and focus becomes extremely important. Moreover, in the era of vibe coding, we can test our hypothesis really quickly, so let's talk a little bit about how we can manage the product strategy.

Product strategy and roadmap

Experienced product managers know that a roadmap is a useful tool for aligning stakeholders and the team on the product strategy. I deeply believe that any ML team should be responsible for a specific product, and that means it should know how to manage and grow the corresponding product. It was not always the case, though, across all organizations, and in the GenAI era, many data and AI teams have realized that they are now a truly product engineering team, and that means it's important to master the corresponding product management skills. If you're new to this topic, I recommend a few starting points:

- An excellent book on strategy and product roadmap is *Inspired: How to Create Products Customers Love*. It is a concise view from a practitioner on developing successful products. This book highlights the importance of choices and the inability to always find the right answers. "*Product management is all about choices—making decisions about what opportunities are worth chasing, which problems are worth solving, what features will provide the most value, what the best time-to-market trade-offs are, and which customers are most important. While you'll never make all the right choices, you have to make most of them right for your product to succeed.*"
- *Jobs to Be Done* is another excellent book that is an example of a product framework. There are many excellent product development frameworks around, and I don't think it's a simple choice to recommend a particular one. But if you're new to the topic, that might be a good starting point.
- The Tesla master plan, written in 2006, is a brilliant example of a very clear and concise product strategy that you can find at `https://www.tesla.com/secret-master-plan`.
- Finally, as a product leader, you're responsible for a strategy for your product. Across many good frameworks, books, and paradigms on strategic thinking, I'd recommend an excellent book called *Good Strategy/Bad Strategy*. It has plenty of practical examples and aspects that differentiate a good strategy from a poor one. This book highlights the importance of a clear focus because "*good strategy works by focusing energy and resources on one, or a very few, pivotal objectives whose accomplishment will lead to a cascade of favorable outcomes.*" At the same time, it should be actionable since "*unfortunately, since*

Kennedy's time, there has been an increased penchant for defining goals that no one really knows how to achieve and pretending that they are feasible."

> **Note**
>
> A product roadmap is a shared strategic plan that describes where and how the product is going. It helps to align team members and stakeholders on common goals, to keep focus, and to give everybody some visibility about when to expect certain product deliverables. In his book *Inspired: How to Create Tech Products Customers Love*, M. Cagan cites General Patton: "*Never tell people how to do things. Tell them what to do, and they will surprise you with their ingenuity*," which illustrates the importance of a shared vision to align team members and foster their creativity.

A product roadmap is one of the key tools that you can use to strategically manage your product. The question of what and why we are going to build is one of the most important and difficult in product management, and an exercise in developing and regularly updating a roadmap gives you a space to analyze the market and the competitors, think about how your product differentiates from many others, and what value you bring to your users.

> **Note**
>
> Sometimes people are hesitant to change the roadmap. I should admit, in the b2c sector, I've never seen a roadmap that has been fully executed (a b2b roadmap is different since, typically, you communicate a short-term roadmap for 2-3 quarters to your customers, and that means you commit to deliver what you have promised). Things are changing quickly; hence, don't be afraid to regularly update your roadmap. It's only the model of the world and your product; use it accordingly. The value is in the thought exercise and stakeholder alignment, and markets are changing quickly; so are roadmaps.

What makes it more challenging to manage a product based on a GenAI? Let's discuss four key changes introduced by GenAI that make the life of a product leader more challenging. However, these challenges are the beauty of what we're doing:

1. Managing uncertainty. Due to the rapid development of the industry, things are changing fast and sometimes unpredictably, but it doesn't mean we should stop working on product strategy. My advice is to clearly communicate to your stakeholders that things will probably change and not to be afraid of these changes. Constantly challenge your assumptions, invest a substantial amount of your time in reading fresh

papers and studies, and constantly try out new tools that come out every day. This is nothing new. The ML community went through a similar experience when deep learning was rapidly being adopted. But it might be a slightly new setup for application development teams, so you need to get used to it! And rapid changes should not be an excuse not to plan ahead. You need to develop the vision and build a plan, at the same time, stay agile and correct your actions if needed.

2. Data is the key, as we discussed in *Chapter 2* and other places in the book. You should invest in collecting high-quality labeled datasets and make this activity a part of your roadmap. As a technical leader, you need to put substantial effort into educating business stakeholders on the importance of this. And you need to secure investments in tooling, such as developing annotation tools and adjusting the existing UI. Let me give a simple example. A large medical company has a division that verifies medical bills. The process includes manually going through related PDF documents and approving or denying the claim. The company tracks only the final decision, and often, it believes it has plenty of labeled data. But this is not enough! We miss the underlying data required to develop a good agent. First, the actual medical history as it looked at the moment when a decision was made is often missed. Only the current state of the patient is known, but since it's constantly changing, a company might not keep track of it. Secondly, to train an agent, we need intermediary data such as citations from underlying medical documents that were relevant to make a decision.
3. GenAI is a lot about research and experimentation. Results are not guaranteed, things are changing, and the performance of techniques depends on specific datasets and use cases. You might read a paper on a new agentic approach, but it would not work well in your case. I can give you three tips that worked well for my team in a similar setup:
    - **No result is also a result**: Praise the negative outcomes of the research across the team. Share these results and learn from them as a team. E. Bik, in her paper *Publishing negative results is good for science*, describes a similar initiative in microbiology to make it easier to report failed experiments. In business, it might be difficult to convince your business leader to express any gratitude for failed experiments, but we should keep trying and educating them.
    - **Limit the amount of time you invest in a single experiment and maintain a backlog of things to try**: We're working in industry, not in academia. We need to deliver business results. Hence, a new agentic architecture or a new fine-tuning method might eventually work if you figure out how to cook it right. But maybe there are other low-hanging fruit. Keep a long list of potential experiments and iterate quickly. For example, our ML team working on developing search models had the rule "*don't spend more than 1 sprint (2 weeks) on a new experiment.*" If a new

architecture doesn't show promising results after 2 weeks, we switch to another hypothesis. To reiterate, we didn't quite say "*it's not working*"; we simply stated that we were not lucky enough to figure out how to make it work fast enough, so we moved on!

  - **Invest time in managing expectations of your stakeholders**: Engineering leaders often underestimate the importance of this part. We love working on solving technical challenges and writing code, don't we? The fact is, if you're becoming a senior technical leader and you're driving GenAI adoption across your organization, communication and expectation management become part of your job, maybe even more important than your technical skills. Hence, I continue to reiterate the importance of expectation management in different places in this book.

4. Last but not least, when developing your GenAI roadmap, take into account ethics and considerations related to Responsible AI discussed in *Chapter 7*.

Summary

We began this chapter by acknowledging that the life cycle of a successful application rarely ends at deployment. In fact, in enterprise GenAI, a successful launch of one GenAI product often leads to fast expansion from a single application to multiple use cases across the organization. To scale in such a way, you might need a foundational GenAI platform that can support multiple use cases across an organization. We discussed how a platform team differs from a traditional product engineering team. The former builds foundational tools for developers, and the latter focuses on the end-to-end life cycle of a specific application for end-users. The platform team's value is measured by its ability to influence other teams' velocity and quality of delivery.

We then dove into the essential architectural building blocks for a scalable and secure GenAI platform. We covered components such as the *model gateway* for managing access and cost, the *prompt store* and *session store* for decoupling logic and providing external memory, the *tool registry* for making agents and functions discoverable, and the *execution sandbox* for safely running LLM-generated code. Furthermore, we explored the critical role of the *feedback service* in gathering high-quality labeled data and the need for HITL components.

Finally, we looked at how to approach a product strategy and roadmap in this rapidly changing field. We learned that due to high uncertainty, data remains the key differentiator, and that embracing research and experimentation, where "*no result is also a result*," is crucial for long-term success. Also, we discussed the importance of keeping the focus and answering very clearly what and why you're building.

In the next chapter, we will look at online experiments and statistical testing, and how we can validate small changes in complex systems.

> **Note**
>
> There are three key outcomes to remember:
>
> - The success of your first GenAI application triggers the adoption of GenAI across the organization, and more and more use cases come to life. To maintain all these different solutions efficiently, you might need a GenAI platform.
> - A platform team's core mission is to provide foundational tools and infrastructure for developers and builders. With the rise of GenAI, anyone in the organization can become a builder. That brings a lot of opportunities, but also requires a central platform that takes care of efficiency, security, evaluation, robustness, and other aspects of GenAI applications deployed across the organization. Such platforms differ from existing MLOps platforms and hence require additional effort to create.
> - GenAI has plenty of interesting technical challenges. Nevertheless, the very first thing to care about for a product leader is to figure out clear requirements and develop an actionable product strategy. Quoting Stephen Covey, "*The main thing is to keep the main thing the main thing*." One instrument you can use is a roadmap, but any framework would work well if it makes the problem the team is solving crystal clear, and how this problem is to be solved.

Further reading

- HashiCorp. *Platform Teams Best Practices*, `https://www.hashicorp.com/en/resources/platform-teams-best-practices`
- Eisele, M. *5 myths about platform engineering, debunked* `https://developers.redhat.com/articles/2024/07/22/5-myths-about-platform-engineering-debunked`
- Kale, A., Lindeman, L. *Building a Successful Enterprise AI Platform* `https://engineering.salesforce.com/building-a-successful-enterprise-ai-platform-197a3c4d8b60`

- Khanna, S. *Griffin: How Instacart's ML Platform Tripled ML Applications* https://www.instacart.com/company/how-its-made/griffin-how-instacarts-ml-platform-tripled-ml-applications-in-a-year
- Xu, Z. *Intelligent Automation Platform: Empowering Conversational AI and Beyond at Airbnb*, https://medium.com/airbnb-engineering/intelligent-automation-platform-empowering-conversational-ai-and-beyond-at-airbnb-869c44833ff2
- Romera-Paredes, B., Barekatain, M., Novikov, A., et al. (2023) *Mathematical Discoveries From Program Search with Large Language Models*, Nature 625:468–475, https://www.nature.com/articles/s41586-023-06924-6
- Tan, Z., Yan, J., Hsu, I-H., et al. (2025) *In Prospect and Retrospect: Reflective Memory Management for Long-term Personalized Dialogue Agents*, https://arxiv.org/abs/2503.08026
- DeepSeek-AI. Liu, A., Feng, B., et al. (2025) *DeepSeek-V3 Technical Report*, https://arxiv.org/abs/2412.19437
- Bik, E.M. (2024) *Publishing Negative Results is Good for Science*. https://doi.org/10.1099/acmi.0.000792
- Ulwick, A. *Jobs to Be Done: Theory to Practice*, https://jobs-to-be-done-book.com/
- Cagan, M. *Inspired: How to Create Tech Products Customers Love*, Wiley, 2018
- Rumelt, R. *Good Strategy/Bad Strategy: The difference and why it matters* Profile Books, 2017

Get This Book's PDF Version and Exclusive Extras

Scan the QR code (or go to `packtpub.com/unlock`). Search for this book by name, confirm the edition, and then follow the steps on the page.

UNLOCK NOW

Note: Keep your invoice handy. Purchases made directly from Packt don't require an invoice.

10

A/B Testing and Online Experiments

AI and ML development is always about innovating, but how can we make sure we actually provide value for the user? We are continuously updating products, modifying the underlying AI/ML models, and adjusting the UI/UX. The central challenge is simple but profound: how can we be certain that a specific change leads to a positive business outcome? While *Chapter 2* covered offline evaluation, which is a crucial first step, it is only a proxy for real-world performance. In this chapter, we will bridge that gap by exploring online experiments, also known as **A/B testing**, where we deploy our changes to a live environment and measure their effects on real user behavior in a controlled manner.

We will go beyond the basic idea of splitting users into *Control* and *Treatment* groups to build the statistical foundation to understand how data-driven decisions are made. Too often, businesses misuse statistical techniques, leading to "data-inspired" decisions based on random chance rather than scientific rigor. In this chapter, we will learn how to properly conduct a statistical analysis and how to design and run online experiments, starting from the definition of an A/B test and the core principle of isolating external changes through a random split of the audience into two groups, analyzing final results, and making a decision whether the difference can be explained by a random chance or by an actual shift caused by the new change in the produce we're evaluating. We will explore the statistical rationale behind online experimentation, including how to formulate null and alternative hypotheses and how to understand and control **Type I** (false positive) and **Type II** (false negative) errors. We will also discuss the characteristics of effective online metrics, such as robustness and sensitivity, and techniques for increasing the statistical power of experiments, including the use of A/A tests and data transformation methods. Finally, we will examine common pitfalls that can undermine even well-intentioned experiments, such as misinterpreting p-values, failing to adjust for multiple testing, and the risks associated with early stopping. Our goal is to equip you with the knowledge needed to build a robust experimental platform capable of reliably detecting even small product improvements as your product matures.

In this chapter, we'll be covering the following topics:

- What are A/B tests?
- Statistical testing
- Conducting statistical analysis
- Good metrics for online testing
- Increasing the power of your tests
- Common errors when running A/B tests

What are A/B tests?

In *Chapter 2*, we discussed offline evaluation as a crucial piece of the AI/ML development life cycle. Now, it's time to discuss another piece: online experimenting, or A/B testing. We deploy our changes to a live environment and measure their effects on real user behavior in a controlled manner. There is an important distinction between A/B testing and canary releases. A canary release is a deployment strategy used to reduce the risk of failure when introducing a new software version. The new version is exposed to a small, random subset of users, and the focus is on monitoring the system's technical health and stability. A/B testing, on the other hand, serves a different purpose. While it may also involve exposing a small group of users to a new version, its primary goal is not system validation but measuring the impact of changes on user behavior. In this sense, A/B testing is a product strategy rather than an operational one.

There are many advanced forms of A/B tests, but let's look at the simplest one that demonstrates the core idea behind it.

First, we establish the key metrics we want to track. Then we randomly split users into two groups (*Control* and *Treatment*) and instrument both groups with desired metrics. The *Treatment* group uses the new feature (a new recommendation algorithm, a new chatbot implementation, a new ranking or retrieval model, etc.), and the *Control* group uses the old version of the product. The core idea is to isolate all external changes during the test. For example, if we run one version of our recommendation system on a retail website today, and another tomorrow, and we see a spike in sales of umbrellas the second day, there are many factors that we can attribute this spike to. Does the new recommendation system better predict users' needs? Or was it raining on the second day? Or maybe a popular vlogger released a TikTok video where they predicted a rainy summer this year. As we will see throughout this chapter, besides random splitting, it's very important to follow statistical testing procedures such as running your experiments with well-defined metrics for a sufficient time frame and with large enough sample sizes.

After the experiment is finished, we compare results using statistical analysis techniques and determine whether a new feature has a positive impact on users or, in other words, if the metrics we're interested in have improved.

> **Note**
>
> A/B testing, or online experiments, refers to a way of evaluating business impact through controlled experiments with live users. In its simplest form, an A/B test randomly splits users into *Control* and *Treatment* groups, collects metrics from both, and then runs a statistical test to determine whether there's a statistically significant positive change in outcomes.

By running an experiment simultaneously on both groups, we try to isolate external factors, and it becomes crucial that we perform our split randomly. Why should we split randomly? Because we want our samples to be *representative*, or truly reflect the behavior of the entire population. For example, if an e-commerce company checks its new recommendation system only on a single subcategory of luxury watches, it would not be a proper experiment since the population of users involved might be biased. A classic textbook example is a poll on the presidential election in the US that a famous magazine, *The Literary Digest*, ran in 1936. They surveyed more than 2.5 million respondents over the phone and predicted a strong win for Alfred Landon. But Roosevelt was the candidate who won this election. Why? Because, despite the sample being huge, it was biased and didn't represent the entire population. Voters with a high income were disproportionately likely to have a phone, and at the same time, support for Alfred Landon was higher across voters with a high income. You can read more at `https://en.wikipedia.org/wiki/The_Literary_Digest#Presidential_poll`, or you can take a look at the *How to Lie with Statistics* book, which gives an excellent introduction to statistics, including a better understanding of bias (you can find this book in the *Further reading* section).

> **Note**
>
> A *representative sample* is a subset of a population that accurately reflects the characteristics of the entire group.

Reading about how companies such as Airbnb, Uber, or Netflix run A/B tests in their tech blogs (you can find some examples at the end of this chapter) is another great way to understand practical challenges and recipes to develop such an experimental platform. But now, let's look into statistical testing to better understand how we analyze the outcomes of an A/B test.

You might ask why we need offline evaluations. As you will see in this chapter, online experiments are expensive to run. They take time to conduct an experiment and to analyze results, and there's a limited number of experiments you can run because you're limited by the size of the audience you have. Very large companies with millions of daily active users can afford to run multiple online experiments simultaneously (but they still run many more offline ones), and smaller companies need to be very careful with what product or model versions to test. Statistical testing underpins both offline and online evaluations, so let's take a brief look at the core mechanics that drive decision-making with statistics.

Statistical testing

Statistics is a branch of applied mathematics that studies the collection, analysis, and interpretation of data. We live in the world of data, and businesses are expected to make data-driven decisions. The business press is constantly telling us about the importance of "leveraging data" and "gathering data insights" when making decisions, and not being guided by our feelings, emotions, or guesses. But what often happens is that statistics and statistical testing techniques are misused in everyday business life, and we make "data-inspired" decisions instead of relying on scientific methods. Cassie Kozyrkov, an ex-Googler and data scientist, explains this topic in detail in her YouTube series, or you can start with her great blog post on Medium called *Data-Driven? Think Again*.

Let's look at a short explanation of the issue (and refer to additional materials I provided if you'd like to study this interesting and important topic in more detail). Imagine you tested two versions of recommendation systems on a website. The first one had an average revenue of $100 per user, and the latter had an average revenue of $102 per user. You put these numbers on the slides and recommend using the second version of recommendations. Have you made a proper data-driven decision? I doubt it, and the reason is that you haven't analyzed the confidence intervals of your metric. We don't have a constant distribution per user, do we? There's a distribution of revenue per user, and we haven't analyzed its shape. As shown in *Figure 10.1*, a distribution of a random variable can be skewed. It might be a normal distribution (a so-called Bell curve that is symmetrical across a peak revenue), left- or right-skewed with a different degree of skewness. Imagine, in our case, most of the users make small orders of around $50, and some of them rarely make a large order of around $500. Then, the chance of getting a few "high-revenue" users in our test sample influences the average revenue we observe quite a lot. In other words, we might observe a positive difference in our experiment due to a random chance, not because an effect is real. Without understanding how large our testing sample was and how the distribution looks (to estimate the probability of observing such a difference just by a random chance), we can't really judge whether the difference we observe is real.

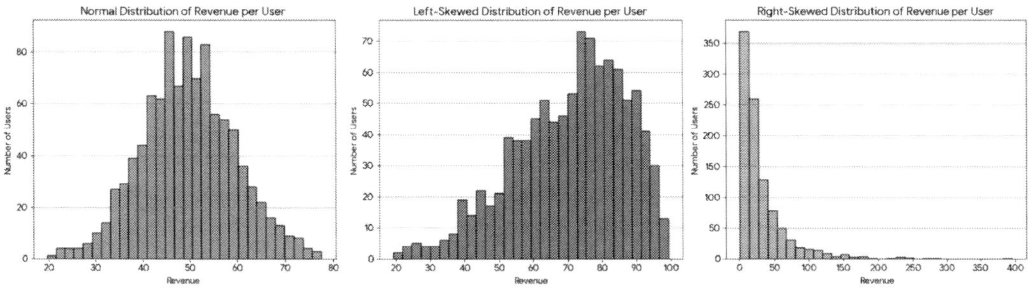

Figure 10.1 – Examples of skewness in a revenue distribution

Statistical testing helps us to make decisions given uncertainty. It gives us a reliable and scientific procedure to quantify the likelihood that the observed effect is real and not due to random chance. It's important to highlight that statistical testing doesn't give us a 100% guarantee that the effect is real. It helps us to make the right decisions in most of the cases.

Statistical testing never gives us ultimate answers, but it allows us to estimate the probability of different hypotheses and pick the most probable one. Let's look at implicit errors that are always included in any statistical test.

Type I and Type II errors

When running online experiments, any evaluations or statistical testing in general, we should be aware of *Type I and Type II errors*. This is also relevant for offline evaluations, and we already touched on this topic when we were talking about metrics for a binary classification problem. Exactly, when analyzing our experiment, we face a classification problem. For simplicity, let's assume we're comparing an existing prompt and a new version of it, and we want to find out which performs better. We need to distinguish between two outcomes:

- The new prompt performs the same way or worse than the existing prompt
- The new prompt performs better than the old one

In the next section, we'll learn that these statements are called statistical hypotheses. As a result of a statistical analysis, we can also make a binary decision.

Let's put this into a table:

	We decided the new prompt is not better than the existing one	**We decided the new prompt is better than the existing one**
In reality, the new prompt is not better than the existing one	CORRECT RESULT	TYPE I ERROR
In reality, the new prompt is better than the existing one	TYPE II ERROR	CORRECT RESULT

Table 10.1 – Type I and Type II errors

In other words, in A/B testing Type I error occurs when we detect a positive change as a result of the release, while in reality, there's no such change. To keep it simple, we release a new version of a model that doesn't bring any impact. In statistics, it is often referenced as α. A **Type II** error is when we miss a positive change while in reality there is one. Or, to formulate it differently, we reject a new version of the model while in reality it did have a positive impact on our users. In *Chapter 2*, we discussed how to evaluate a binary classification task. Making decisions based on an A/B test is an example of binary classification, so you can see that our way of thinking about it is the same. Any evaluation procedure includes an implicit or explicit statistical analysis, and that means we're facing Type I and Type II errors. While we can aim to keep Type I and II errors small, we can't bring them to zero. The probability of making a wrong decision is always there, and we need to control it to make better decisions.

Developing a good A/B testing strategy includes finding good metrics and corresponding statistical tests. By good metrics, I mean the ones with the low Type I and Type II errors, but before we jump into this topic, let's briefly discuss what it means to conduct a statistical analysis.

Conducting statistical analysis

My goal is not to teach you how to run statistical testing. It's worth a separate book or a course. But I want to demonstrate to you potential problems you might encounter without implementing a proper procedure, and give you a sense of what it could look like, so that you can validate whether you're running statistical experiments properly at your organization, and consult a professional statistician to help you to establish best practices.

To reiterate, statistical testing answers the simple question "what is the likelihood of observing the difference between two samples based on random chance?" A classic example is a biased coin. Imagine you've tossed a coin 10 times, and you got 6 heads and 4 tails. Is the coin biased, or is it a random coin and you got slightly more heads than tails because of a random chance?

To run a statistical test, we need to state a null hypothesis and an alternative hypothesis first. In statistical testing, our default assumption is that there is no difference between two samples, and this is our null hypothesis (H_0). An alternative hypothesis is that there is a difference, and our metrics have improved.

Then we choose a specific statistical test to use. A statistical test is a strict mathematical evaluation procedure that has some underlying assumptions on the form of the hypothesis and the shape of the data distribution. There are a few common statistical tests that are used in A/B testing, and we choose an appropriate one based on our specific case. Then we set a significance level for our testing, or the probability of rejecting the null hypothesis when it is actually true. We classify this, as discussed in the previous section, as a Type I error. The following diagram shows the statistical testing workflow, from hypothesis statement to the decision:

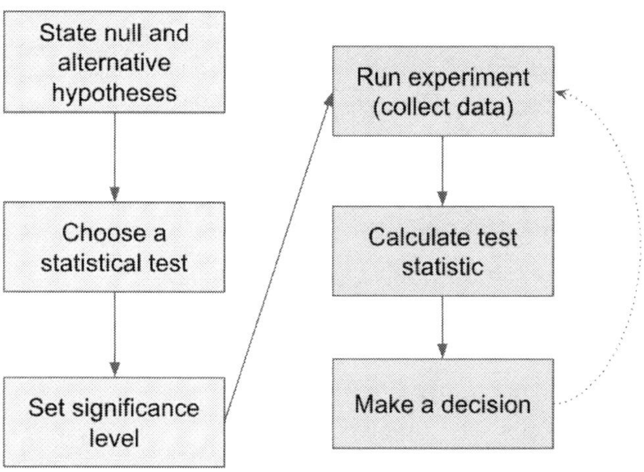

Figure 10.2 – The statistical testing procedure: from hypothesis to decision

Now, we are ready to run an experiment. The previous phase was a preparation, when we identified our hypothesis and how we're going to prove it. Now, we can take different product features, run an experiment, and perform an evaluation. An evaluation typically looks like computing a statistic, or a special value based on metrics we observed, and then computing a p-value based on it (there are some tests that have a slightly different procedure, though). There are a lot of misconceptions about the p-value. It is neither the probability that the null hypothesis is true nor the probability of making a mistake. It is simply a measure of how compatible your data is with the "no effect" scenario of the null hypothesis, or the probability of observing your data (or even a more extreme value) if the null hypothesis were true. If the p-value is less than a predetermined significance level, we reject the null hypothesis and consider our result to be statistically significant.

Myths about p-value

As Greenland et al. state in their paper *Statistical Tests, P-values, Confidence Intervals, and Power: A Guide to Misinterpretations*, "*misinterpretation and abuse of statistical tests, confidence intervals, and statistical power have been decried for decades, yet remain rampant.*" If you're running statistical tests yourselves, or you're interpreting results prepared by analysts, I'd highly recommend that you go through this paper, and maybe take a look at other material listed in the *Further reading* section.

One of the common misinterpretations is that the p-value tells you the probability of the alternative hypothesis being true. This is not the case. People often think that the p-value refers to the probability of the alternative hypothesis being true, given the data you found. But actually, it refers to the likelihood of finding your data, assuming the alternative hypothesis is true. These two statements are very far from being the same. For example, the probability of seeing clouds if it is raining is very high. But the probability that it is raining if you see clouds is not necessarily high, as it's often cloudy without rain. The p-value is like the first case. It assumes the alternative hypothesis (the "rain") and calculates the probability of the data (the "clouds"). We start by assuming the null hypothesis is true, and then we calculate the likelihood that the observed data occurred purely by random chance within that world.

I encourage you to look at the paper suggested to study more than 20 other misinterpretations related to p-values that are common in the research industry, and hence, they can occur in everyday A/B testing. Or, if you'd like to study this subject in more detail, take a look at the book *Statistics Done Wrong: The Woefully Complete Guide*.

Now that we have discussed the basics of statistical testing, let's look at what it means in practice. Are all metrics equally good, and what does it mean for a metric to be a "good" one?

Good metrics for online testing

We want metrics with low Type I and Type II errors. What does this mean in practice? Some product improvements are very easy to verify. Typically, this happens in the early stages of the product when you keep iterating quickly and fix major issues. You have a very clear idea of what you should improve, you're doing it, and you observe how the performance gets better. For example, if the conversion rate increased by two times after some change (all other things being equal), you do not need a sophisticated A/B testing framework to confirm this. The challenge is that as your product matures, you start dealing with a diminishing returns effect.

You need a lot of effort for a small improvement in your product metrics, and this improvement becomes difficult to catch. Since we do not necessarily know what would work and what wouldn't, and our product becomes pretty complex (especially when it's AI-based), we're at risk that by fixing one thing, we might break another. For example, if you end up with a long and complex prompt (which in turn is part of a long agentic workflow), any change to this prompt becomes dangerous since it might influence the whole system unpredictably. You need to introduce a proper testing framework, and this requires a large amount of research and experimentation, which is often underestimated by businesses.

Back in the day, Netflix pioneered ML-based recommendations for practical use cases, and they perfectly explain how practical ML requires not only a dataset and a model, but also metrics and an experimentation system: "*The Netflix Prize abstracted the recommendation problem to a proxy question of predicting ratings. ... Over time we have reformulated the recommendation problem to the question of optimizing the probability a member chooses to watch a title and enjoys it enough to come back to the service. More data availability enables better results. But in order to get those results, we need to have optimized approaches, appropriate metrics and rapid experimentation*" (`https://netflixtechblog.com/netflix-recommendations-beyond-the-5-stars-part-1-55838468f429`).

> **Note**
>
> As the product matures and gets more complex, it becomes less clear how to improve it. You need to invest in a sophisticated A/B testing framework to be able to measure small improvements (and discard bad hypotheses).

Another problem is that statistical decision-making requires a careful setup, and I've seen teams doing this wrong. We will talk about the most common errors in the next section, and I encourage you to read additional material if you're interested. But why is it so difficult to set up a proper approach to statistical analysis? One of the main reasons is that every statistical test has certain assumptions on the underlying data distribution, and one of the common major assumptions is that the events we observe are uncorrelated. In online experiments, this is not the case, and because of that and some other more nuanced reasons, we tend to overestimate the effect sizes. For example, consumer applications often deal with unlogged users, making it difficult to split traffic based on a stable user identity. Instead, users are typically assigned to experiment groups using a cookie ID (or device ID on mobile). However, a single user may interact with the application across multiple devices (such as a phone, laptop, or smart TV). Additionally, behaviors may be correlated among family members or users in the same household or location, further violating independence assumptions.

To recap, finding a good metric for our product is difficult. Such a metric should be robust and sensitive. A robust metric doesn't show positive changes when there's no change (in other words, it has a low Type I error), and a sensitive metric almost always catches positive changes when they occur (in other words, it has a low Type II error).

> **Note**
>
> A good metric is robust (it doesn't show a change when there's no such change) and sensitive (it doesn't miss a change when there is one). When our product matures and becomes complex, we try a lot of experiments, and only some of them lead to positive changes. Since many assumptions common for statistical tests are violated in web experiments, finding a good metric that catches such small improvements becomes a challenging task that requires time, effort, and experimentation.

How do we find a good metric? Finding a good metric is difficult, and it requires a lot of experimentation. We define a metric that the business is interested in (such as user retention or revenue), and it's sometimes called a North Star metric. Then, we look for a so-called proxy metric (or multiple ones) that correlate with our North Star metric but are easier to measure and have good statistical properties. For example, Netflix is interested in long-term user retention, but they use a proxy metric such as a click-through rate when running A/B experiments.

What does this mean in practice? We typically have three ways to develop a metric (beyond our common sense, of course):

- Validate robustness by estimating the empirical variance of a metric with online A/A experiments or historical simulations. An A/A experiment is similar to an A/B test, but as you can imagine, both the *Control* and *Treatment* groups get the same version of the product, and we expect not to reject a null hypothesis (in other words, not to detect any improvement) when analyzing test results. We can scale this analysis by running simulations of an A/A test on historical data when we know there were no product changes deployed. Do this for metrics you have in mind, and you might be surprised by how unexpectedly high the empirical variance of your metric is.
- Run ablation studies to validate sensitivity. Think about something that should definitely decrease the quality of your product (for example, reduce the size of the knowledge base of your RAG twice) and check whether you observe a difference during

A/B testing. Ablation studies are expensive, and they harm user experience, so we should be very careful when we run such studies.

- Iterate on your metrics and try to transform them or use advanced techniques to increase their sensitivity and robustness.

Why does it matter so much? Because when you adopt A/B testing, you typically start running a lot of experiments, and only a part of them is winning. A very simple example is prompting. How many versions of your prompt do you typically try until you get one working? Let's imagine you try different versions of the prompt indefinitely, until you see an improvement. Sooner or later, you'll see one, but it will only be because of chance. If you toss a coin for a long period of time, you'll end up with a sequence of tails only with an arbitrary length N (yes, you just need to try long enough). You can search on YouTube for videos demonstrating exactly this effect. To reiterate, getting $N = 100$ sequential tails in a row is very unlikely if the coin is unbiased, but only if your trial is limited. This is a very common error in A/B testing, where we tend to treat each experiment completely independently from others.

Now, let's make some assumptions. Let's imagine our significance level is 0.95, and our beta is 0.9, and only 1 out of 10 changes we try have an actual impact. Now, let's ask ourselves a question: what is the probability that our changes are truly impactful if we have detected an impact when running the A/B test? We can apply Bayes' theorem:

The number of changes tried (experiments run)	1,000
Impactful changes (1/5)	100
Impactful changes detected	100*90% = 90
Changes without actual impact	1,000-100=900
Changes where we erroneously detected an impact	900*0.05=45
Changes where we detected an impact during A/B testing	90+45=135
Probability that there's an actual change if we detect an impact during the A/B test	90/135 = **66%**

Table 10.2 – Example of how the number of trials influences the A/B test outcomes

As you can see, only two-thirds of deployed changes would be truly impactful given our realistic assumptions. In practice, your empirical beta might be lower than 0.9, and you might have a lower ratio of truly successful changes, and that would make your situation even worse.

Now, let's discuss how you can change a metric and increase its statistical properties.

Increasing the power of your tests

Before we look into some examples of increasing the sensitivity of our experiments (and you'll find a list of additional links to papers and studies if you're interested in learning more about the topic in the *Further reading* section), let me reiterate a very important aspect. The power of your statistical test depends on the following four factors:

- The distribution of your data.
- The specific statistical test you've chosen.
- The effect size. It's much easier to detect a statistically significant increase in a click-through rate from 10.0% to 16.5% than from 10.0% to 10.1%. In the first case, the effect size, or the difference in the metric, is 6.5 percentage points, while in the second case, it's only 0.1 percentage points.
- The size of your test group. This has certain diminishing effects, but if you have hundreds and even thousands of users, you are limited in the sophistication of A/B testing that you can run, and you would be limited in the effects that you can detect.

That means the power of your test depends a lot on the effect size. In practice, we typically reach the area of diminishing returns very fast. In product development, our typical situation is that changes bring only a small improvement, and we need to run a lot of experiments until we find a change that actually moves the needle. This is where making a good evaluation system becomes very challenging and important, but only if you operate at a large enough scale, because when you don't have many users, you have the issue of attaining significance in your A/B testing. In fact, you can do A/B testing only if you have enough traffic, or if your effect sizes are large enough that you can observe them even with a small sample.

When we're talking about A/B testing, we typically mean web experiments in the b2c (business-to-consumer) domain. It's possible to run A/B testing in the b2b (business-to-business) area, where you sell services to enterprise customers, or in the offline b2c business (such as offline retail). The setup becomes more complicated, although it's based on the same principles we have discussed in this chapter.

In short, it is possible to increase the power of your tests. What can you do? In the pre-experimental phase, you can experiment with different hypothesis statements and choose across multiple tests available to determine which ones work better in your domain and on your data. You can choose the right metric. In practice, we iterate across multiple metric definitions, experimentally check their statistical properties, and determine how they are correlated with the main business metric that we have in mind.

Consider altering your metric to proportions for a simpler approach. In statistics, a *Bernoulli trial* is a random experiment with only two outcomes: *success* (1) or *failure* (0). If the probability of success (p) is constant and trials are independent, the number of successes in n trials follows a *binomial distribution*, which is simpler for statistical analysis.

Please note that there's a very important assumption under a binomial distribution called **i.i.d.** In statistics, i.i.d. stands for **independent and identically distributed**. It's a fundamental assumption made about a collection of random variables, meaning that each variable in the collection meets two key conditions.

Outcomes being independent means that the outcome of one random variable doesn't influence the outcome of another. They are statistically unrelated. Let's imagine we're testing a new sharing mechanism on a social media platform, and our target metric is actually a click-through-rate in the recommendation feed (that we believe to be a proxy for user engagement). *User A* (who is in the *Treatment* group) starts sharing more engaging content, and this content lands in the news feed of *user B*, who is in the *Control* group. This is called a network effect and can influence your A/B testing results.

Outcomes being identically distributed means that all the random variables in the collection are drawn from the same probability distribution. They have the same mean, variance, and overall shape. A simple example of how this assumption is violated in online experiments is online retail. Imagine you're testing a new recommendation feed that suggests to users what they might want to add to their basket during checkout. Your test has started in the second part of November, and it takes three weeks until it converges. That means, your test runs through Black Friday, and your events are not identically distributed anymore, since Black Friday changes the users' behavior, and it also might be related to marketing activities that bring other types of users to your website. Yes, you try to compensate for this by running an A/B test, which means both the *Control* and *Treatment* groups are expected to be affected in the same way, but it still violates assumptions for statistical testing.

As we have discussed, such violations make it necessary to estimate the empirical variance of our metrics and not blindly rely on a statistical test from a textbook or the internet.

There are many other more advanced methods to reduce the variance of metrics when running A/B experiments. For example, Rohani et al. demonstrated that a **Controlled-experiment Using Pre-Existing Data (CUPED)** approach helped to "*reduce variance by about 50%, effectively achieving the same statistical power with only half of the users, or half the duration.*" This approach is based on a trick that uses pre-experimental data for every user participating in the experiment. There are many other more advanced approaches and techniques that you will become aware of if you start studying this topic more deeply.

Common errors when running A/B tests

As you can imagine, getting a proper A/B testing setup at your organization is a complicated task. With the growing adoption of GenAI and by incorporating it within our products, more and more organizations need to adopt the right approach to running online experiments. Let's look at some common mistakes reported by field teams in tech companies that have been doing this for years, and please explore the additional resources you can find at the end of this chapter.

First, you need to always think about comparing confidence intervals for your outcomes. It is not enough to observe a difference between two values; you need to check whether this difference is caused by random chance or not. For example, if an average revenue per user equals $100 in version A and $105 in version B, this difference might not be large enough to exclude a random fluctuation.

Tip

Tip 1: Do not compare absolute values only; use statistics to determine how likely it is that a difference is caused by random chance.

As we already know, do not blindly trust a random statistical test from a textbook. Most probably, you'll need to iterate to pick the best working statistical test and adjust the metric for your specific data distribution.

Tip

Tip 2: Always check what statistical test you use when analyzing A/B tests, and whether the assumptions behind this test match your data.

Another common misperception that we are already aware of is the belief that you can just test any hypothesis with A/B testing. For example, throw 100 versions of a different web page design into an experimental pipeline, and pick the winner. As we saw in the previous section, it doesn't work that way, unfortunately. You might pick the winner by pure random luck.

Tip

Tip 3: Know the Type I and Type II errors behind your experiments. Do not misinterpret p-values. Remember that you always need to have a strong product hypothesis behind the change you're implementing.

As we have discussed, not all metrics are equally good for A/B testing. Validate empirical variance of the metric you're going to use, and be prepared to transform it to a metric with lower variance (or pick another one).

> Tip
>
> **Tip 4**: Metrics that have a similar business sense might have a very different variance. Always check the empirical variance of the metric you choose, and be prepared to iterate on the metric definition.

Another common problem that I often observe teams and businesses run into is not adjusting for multiple testing. What happens in practice is that we (or our boss) have a brilliant idea. We implement it, and maybe they ask us to run an A/B test to confirm that this idea was great. Then an analyst collects the data and starts looking for a metric that has improved. Sometimes, I've even observed the question being honestly asked in such a form:

"*Let's study what exactly we have improved with this change, and in which way users have positively reacted to it.*"

As you know by now, it has nothing to do with statistical analysis. If we take a large enough number of user segments and try many different metrics instead of a single one, we will eventually find some metric or segment that was positively impacted, but because of multiple things we compared before, most probably this would be just noise.

As Mark Twain allegedly said (though the attribution is debated), "There are lies, damned lies, and statistics." What he likely meant is that statistical reasoning is often misapplied, largely because it can be counterintuitive compared to our everyday common-sense thinking.

Similarly, if we toss a coin for a large enough time, we will eventually observe an interrupted sequence of heads of any length. In statistics, it's called a multiple comparison problem. Let's imagine there are independently distributed metrics that we're testing across (in practice, they are most likely correlated, but we use them only as an illustration).

If each metric has $\alpha = 0.05$, and we test 10 metrics, the probability of observing at least one false positive is now much higher, or roughly 0.4:

$$p = 1 - (1 - \alpha)^{10} = 1 - 0.95^{10} = 0.40$$

> **Tip**
>
> **Tip 5**: Always define a clear hypothesis upfront: which metric should improve, how it will be tested, what the null and alternative hypotheses are, and how long the experiment will run. In other words, explicitly state your expected outcome (for example, "We believe the conversion rate across all users will increase") and do not revise this expectation after the experiment has started.
>
> A common pitfall is to look backward after the fact. Product teams may say, "This is a great feature, we know that. Let's find a metric that improved." This kind of retrospective justification undermines the validity of the experiment.

If you do not fix the duration of a test and run it until you observe a convergence, you face an *early stopping* issue that is related to the previously mentioned issue. I once witnessed an experiment that had been running for half a year. When I asked the team about it, they told me, "our PM really loves this feature, and they're waiting for a convergence." As you know now, if you wait long enough, you'll observe it, but it has very little to do with reality.

These are a few examples of problems that you can run into, and if you look into the papers provided in the *Further reading* section, you will find more examples and things to keep in mind.

Summary

We started this chapter by tackling a profound challenge: how can we be certain that a product change truly leads to a positive business outcome? We learned in *Chapter 2* that an offline evaluation is only a proxy. To bridge this gap, we can use online experiments, or A/B testing, where we deploy our changes to a live environment to measure their effects on real user behavior in a controlled manner. The core principle is that we must isolate all external changes by randomly splitting users into *Control* and *Treatment* groups to ensure we have a representative sample that accurately reflects the entire population.

Then, we learned about the importance of a statistical foundation that is required for making truly data-driven decisions, rather than falling for "data-inspired" decisions. We learned how to properly conduct a statistical analysis, starting with stating null and alternative hypotheses. Critically, we discussed the unavoidable reality of Type I (false positive) and Type II (false negative) errors, highlighting that a proper A/B testing strategy minimizes both. A large part of this strategy relies on identifying good metrics, which are both robust (low Type I error) and sensitive (low Type II error).

Finally, we talked about common, costly mistakes that undermine experiments, including the misinterpretation of p-values, the danger of not adjusting for multiple testing, and the fallacy of early stopping. Additional papers and books that you can find in the *Further reading* section will help you to learn how to establish a proper, robust experimental platform that reliably detects even small product improvements.

> **Note**
>
> There are three key outcomes to remember:
>
> - There are offline and online experiments in AI. With offline experiments, you test your workloads without putting them in front of the user (using a labeled dataset or annotators). Such experiments are only a proxy of real-world performance, but they are relatively fast and cheap. With online experiments, you put your workflow in front of the actual user. A/B testing is an example of a controlled experiment that splits traffic into two random groups to isolate external changes, and then it uses statistical methods to determine whether a new feature or a new model positively impacts user outcomes.
> - A statistical experiment always has an implicit assumption of how the data distribution looks, which statistical algorithm to use, and it never gives the result with 100% certainty. It involves unavoidable Type I (false positive) and Type II (false negative) errors, and you control only the probability of such an error (which you can never drive to zero). A very common issue with statistical testing is not setting your bet before the experiment, and looking for a positive change after that.
> - An A/B test requires a special procedure to design. The validity of A/B tests depends on whether you run them according to statistical guidelines. In online work, some assumptions behind statistical tests are often violated; hence, you always need to validate your Type I and Type II errors, and it requires some time and iteration through different metrics, experiment setup, etc.

Further reading

- Reinhart, A. *Statistics Done Wrong: The Woefully Complete Guide*, No Starch Press, 2015, 227 p.
- Huff, D. *How to Lie with Statistics*, W. W. Norton & Company, 145 p.
- Wheelan, C. *Naked Statistics: Stripping the Dread from the Data*, W. W. Norton & Company, 2014, 304 p.
- Netflix Technology Blog, *What is an A/B Test?* `https://netflixtechblog.com/what-is-an-a-b-test-b08cc1b57962`
- Airbnb Tech Blog Experiments at Airbnb, `https://medium.com/airbnb-engineering/experiments-at-airbnb-e2db3abf39e7`
- Uber Tech Blog, *Under the Hood of Uber's Experimentation Platform*, `https://www.uber.com/en-DE/blog/xp`
- Kozyrkov, C., *Data-Driven? Think Again*, `https://kozyrkov.medium.com/data-inspired-5c78db3999b2`
- Greenland, S., Senn, S.J., Rothman, K., et al. (2016) *Statistical Tests, P Values, Confidence Intervals, and Power: A Guide to Misinterpretations*, European Journal of Epidemiology 31:337–350, `https://link.springer.com/article/10.1007/s10654-016-0149-3`
- Lewis, R., Rao, J., Reiley, D. (2011) *Here, There, and Everywhere: Correlated Online Behaviors Can Lead to Overestimates of the Effects of Advertising*, `https://doi.org/10.1145/1963405.1963431`
- Bibaut, A., Chou, W., Ejdemyr, S., et al. (2024) *Learning the Covariance of Treatment Effects Across Many Weak Experiments*, `https://arxiv.org/abs/2402.17637`
- Dmitriev, P., Gupta, S., Kim D-W., et al. (2017) *A Dirty Dozen: Twelve Common Metric Interpretation Pitfalls in Online Controlled Experiments*, `https://doi.org/10.1145/3097983.3098024`
- Deng, A., Xu, Y., Kohavi, R., et al. (2013) *Improving the Sensitivity of Online Controlled Experiments by Utilizing Pre-Experiment Data*, `https://doi.org/10.1145/2433396.2433413`
- Budylin, R., Drutsa, A., Katsev, I., et al. (2018) *Consistent Transformation of Ratio Metrics for Efficient Online Controlled Experiments*, `https://doi.org/10.1145/3159652.3159699`

- Deng, A., Knoblich, U., Lu, J. (2018) *Applying the Delta Method in Metric Analytics*, `https://doi.org/10.1145/3219819.3219919`
- Robinson, E., *Guidelines for A/B Testing*, `https://hookedondata.org/posts/2018-08-07_guidelines-for-a-b-testing`
- Miller, E. *How Not To Run an A/B Test*, `https://www.evanmiller.org/how-not-to-run-an-ab-test.html`
- Stucchio, C. *Multiple Comparisons - Make Your Boss Happy with False Positives*. `https://www.chrisstucchio.com/pubs/slides/crunch_conf_2015/slides.html#1`. Accessed 23 Jul 2025

Subscribe for a free eBook

New frameworks, evolving architectures, research drops, production breakdowns—*AI_Distilled* filters the noise into a weekly briefing for engineers and researchers working hands-on with LLMs and generative AI systems. Subscribe now and receive a free eBook, along with weekly insights that help you stay focused and informed.

Subscribe at `https://packt.link/8Oz6Y` or scan the QR code below.

11

Unlock Your Exclusive Benefits

Your copy of this book includes the following exclusive benefits:

DRM-Free PDF Version

Download DRM-free PDF and ePub copies of this book.

7-Day Packt Library Access

Get 7-day unlimited access to 8,000+ books and videos. No credit card required.

Available for first-time Packt+ trial users only.

Next-Gen Reader Access

Read this book on Packt Reader with progress sync, dark mode and note-taking.

Follow the guide below to unlock them. The process takes only a few minutes and needs to be completed once.

Unlock this Book's Free Benefits in 3 Easy Steps

Step 1

Keep your purchase invoice ready for *Step 3*. If you have a physical copy, scan it using your phone and save it as a PDF, JPG, or PNG.

For more help on finding your invoice, visit `https://www.packtpub.com/en-us/unlock?step=1`.

> **Note**
>
> If you bought this book directly from Packt, no invoice is required. After *Step 2*, you can access your exclusive content right away.

Step 2

Scan the QR code or go to `packtpub.com/unlock`.

On the page that opens (similar to *Figure 11.1* on desktop), search for this book by name and select the correct edition.

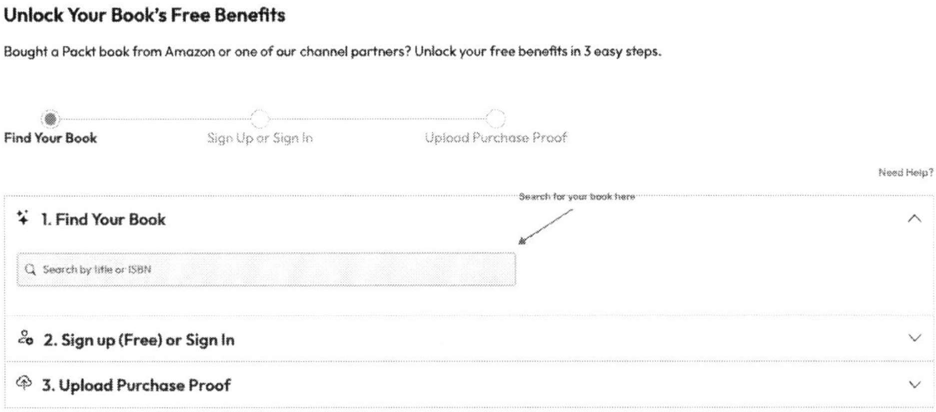

Figure 11.1 – Packt unlock landing page on desktop

Step 3

After selecting your book, sign in to your Packt account or create one for free. Then upload your invoice (PDF, PNG, or JPG, up to 10 MB). Follow the on-screen instructions to finish the process.

Need Help

If you get stuck and need help, visit `https://www.packtpub.com/unlock-benefits/help` for a detailed FAQ on how to find your invoices and more. This QR code will take you to the help page.

> **Note**
>
> If you are still facing issues, reach out to `customercare@packt.com`.

Other Books You May Enjoy

If you enjoyed this book, you may be interested in these other books by Packt:

Generative AI for Leaders Playbook

Adrián González Sánchez

ISBN: 9781806388493

- Understand Generative and Agentic AI capabilities and business value
- Build organizational AI literacy and cultural readiness
- Craft an enterprise AI strategy aligned with business goals
- Design and scale high-performing AI teams and structures
- Evaluate AI platforms and vendors for transparency and reliability
- Embed responsible AI governance and compliance frameworks
- Prepare for emerging trends in AI and build organizational foresight

Agentic Architectural Patterns for Building Multi-Agent Systems

Dr. Ali Arsanjani, Juan Pablo Bustos

ISBN: 9781806029570

- Apply design patterns to handle instruction drift, improve coordination, and build fault-tolerant AI systems
- Design systems with the three layers of the agentic stack: function calling, tool protocols (MCP), and A2A collaboration
- Develop responsible, ethical, and governable GenAI applications
- Use frameworks such as ADK, LangGraph, and CrewAI with code examples
- Master prompt engineering, LLMOps, and AgentOps best practices
- Build agentic systems using RAG, fine-tuning, and in-context learning

Packt is searching for authors like you

If you're interested in becoming an author for Packt, please visit `authors.packt.com` and apply today. We have worked with thousands of developers and tech professionals, just like you, to help them share their insight with the global tech community. You can make a general application, apply for a specific hot topic that we are recruiting an author for, or submit your own idea.

Share your thoughts

Once you've read *Architecting Generative AI Applications*, we'd love to hear your thoughts! Scan the QR code below to go straight to the Amazon review page for this book and share your feedback.

`https://packt.link/r/1806678659`

Your review is important to us and the tech community and will help us make sure we're delivering excellent quality content.

Index

A

A/B testing 27, 223 - 225
- running, errors 236, 237

AI Principles 161

AI products
- developing 12 – 15
- developing, misconceptions 15 – 18

AI prototype
- proof of concept, starting as start-up 8, 9
- proof of concept, starting at large company 5 – 8
- success, secrets 2 – 5

AI safety 168
- GenAI safety 170 – 172
- in classical ML era 168 – 170

AgentOps 124

Application performance monitoring (APM) 194

Asynchronous Server Gateway Interface (ASGI) 141

abstract syntax tree (AST) 150

acceptance tests 96

agent registry
- reference link 210

agentic architectures
- exploring 69
- external orchestrator 77, 78
- memory 79 – 81
- multi-agentic systems 75 – 77
- task decomposition 73 – 75
- tool calling 70 – 73
- tool-calling pattern, operationalizing 78, 79
- tree of thoughts 73 – 75

application deployment 139
- code wrapping, as web API 139 – 143
- container deployment, on Kubernetes 143 – 146
- LangSmith Deployment 147, 148

application scaling, best practices 148
- caching 148 – 151
- graceful failures 153

approximate nearest neighbor (ANN) 59

B

Bell curve 226

binary classification 29 - 31
- accuracy (acc) 29
- F1 score 30
- precision (P) 30
- recall (R) 30

bulkhead pattern 155

C

CAP theorem 133, 151

CRUD operation 136

California Consumer Privacy Act (CCPA) 172

Cluster Autoscaler 146

Controlled-experiment Using Pre-Existing Data (CUPED) 235

cache-augmented generation (CAG) techniques 152

caching 148, 149
- CAP theorem 151
- context caching 152
- examples 150
- semantic caching 150

cascading failure 154 - 156
- patterns, for preventing 155

circuit breaker pattern 155

classification 28

code readability 89 - 91
- Don't Repeat Yourself (DRY) 94
- extension 92
- in Python 91, 92
- loose coupling 95
- Single Responsibility Principle (SRP) 93

comparing texts 32 - 34

complex evaluation scenarios 48
agent, evaluating 50
RAG applications, evaluating 48, 49

concept drift 122

configuration management 138, 139

confusion matrix 29

constitutional AI 171

containerization 144

context caching 152
explicit context caching 152
implicit context caching 152
prefill cache 152
preprocess cache 152

continuous batching 102

continuous delivery 115

continuous deployment 115

continuous integration (CI) 115

continuous integration/ continuous delivery (CI/CD) 113 - 117

D

DevOps 114
code delivery processes, automating 114, 115
continuous integration/continuous delivery (CI/CD) 115 – 117

Don't Repeat Yourself (DRY) 85, 94

data drift 122

data governance 173

data leakage 24

deanonymization 173

dense embeddings 63

deployment best practices 135
configuration management 138, 139
infrastructure as code 135 – 137
secret management 137, 138

discounted cumulative gain (DCG) 36

E

Explainable Artificial Intelligence (XAI) 166

embeddings
storing and retrieving, with vector databases 58 – 61

engineering
best practices 105, 106

example-based explanations 166

execution sandbox 211
reference link 211

explainability 164
improving 165, 166
of LLMs 167

explicit context caching 152

F

FastAPI 141

Flask application 141

fairness ML models, Responsible AI 162
fairness, improving 162
fairness, in GenAI 163

fairness indicator 162

fan-out pattern 156

fear of missing out (FOMO) 10

feature-attribution method 166

federated machine learning (FML) 174

feedback service 212, 213

first-in, first-out (FIFO) 154

frequency-inverse document frequency (TF-IDF) 64

G

GenAI applications 99, 100
developing 125, 126
evaluating 22
LLMOps tools, selecting 126, 127
ML development lifecycle 26, 27
ML generalization 22 – 25
observability, instrumenting 198, 199

GenAI platform building blocks 208
execution sandbox 211
feedback service 212, 213
model gateway 208, 209
prompt store 209
session store 212
tool registry 210, 211

GenOps 124

General Data Protection Regulation (GDPR) 172

Generative AI (GenAI) 1
impact 9 – 12

platform teams, versus regular platform teams 205 – 207
safety 170 – 172

GitHub 138

GitLab 138

Gradio 133

garbage in, garbage out (GIGO) 14

generalization 22

H

HashiCorp Configuration Language (HCL) 136

HashiCorp Vault 137

HorizontalPodAutoscaler 146

Human-in-the-loop (HITL) 43, 212, 213
human evaluation, scaling and operationalizing 46, 47
implementing 43 – 45

Hydra 139

hit ratio 149

human evaluation
operationalizing 46 – 48
scaling 46 – 48

human-in-the-loop (HITL)
serving infrastructure 214
training infrastructure 214

human-on-the-loop (HOTL) 213

human-over-the-loop (HOTL) 213

hybrid search 61, 62
inverted index 62, 63
results, re-ranking and merging 64 – 66

hyperparameter optimization 24

hyperparameter tuning 24

hyperparameters 23

I

implicit context caching 152

incident 168

independent and identically distributed (i.i.d) 235

infrastructure as code (IaC) 133 - 135

integration testing 101

inter-rater agreement 46

inter-rater reliability (IRR) 46

J

jailbreaking 170, 171

K

Kubernetes 133
rollout patterns 145

kubectl 144, 145

L

LLM-as-a-judge
consensus mechanism 42, 43
using 38 – 41

LangChain
reference link 213

LangSmith Deployment 147, 148

LoadBalancer 145

large language model operations (LLMOps) 113, 124
case study 127 – 129
GenAI applications, developing 125

large language models (LLMs) 1
inference 175

large vision models (LVMs) 1

last-in, first-out (LIFO) 154

lazy loading 149

least recently used (LRU) cache 149

lexical similarity 33

limited context window
used, for dealing with MapReduce 67, 68

linter 91

load testing 102 - 104

logs 190 - 192

loose coupling 95

M

ML pipeline 119 - 123
reference link 119

MapReduce 55
used, for dealing with limited context window 67, 68

Model Context Protocol (MCP) 78

Monk Skin Tone (MST) scale 162

machine learning (ML) 1, 21

development lifecycle 26, 27
generalization 22 – 25

machine learning operations (MLOps) **113, 117 – 119**
metrics 124
ML pipeline 119 – 123

macro-averaging **32**

mean average precision (MAP) **36**

mean reciprocal rank (MRR) **36**

mechanistic interpretability **167**

metrics **192, 193**
types 192

metrics-based evaluation **28**
binary classification 28 – 31
multi class classification 28, 31, 32

micro-averaging **32**

model gateway **208, 209**
reference link 209

multi-agentic systems **75 – 77**

multi-class classification **31, 32**

multi-label classification **31**

multiple comparison problem **237**

N

North Star metric **232**

normalized discounted cumulative gain (NDCG) **36**

O

observability **196, 197**
instrumenting, for GenAI applications 198, 199
instrumenting, in application 199, 200

onboarding users **107, 108**

online testing
good metrics 230 – 233

operationalization
need for 86 – 89

P

PACELC design principle **152**

PEP-0333 **141**

Personal Information Protection Law (PIPL) **172**

Python
unit testing 99

p-value
myths 230

parameter-efficient fine-tuning (PEFT) **214**

platform team **204, 205**
human-in-the-loop (HITL) 213
reference link 205

positional bias **44**

preference bias **163**

prefill cache **152**

preprocess cache **152**

privacy, Responsible AI **172**
deanonymization 173
differential privacy 173
federated machine learning (FML) 174
improving 172 – 175
privacy concerns 175, 176

product strategy and roadmap **215 – 218**

production application
alerting 195, 196
managing 106, 107, 189
monitoring 194
telemetry data 190 – 193

prompt store **209**
reference link 209

prompt template
organizing and versioning 56 – 58

proof of concept
starting, as start-up 8, 9
starting, at large company 5 – 8

Q

query expansion **66, 67**

R

Reason-Act (ReACT) pattern **70**

Representational State Transfer (REST) API **140**

Responsible AI **159 - 161**
explainability 164
fairness. ML models 162
privacy 172
safety 168

reciprocal rank fusion (RRF) **65**

red team **171**

regression tests 96
representative sample 225
request throttling 153, 154
retrieval components 34 - 37
retrieval-augmented generation (RAG) 55, 127
root mean square error (RMSE) 28

S

Single Responsibility Principle (SRP) 85, 93
Streamlit 133
secret 137
secret and configuration management 133
secret management 137, 138
semantic caching 150
semantic search 63
semantic similarity 33
service-level agreement (SLA) 183, 184
service-level indicators (SLIs) 181 - 185
service-level objectives (SLOs) 181 - 185
session store 212
site reliability engineering (SRE) 114, 181, 182
- achieving 182, 183
- error budget 185 – 187
- principles 187 – 189
- SLAs 183 – 185
- SLIs 183 – 185
- SLOs 183 – 185

software-as-a-service (SaaS) 147
state-of-the-art (SOTA) 9
stateful application 133, 134
stateless application 133, 134
static evaluation 27
statistical analysis
- conducting 229
- p-value, myths 230

statistical hypotheses 227
statistical testing 226, 227
- Type 1 error 227, 228
- Type II error 227, 228

stereotypical toxicity 163
stock-keeping unit (SKU) 65
subject matter experts (SMEs) 16

T

TabNet 166
TensortRT 214
Terraform 133 - 135
- provider 136

Type I error 227, 228
Type II error 227, 228
telemetry data, pillars 190
- logs 190 – 192
- metrics 192, 193
- traces 193, 194

test coverage 98
testing 96
- integration testing 101
- load testing 102 – 104
- unit testing 97, 98

testing set 24
tests
- power, increasing 234

time to live (TTL) 149
timeout pattern 156
tool calling 70 - 73
tool registry 210, 211
- reference link 210

tool-calling pattern
- operationalizing 78, 79

toxicity 163
- stereotypical toxicity 163

traces 193, 194
training set 23
type checker 92

U

unit testing 97, 98
- GenAI applications 99, 100
- in Python 99

V

VerticalPodAutoscaler 146
vLLM 214
validation set 23
vector databases

used, for storing and retrieving embeddings 58 – 61

vibe coding **97**

W

Web Server Gateway Interface (WSGI) **141**

web API wrapper **139, 140**

Made in the USA
Monee, IL
13 September 2026

63137529R00153